Fuel

Fuel

SEÁN O'BRIEN

SANDYCOVE

an imprint of

PENGUIN BOOKS

SANDYCOVE

UK | USA | Canada | Ireland | Australia
India | New Zealand | South Africa

Sandycove is part of the Penguin Random House group of companies
whose addresses can be found at global.penguinrandomhouse.com.

First published 2020
001

Set in 13.5/16 pt Garamond MT Std
Typeset by Jouve (UK), Milton Keynes
Printed and bound in Great Britain by Clays Ltd, Elcograf S.p.A.

A CIP catalogue record for this book is available from the British Library

ISBN: 978–1–844–88459–9

www.greenpenguin.co.uk

Penguin Random House is committed to a
sustainable future for our business, our readers
and our planet. This book is made from Forest
Stewardship Council® certified paper.

Contents

CONTENTS

Prologue: 11 May 2019

We lost.

I was home in bed by 2.30am. There was nothing to celebrate. Saracens were champions of Europe. We'd already begun to talk about Munster. We'd lost one final, and we didn't want to feel like that a second time.

I was pretty sore when I woke up the next morning, so I went in to Riverview for a quick swim. It had been a constant fight with my right hip. I can't even begin to explain some of the evenings, and especially the nights, I'd had with this. Breaking down crying with pain. Breaking down in front of Sarah after coming home from training. For two years this hip had been the bane of my life. It had put me in bad form with everyone. All I wanted to do was train and play to the best of my ability, and I couldn't.

Matters came to a head the week after that defeat in the Champions Cup final. I'd taken a kick, or stamp, on my right calf during the game. It had made my hip very angry. The resulting haematoma in my calf meant everything was going through my hip and glute.

On the Monday, I began doing what I usually do at the start of a week between games. I got my hip moving and had a bit of physio. But I couldn't even manage the unit sessions with the forwards on the Monday or Tuesday, never mind the full squad run.

On the Tuesday, I walked into UCD with a limp. It was purely because of my hip. There was nothing else wrong

1

with me. That morning our rehab physio, Fearghal Kerin, who worked with me every single morning, looked at me and shook his head.

I said to him: 'Yeah, I know. This isn't good today at all.'

He said: 'They're giving you until Thursday to get yourself right. Hopefully, you'll be good.'

Later that morning Leo said to me: 'What do you want to do?'

'I want to give it until Thursday.'

'Grand,' he said. 'A1. Whatever you want to do.'

I desperately wanted to play against Munster in the League semi-final. It would be my last game for Leinster at the RDS, potentially my last game in Ireland. This would be my final moment in the jersey I loved and I wanted to live it.

After the pool on the Tuesday, I did a stretch. That evening at home I used a foam roller and had a massage machine on me for a few hours.

I stayed at home on Wednesday, repeating that process with the massage machine. I loosened myself out and was pain-free for the day.

Pain kept me awake most nights, and that was worrying me because it meant I wasn't recovering well. I'd often be awake for two hours or more in the middle of the night. I'd maybe prop two pillows under my knee, which would bend my knee up a little and ease the pain. Then I might drift off. Sometimes I'd sleep on my back, sometimes on my side with my knees bent to relieve the pain.

In recent years, I'd set the alarm on my phone for 6.50am because I was always in the Leinster training centre in UCD for 7.30am to work with Fearghal. My body clock usually woke me up about five minutes before the alarm went off anyway. Some mornings I'd wake up at 6.45am in a state of panic, convinced I'd slept through the alarm.

Waking up and getting out of bed, I usually knew straight away what kind of day it was going to be. I'd invariably have an ache. It just depended how bad it was. Some mornings it was worse than others. Or it could get worse when I started walking around.

On the Thursday morning before the Munster game, it was a very mild ache. Barely there, but there all the same. At least I felt a good deal better than I had on the previous three mornings.

I went to UCD for 7.30am and did my rehab with Fearghal for about forty-five minutes. Fearghal knew me as well as I knew myself at that stage, and he knew how to deal with me.

We got to work. I didn't feel too good doing the single-leg bridges to get my glutes and hips switched on. They were making my hip angry. I felt weak. So we stopped them and did stretches and exercises that didn't make it angry. After that, I took my painkillers. We had meetings for a couple of hours, and then went out onto the training pitch. I didn't feel too bad warming up, although the hip was biting at me every now and again.

We started with twenty minutes of unstructured stuff, a game of Attack and 'D' in which we alternated between the two. With Munster coming in three days' time, training was intense. It was fast, like a game.

I was in 'D' for the first few minutes and turned quickly to tackle someone, but just couldn't run. I pulled up. I was going to pull out of the session, but then I reasoned with myself, you're only in the session a couple of minutes. This might warm up again. That was often the case. It could take fifteen minutes of movement, but as I'd get into the session and get up to speed, I'd generally be okay. The heat and the adrenalin would loosen it up.

About four minutes later one of the backs, I think it was Ringer, made a half-break and I was tracking him. Both of us were sprinting and as he turned back inside me, I went to turn as well, and my whole right leg went from under me.

I thought, what the fuck was that?

The pain fired up into my groin. In fact, it felt like someone had shot me. I was only on the ground for about five seconds, but then it became a constant, hard ache. I had no power in my right leg.

I was on the side of the pitch where there were no coaches, or players. The only person nearby was Johnny. I limped off on the opposite side of the pitch, away from the other players who were carrying knocks from the Saracens game and the staff. I didn't want to be near anybody else. Max Deegan swapped in for me straight away.

I knew it then. I knew that I was fucked. I knew that I wasn't in with a shout for Saturday, and that I wouldn't be involved for the final in Glasgow the following week if we beat Munster. I knew that there was only one way left to deal with this: an operation. I was pretty upset. There were tears streaming down my face.

I didn't want to go over to the rest of them. I wanted to be on my own until I'd got myself together. Johnny was being managed after picking up a knock in the European final, coming in and out of training. He walked around the pitch and could see I was upset. He said to me: 'If it's not right, it's not right. Don't be the hero. Don't make it worse. It's not worth destroying yourself.'

I went back to the other side of the pitch and up to Leo.

'It's not right.' That was all I said to him. I could see he knew. We didn't need to talk.

Walking off the field, various thoughts and emotions flooded through me. I immediately thought of London Irish. I had signed to join them after the World Cup. Now I was going to have to tell them that I was retiring, which I didn't want to do. I thought of the World Cup being gone, even though I desperately wanted to make amends for what had happened in 2015. And I thought of my Ireland career being over. My Leinster career was done too, and not the way I wanted it to be done.

I came home to Dundrum. Sarah was coming back up to Dublin later that night. I rang her and said: 'This has to stop. I can't keep fighting this battle. Mentally, it's been wearing me out for a year and a half.'

The next day, I went back to UCD and called in to Leo's office.

Leo had been a little emotional around me in the last few months. My move to London Irish, and the way my time at Leinster had come to an end, had clearly got to him. I could see that it was bugging him. He could also see that I was trying everything to be ready to play. But I'd say he could also see how it wasn't working, not to the level required anyway.

I said to him: 'I'm going to have to see what the next option is.'

He said: 'Look, it's not the way I wanted you to go out either.'

I love Leo. He was one of my favourite players to play with. An exceptional captain. I learned a hell of a lot from him. A serious coach. Highly knowledgeable. Great with people. I always had an excellent relationship with him. What you see is what you get with Leo. He can be blunt, but that's the way he is, and the way he played. Hard and straight. He probably never got the recognition he fully deserved as a player, but he was phenomenal.

There wasn't much else to be said. I didn't want to get into it all again. So much had pulled at me emotionally in the last few months, more than at any other time in my career. I was drained.

On the following Monday and again on Wednesday I Skyped with Professor Damian Griffin, the orthopaedic surgeon who had done my two previous hip operations. I told him everything that had happened to me since the last operation. All the symptoms and incidents I could recall. The whole story.

He told me I had two options left. I could have the 'resurface', the operation the tennis player Andy Murray had undergone, and see if I could still play afterwards. Or else I could have a full hip replacement and retire from rugby.

'I'm not finishing,' I said.

He asked me why not.

'I haven't done what I wanted to do in the last two years. I'm feeling great apart from my hip. I've played very little rugby and I still have goals, and I still have a lot to achieve in rugby. I personally just can't go out like this. I need to go out somewhat on my own terms. This might break me but, if it does, so be it. Then it's broken me. But at least I can then say I fired everything at it.'

That's what I said to him: 'I want to fire every single thing at this.'

Once we had made a plan to go ahead with it, I contacted London Irish and the IRFU. I met with Joe Schmidt in the Ballsbridge Hotel for a coffee on the Thursday before the Pro14 final and told him the plan. I'd say he knew it was coming.

'I can't even train the way I want to train, never mind play the way I want to play,' I told him. 'I'm way off where I know I can be. I'm just in complete pain. The faster I'm running, the better I am, but stopping and getting going again is a problem. Getting up off the ground is terrible. I can't get up off the ground quickly.'

Joe's thinking was that I should put rugby aside, that being able to run around with kids in ten years' time was the most important consideration. He wasn't trying to persuade me to have the full hip replacement and pack in rugby. 'But rugby is not the most important thing here,' he told me. 'You are.'

I hadn't been involved as much with Ireland in recent years, but I'd known Joe for over ten years and he'd taught me so much. He was the most influential coach in my career. I hadn't had a good chat with him in some time. It was nice to have a catch-up and a conversation about things other than rugby. I'd say it was only the second time we'd had a chat like that. We did talk rugby too, though, and I had a bit of a laugh with him.

'I suppose I wouldn't have been on the fecking World Cup squad anyway, the way I'm playing?'

He hummed and hawed. He didn't want to admit that to me, but it might well have been the reality. I think I would have made the training squad all right, but as for the thirty-one-man World Cup squad, I don't know.

I was pissed off that I wouldn't even have the opportunity to find out, but it was also a relief to know that I'd made the decision and that, more than likely, I was going to be pain-free and possibly, maybe, have at least a shot at getting back to being myself.

If I get this right, I think I can get back to myself again. I haven't put too many miles on the clock in the last two years.

I've started just nineteen games for Leinster and Ireland since the Lions tour, and another four appearances off the bench. That's twenty-three games in two seasons.

Of course, I think long and hard about the consequences of the operation going wrong. If it goes bad, it could be very bad, and how would I manage that? The worst-case scenario is that the hip breaks and I have to undergo a full hip replacement. In other words, go through all that again. That's a difficult thought to wrap my head around.

I think about retiring. It would be done then. No more battling, no more rehab. But I know I'd never be happy leaving the game when I could have tried something, when I hadn't fired everything at it.

That's the biggest motivation for putting myself through this at the age of thirty-two. If I can get back to myself and show people that I still have what they've seen before, I'll be happy, because I know that no one has seen the real me for almost two years.

1. Beginnings

I was born on St Valentine's Day in 1987, in the Coombe Hospital in Dublin. I'm the third of five children, after Stephen and Caroline, and then William and Alexandra came after me. We grew up on the family farm in Ardristan, just outside Tullow in County Carlow, on a road known as the Bog Lane. We own a bog there, as do two neighbours. Hence the name.

Dad played Gaelic football with Grange and Tullow as well as with the Fighting Cocks in Rathoe, which is my intermediate club, and played rugby with Tullow. There are junior, intermediate and senior adult Gaelic football teams where I'm from. The Fighting Cocks is the club for my area, and has been in the intermediate championship for as long as I can remember, except for one season in the senior championship a few years ago. Then they came straight back down. But, for the size of the parish, they're batting well above average.

Dad was a full-back in the football and a number 8 in rugby. He wasn't really a first-team player, more of a social rugby player. He played mostly for the Seconds and a bit of Firsts, and then moved to prop in his later playing days.

I only remember watching him play once. I'd say I was eight or nine at the time. I'd run around with a ball, but I hadn't actually played a game of rugby by then. It was one of his last games. The game was in Tullow, against Old Wesley from Dublin, and I was standing on the sideline with

William. Dad was tighthead and packing down at a scrum. The Wesley flanker punched him in the face and split him – and I mean split him, from ear to ear.

'Cas' was Dad's nickname. Someone said to Mam: 'Cas has gone off.'

Mam said: 'I knew he shouldn't have been playing. He's gone too old for that now.'

Now, my father would have been known for fighting and being able to handle himself. And I remember how mad he was that day. There were ten lads trying to get him off the field. He was going to kill yer man from Old Wesley. Instead, he had to go to hospital to get stitched up. He was cut deep to the bone and the blood spewed out. I went home crying.

The story went that Dad came back to the club that night, but the Old Wesley team had left. The following weekend, Dad and one of the other lads on the team went to Dublin. He was still that thick over it. Luckily for yer man, Daddy couldn't find him. But Dad would be an awful man for holding a grudge.

The farm was small, and with the sand quarry rented out there was little to do. Still to this day, Dad would be of the view that the cows should calve out. He'd be old school that way. For him, it was a priority to be working the whole time, more often on sites than on the farm.

He worked in Dublin and locally, including a long stint at Clonegal Castle, on the Wexford/Carlow border. It's a big tourist attraction now. They refurbished every room inside and landscaped the external face of the castle outside. Every year they go at something else down there, to improve it. There's been a phenomenal amount of work done over many years, and I think it's reached the point where there's not much more they can really do.

While he was working, Mam had her hands full, rearing the five of us. When I was about twelve or thirteen, she started doing the books in an agri store in town to make ends meet and help pay the bills. She did that until about six years ago, when she had to stop due to a back problem.

How would I describe my mam? She was very good to us, but if she lost her temper your pants would be coming down and you'd be getting a belt of the wooden spoon. Then again, we knew that at the time, so we probably deserved it. We used to get the 'sally swootch' as well. It was a sally plant, a really thin, bendy stick, and I remember getting a few flakes of that all right over the course of my childhood. We all got it. If you misbehaved really badly, you got a belt of the stick, and that was usually more as a result of fighting than anything else.

Mam is a very caring person. She was probably frustrated that she wasn't able to provide everything she wanted for us because of finances. She was devoted to us and certainly did everything possible for us all. And I'll always be grateful to her for that.

Dad is a real man's man. He'd be a Jack the Lad and up to devilment when he'd be out. He'd work hard during the week and he'd love his weekends. Friday and Saturday would be his nights out. Mam doesn't drink much. Never has. So it was a slightly weird dynamic. He was out a good bit and she wasn't. And I'd say that was frustrating for Mam, too.

Dad's half-brother Billy lives in Ashbourne, County Meath, and I used to visit him regularly. Billy kept Alsatians and I loved helping out with them. Pretty much as soon as I was able to walk, I was out hunting and shooting with Dad. He'd shoot rabbits and we'd have rabbit stew once a week. I started school at the age of four and I started hunting with Dad around the same time, heading out in the jeep. A neighbour, Raymond Kane, took me under his wing. On holidays, and even during school days, I'd call in to Raymond and his wife, Marie, almost every day, and I still go shooting with him every now and again.

Some of my best childhood memories are of going hunting. I've always loved being out in the open air, and I still do because it relaxes me. I probably didn't realize back then that it relaxed me, but looking back now I was getting away from all the madness in the house and I enjoyed being on my own, or at any rate with someone else who was doing exactly the same thing. When you're hunting, you don't do that much talking. It was quality time with my dad as well. I remember going to a few local clay shoots with him and Stephen and Caroline. Caroline was a very good shot, but she didn't stay with it.

There was permission to hunt agreed between all the neighbours. There were 2,000 or 3,000 acres which were owned by just three or four people, and there were several of us into hunting. We'd mostly hunt rabbits, a few pigeons maybe, and pheasants when it was pheasant season. Pretty much everything would be cooked.

Our local village, Rathoe, lies between Tullow and Ballon. Rathoe hasn't changed much over the years. Today there is just a shop, a church, a crèche and a school. It used to have a post office as well, but that's been moved to Ballon. There isn't even a pub.

Scoil Phádraig Rathoe National School was my school from the age of four to twelve. The bus passed by our house each morning, but it would have to do a loop and had so many stops it could take forty-five minutes to reach the school, whereas I could cycle there in twenty minutes. In the middle of winter, though, I'd take the bus.

It was a lovely school. The teachers were nice, but strict. My first classroom was at the front, to the left of the main door. It was Mrs Maher's class for junior infants. Sadly, she's dead now. She was an old-school type of teacher – very stern, but caring, too. She'd give you a rap on the knuckles if you needed manners, but she praised us as well, and would reward us by dipping into her box of penny sweets, or *milseáin*, in the top drawer of her desk. When she walked out of the room, we'd rob them continually.

She was one of only three teachers in the school when I was there, and there were no more than nine in my class and no more than fifty kids in total. The school has doubled in size since then, with extensions to the side and back, and there are over 175 pupils there now.

As well as Mrs Maher, there was Mr Folan, who taught third and fourth classes, while fifth and sixth were taught by Mr Dowdall.

I enjoyed the fun factor in school more so than studies. We had a sports hall and a half-sized outdoor pitch, which was forty yards wide, and I couldn't wait to get out at break-time to have a run-around or play with a ball. We had one basketball net as well.

At the end of each school year we had our sports day. The main race was ten laps around the pitch, and I remember that when I was in fifth class I was sure I was going to win it. You had to go through the goalposts on the last loop and then run straight up the middle of the pitch to finish between the opposite posts. I hared off, but I turned into the middle of the pitch on the ninth lap – a lap too early! I was about forty yards clear, and I'd say I was forty yards up the pitch when I heard one of the teachers shouting at me to go back. One of the girls in the class took over the lead and won the race. I was thick about it afterwards. The following year, my last at Rathoe National School, I made sure I counted to ten correctly and won the race. Even back then, I was very, very competitive.

One day a few of us were out at the backyard, behind the oil tanker, playing with a ball. One of the other boys was Seamus O'Reilly, who used to be a fecker, and one day I decided, I'm not going to stand for this abuse. We had a full-on fight, throwing punches. It was a good old row. We went back inside to Mr Folan's class and got an awful grilling. I'd say we were eight or nine. Seamus is actually a lovely fella and is an engineer now. He's one of the best Massey Ferguson mechanics in the whole country. He could strip down a tractor with his eyes closed and put it back together.

My last primary-school teacher, Mr Dowdall, absolutely loved football and soccer. He had us practising in a tiny area at the back and gave us a good grounding in basic skills – kicking, catching and passing. We used to have shooting tournaments as well. We had timber goalposts, but no nets, so if a ball went across the road, Mr Folan would have to fetch it.

Once, and only once, when I was in sixth class, I jumped the wall and mitched from school. I went to the shop to buy some sweets. You could be seen from anywhere, so I sat in the ditch behind the church for the whole day. I was too afraid to do anything else because I knew that if Mam found out, I'd get a belt of the wooden spoon or the sally swootch.

I never took my education seriously, and I wasn't pushed

at home to do my homework or do well in exams. Even though Mam and Dad would say, 'Go and study now', they were probably a bit too relaxed about that. We were largely left to our own devices, which was nice, although if I have kids, they'll do their studies and that will be the end of the matter.

The minute I would get home from school, all I wanted to do was go out and work on the farm, the whole way through National School, and then I'd go training, or I might go shooting. Whatever the season, I'd be out there with Dad. We had sheep at that time, so we could have been lambing ewes or there could have been something to do with the cows and calves. Or it could have been that there was actually very little to be done, but when school ended I was still thinking, great, I'm going home now, to work, and that was the whole way through school.

From the age of twelve, in sixth class, I'd even take the odd Tuesday off school altogether. I'd say to Mam and Dad, 'Can I go in and work on the mart?' Tuesday would be sheep day, and I got a good bit of work out of that as well. After the mart, lads would bring me with them to load up or pen sheep on their own farms, and they'd throw you a tenner or twenty. Sometimes I'd give Mam some of my pay cheque as it would help with bills at home.

2. GAA roots

My first sport was Gaelic football. Next was soccer. Soon enough I was playing everything, a bit of hurling and rugby too, but Gaelic football came first. Ballon GAA was my juvenile club, and Burrin Celtic in Ballon was my soccer club. It wasn't until the Community Games, when I was on the Ballon/Rathoe under-11s, that rugby kicked off.

Myself and my buddy James Foley, as well as the Nolan twins, Padraig and Eoin, started playing football at under-8s with Ballon GFC. They all went to Ballon National School, so it was through football that I first met them and became good friends with them.

Padraig and Eoin grew up on a dairy farm in Carrigslaney, and were born two days before me. My mam and their mum, Mary, were three hospital beds down from each other in the Coombe. The Nolans are actually related to us in some way. James, like his dad, is a staunch Kilbride man, to his very core. But his address is Connaberry, Ballon, where my grand-dad Thomas lives, and Ballon and Kilbride hate each other.

Thomas Murphy was another of my good friends growing up who played with Ballon. We used to do everything together and stay over in each other's houses regularly.

The Ballon pitch was the first I ever stood on, in any sport. It was a good pitch, although it could get a little wet along one side. There were always two little dugouts, which are still there today. I played with an oversized pair of gloves, but at that stage it was just a bit of craic. Joe Whelan and Pat Doyle were our first coaches, and Padraig and Eoin's father, Pat Nolan, was also involved in the under-10s and under-12s. Joe had a hearing aid and when he thought he was talking to us, he was actually roaring. He's also a very good singer and sings in the choir in Ballon. Pat Doyle was an army officer and a strong-willed man. He liked to push us. He was old school. He'd have us running laps around the pitch at the start of training and I can still vividly hear him shouting: 'Lift your feet, they will fall themselves.' Another of his favourites was: 'Take your points, the goals will come.' That's because lads would always be trying to score goals, six-yard-box fever, and drive it wide.

I loved playing Gaelic football, and I thought I was quite good at it from a young age. I was able to read where the ball was going to go next, and I was fit and athletic as well. From around the age of eight, I was well able to run and I was a little stronger than most lads. That was probably because I was hauling buckets of water around the farm. I'd have a bucket in each hand for several hours some days.

The juvenile team of Ballon/Rathoe, which is now called St Martin's, was made up of players from Ballon, Kilbride and the Fighting Cocks. Myself and James Foley played together all the way up to minors with Ballon/Rathoe. Most of the time we barely had fifteen players, which was fine. It meant we all played every minute. We rarely had subs, but they were good players and that team loved winning. We trained twice a week and the matches were on evenings during the week, usually around 7pm. They were twenty-five minutes each way up to under-14s, when they became thirty minutes each way. Mam, and then Caroline, brought me to virtually every training session and match.

The first tournament I remember playing in was the

under-9 Éire Óg tournament, which we won. That was the start of it. I played in midfield, I loved catching high balls, toeing it the length of the field and scoring points. Padraig and Eoin's dad, Pat Nolan, remembers me playing as an eight-year-old for the under-12s in a match in Tullow, at right half-back, with my sleeves rolled up. He says he asked someone on the sideline who I was.

'That's Seán O'Brien from Bog Lane.'

He said: 'Bejaysus, that lad is going to be a quare one.'

We also won the under-10 Maurice Nolan tournament in Carlow, when we beat what was regarded as the Éire Óg dream team. I remember Pat Doyle telling me before the match not to kill myself by toeing the ball the length of the field, as I had been doing, but to kick it towards Padraig. I did this for the first half, and at half-time we were behind by a point or two, but we were going grand. Mr Doyle told us to keep going and we'd win this match. As we walked back out for the second half, Padraig's dad, Pat Nolan, recalls me saying to him: 'I completely understand what Mr Doyle is saying, but if the field opens up in front of me, I'm going to go for it.'

'By all means, Seán. If the field opens up, put the head down,' said Mr Nolan.

The field did open up with about ten minutes to go and I did put the head down. Although I couldn't have hit my shot any harder, somehow the keeper got his hand to the ball, but Mark Doyle tipped the rebound into the net and we won.

Our first year as under-12s was our weak year, but the following year we won the under-12 A, beating Michael Davitts in the final. We had a fierce rivalry with Michael Davitts all the way up, taking lumps out of each other.

In the under-14s, we lost in the semi-finals against Éire Óg in the first year, and in the second we reached the under-14 final against Michael Davitts. I played centre-forward and scored an important goal with about fifteen minutes left, and we won.

By that stage, I was attending secondary school at Tullow Community School. The school has always had two football pitches and two soccer pitches, and it has a mini Astroturf pitch now, but otherwise everything else is the same.

There were around 750 kids, boys and girls, at the school when I was there. It was a good school, the only secondary school in Tullow, and the pupils came from all over the county and beyond. When I was there, the school had thirty-five classrooms in total. We also had a gym, with four basketball courts, and that was where we sat our exams.

Tullow CS was a very sporty school, which was just as well because if I wasn't doing farm work or shooting, I was playing sports. At that stage, from around under-14s, the games were starting to become physical, but that suited me fine.

In our second year at under-16s with Ballon, with our good team, we won all seven matches in the round-robin part of the championship with at least two goals to spare, including wins against Michael Davitts and Éire Óg. We were on fire. I played mostly at full-back.

But then in the semi-finals, against Rathvilly, Jimmy O'Brien was harshly sent off, with two yellow cards. The club appealed successfully and he played with us in the under-16 County Carlow final against Éire Óg.

The final was tough. Jimmy hardly got a kick, Padraig missed a penalty and we conceded too many goals. Éire Óg caught us on the hop that day. But they were a good team.

The game was played in Dr Cullen Park, the county grounds in Carlow, and it made the front page of the *Irish*

Independent – for the wrong reasons, unfortunately. This was due to a huge row on the pitch, with supporters of both teams joining in from the stand and the sidelines.

Padraig had a bit of a beef with one of the Éire Óg backs, who had been giving him verbals and digs. A few seconds after the full-time whistle, Padraig went through with his hit on yer man after he caught the ball. He never saw Padraig coming.

Padraig turned and walked over to the referee, Pat Keogh, and shook his hand. As he did that, yer man started unloading punches left, right and centre at Padraig in front of the ref.

I was the first in, all the way from full-back. I lost the head completely. Punches were being fired everywhere. All hell broke loose. I'd say almost all the thirty players and at least ten people from the sideline quickly became involved, with others gradually joining in.

A few lads came running at me and I started to unload! I'm not sure I caught any of them really, although it did make them back off. An ould lad from Éire Óg grabbed me to pull me out of it, but he pulled me out of it fairly aggressively and my father saw this. Then we were trying to calm down Daddy because he was going to take the head off yer man. It all got a bit heated and it was fortunate that no one was badly hurt.

When the dust settled, the awards ceremony was held. I was called up to accept the Man of the Match award, with what was left of my ripped jersey, which wasn't much, hanging off me. At the disciplinary hearing that followed, they threatened to take back the Man of the Match trophy because I'd been sent off after the final whistle.

On balance, I'd say there is more fighting in under-age Gaelic football than in rugby. I was more of a protector than an enforcer. I'd never start a row, but I'd always have the lads' back if something did kick off. I didn't ask any questions, I just bailed in.

It's not a characteristic I like having. I've done the same at training sessions in rugby. I've struck first and then asked questions or said sorry later. The switch would go, the red mist would descend, and that would be it.

Back in my Tullow days with rugby, I came up against country lads more often. With Gaelic football in Carlow, you were coming up more against town lads and they'd be trying to give you banter, calling you a 'bogger' or whatever. That's what most of the rows were caused by, lads abusing each other, or sledging. Town lads were usually trying to get a little dig at you, and we didn't take too kindly to that.

More often than not, town lads weren't able for us either. We were definitely hardier. At Ballon/Rathoe, we were a country team, whereas a town team would be anything in Carlow town, like Éire Óg, Bagenalstown, Hacketstown. Very few of them would be out doing farm work, whereas that's what the majority of our team did.

At under-16 level we all went on to play with St Patrick's Tullow, and in 2003 we won the Leinster (under-16) Junior Championship. We played Gorey in the first round and beat them convincingly. They couldn't believe it. They thought they were going to walk Leinster. Then we beat Baltinglass and Maynooth to reach the final, where we played Ferbane on a lovely spring day in Mountmellick. They were a right good team, but we beat them by three points.

Even though I was only sixteen, I was also full-back on the Tullow Community School's senior team, so there was plenty of Gaelic football to keep me occupied.

Two years later, Ballon would lose the minor-county final

at Dr Cullen Park against Rathvilly. We might have had a better chance if I hadn't played a rugby match for the Leinster Youths the day before, against Munster in Musgrave Park.

I had started playing mini rugby with Tullow from the age of eleven on Sundays, and the football was on Saturday. While in soccer, I played for Burrin Celtic in Ballon. I was mostly a centre-half, although one year I played up front for Carlow in the Kennedy Cup in Limerick. And I scored two goals in three games.

But Gaelic football always came first. The Ballon/Rathoe community has two clubs, Ballon and the Fighting Cocks, which is five miles down the road in Rathoe. There's also Kilbride, where my sister Caroline and her family live, which is another four miles down the road. So within three parishes there are three football clubs, and there's also Tullow and Grange.

I started out playing juvenile football with Ballon when I was nine, because there was no juvenile team in the Fighting Cocks or Kilbride. From under-9s to under-16s all the lads played together with Ballon, before we were divided into our local clubs when we got to Minor level. Even though my parish, and hence my club, was the Fighting Cocks, I started to train with James, Eoin and Padraig in Kilbride, and I could have ended up playing with them.

But one day I arrived home from work or school, I can't remember which, and there were three men from the Fighting Cocks sitting in the kitchen at home. Austin Donoghue and John McDonald, both of whom have since passed away, and Mick Byrne were talking to my father. I knew right well what was going on. They must have got wind that I was training with the boys in Kilbride and they were adamant that I would sign for the Cocks.

My first contract!

Although myself, James, Padraig and Eoin are all very close, when it comes to football you play for your parish, and where your family played. So, like Dad and my older brother, Stephen, me and my brother William played in the Inter-mediate Championship for the Fighting Cocks, where I'm still a member.

The ground is beside the Fighting Cocks pub, which is also known as Radfords. Two weeks after the three men were in the kitchen when I came home, I played my first match for the Cocks against Grange, another local team. I was seventeen years old. I'd say I played no more than ten or twelve games for them, but one day stands out.

We were playing a practice game against Railyard, a team from Kilkenny, and they were filthy! William was playing half-back and I was playing full-back. The fella I was mark-ing was pucking at me the whole game. I did nothing about it. I just laughed at it. He roamed around and if a full-forward was going way out, I'd let him go.

Anyway, this ball broke between himself and William, who got to it first and fisted it on. But yer man absolutely destroyed him with a late challenge that was actually a full-on punch. He left William on the ground and walked away sniggering, obviously not knowing he was my brother.

I said to him: 'What's so funny with you?'

He goes: 'Ah, I got yer man there.'

I said: 'You did, yeah.'

Bang. I caught him square between his two eyes and dropped him like a heap on the ground.

The referee came over and said: 'What's after happening here?'

I said: 'I don't know. I think he just fell over.'

But the ref took out his book and sent me off anyway.

'Off you go,' he said. 'This is a friendly game. You can't be doing stuff like that.'

Yer man was still on the ground. He wasn't in a good way. Going past him I said: 'Now who's laughing, you little fuckin' bollix, ye?'

As I was walking off, I looked back and saw that William was following me.

'What did you get sent off for?'

'Ah, I abused the shite out of the referee,' he said.

Things began to happen for me in rugby soon after that, and I was only able to manage a game or two with the Cocks every year. But there are great lads driving the club on and there's a good group of young players there now. For the size of the parish, they're still batting above average. They're like any small GAA club. There's a real community spirit around there and good people involved in it. I'm not as involved as I'd like to be. I've given more to the Tullow Rugby Club, but I've taken the odd training session with Cocks, as I have with Kilbride, and I give the Carlow football team a talk every now and then. Coming from the county is more important than what sport you play. There's still a sign outside the Fighting Cocks ground saying: 'Best of luck Seán from the Fighting Cocks GFC – World Cup 2015.'

Mad.

There's always been serious support back home at the time of Heineken Cup finals or World Cups. Every second or third house would have Leinster or Irish flags flying, or have signs made up. The GAA clubs really got behind me in 2011 and 2015.

In football, like Dad, I played full-back. Sometimes I was moved to midfield, but mostly I played full-back. I'd also usually hold my own with any kind of high ball that came in, and I loved going up for them. We played in loads of blitzes and *féiles* around Carlow. A young lad running around the pitch and loving life. Great days and, yes, bad days too. Even at a very early age, I quickly began to hate losing.

Some of the great days were with my school, Tullow Community School. The pitch is quite exposed and training there in the winter months was tough. It could get very sodden. Paddy Quirke, our trainer, was old school. Even wearing wellies when he trained us, he could still kick points from the corner flag. He was probably one of the best players ever to play for the county and was a Carlow all-star at both hurling and football. He was 6 foot 3 inches and hard as nails, but there was no dirt in him. He also taught engineering at the school. He was a nice man, one of those teachers you actually wanted to do a bit of homework for.

The school had reached a few All-Ireland Senior schools football finals before, and had won it in 1992. In 2003 we reached the Junior final after we beat Ferbane in the Leinster decider by two points. That put us into the serious stuff, against good teams. We beat Coachford, from Cork, in Carrick-on-Suir in the semi-finals, but we lost the All-Ireland Junior schools football final against St Ciaran's HS Ballygawley, in Tyrone, who were managed at the time by Mickey Harte. They were also the defending champions, and some fella who went on to play for Tyrone ran the show that day in midfield.

I started that match at full-back, Padraig was full-forward, Eoin was corner-forward and James was on the bench that day. Harte came into our dressing-room after the game and said: 'You have a star in the making in your full-back'.

Although I only turned sixteen that February, I was also on the senior panel in 2003, but Mr Quirke wouldn't play me.

I thought I was worth my place in the backline that day, and I remember being quite annoyed about it, but, then again, I was very young.

After my school years ended, I played a few sneaky games with the Fighting Cocks until I was twenty-one. In 2007 I came back from the Leinster Academy to play a first-round county championship game against Kilbride in Dr Cullen Park. There was a lot of talk around home that week about how the Fighting Cocks would have to contain a fella called Paddy Waters, whom I knew pretty well. He and his brother Joe were playing for Kilbride, with Paddy at full-forward.

My old friend James was also playing for Kilbride, and he was getting on to me in the days before the game. 'Oh, we've the job for you now if you do play,' he kept telling me.

They weren't sure whether I was going to be playing or not, because by rights I shouldn't have been. But I rocked up at full-back and Paddy Waters didn't get a kick of the ball all day. I couldn't understand what they were at, but they kept kicking high ball after high ball in to him. He's a big lump of a man, and I sailed over him, catching balls and running up the field. We won, and the Kilbride boys were pretty sick afterwards, especially James. I laughed my head off at him.

'Where's your tactics gone now?' I said to him. 'What was that job you had for me?'

I think my last competitive game for the Fighting Cocks was in the second round that year. I played in another practice game for them against Kilbride one day, just to keep up my fitness. James tried to do me. He came across me one time with his elbow. He was a fierce man for doing that. He missed the bridge of my nose by a whisker. I could feel the air coming across my face. I fucked the ball away and said to him: 'If you ever do that again, I'm gonna kill ye.' Jim, his father, started laughing on the sideline, and it was funny, but I was genuinely furious. James could have done a serious number on me. You couldn't meet two nicer men off the football field than Jim and James, but on it they're crazy.

If I hadn't become a professional rugby player, I'm sure I'd have played Gaelic football, and once I finish my rugby, I'll play a bit of junior football if I can, just for the craic, as well as playing a season with Tullow.

Compared to football, in hurling I was a bit of a hacker. My club, Ballon, didn't play hurling. In fact, there are only four senior hurling clubs in the whole of Carlow. As St Patrick's Tullow was one of them, that's where I played. I was basically put in there to win the ball because I was relatively big and strong. I wasn't great at hurling, but I enjoyed it. It's a great game to play and a savage game to watch.

To be good at hurling you have to be playing from a young age. When I first picked up a hurl, I held it with a golfer's grip and I had fierce difficulty in striking the sliotar on the run. I could catch it, I could scoop it up, I could run with it on my hurl, but striking it was when the problems arose for me.

We were playing everything at this stage – football, rugby, basketball, soccer and hurling. Too many sports really. I eventually stopped playing soccer when I was fifteen. I hated the amount of mouthing that went on, even at that level. I wasn't one for giving out, or mouthing, even on a Gaelic football field. But soccer was different gravy. It really bugged me. The referees were on the receiving end of continuous abuse, not only from the kids and the coaches but from the parents on the sidelines as well. I'd look over at the sidelines and shout: 'Will you ever leave us to it! Let us play. Don't be shouting and roaring!' It wasn't too bad at Burrin Celtic, but it could be terrible with some of the opposing teams.

As well as playing four sports, I was also working a lot. At the Tuesday mart I got to know a farmer by the name of David Leybourne. He said to me: 'If you want to work after school, come up to me', so I went up there after school to earn a few quid.

In first and second year at Tullow CS, I used to go into the Tara Arms, beside the cottage where I now live, or Flynn's shop for lunch. Chicken fillet rolls, with spicy wedges and red sauce. I'd also stop the odd time in the Pit Stop, a take-away in the village, for a chip butty. Scandalous when I think of it now. I put on way too much weight.

Later on, I stopped eating rubbish food out of the shop at lunchtime. If you look out from the back of Tullow CS, there's a lane leading to a fence and the gap in the fence is still there now. The first house you come to is my god-parents', Seanie and Bernie Fleming, and I used to have my lunch there most days.

After school, I'd go back there to get changed and then I'd walk to David Leybourne's to work on his farm, which you can also see from the back of the school. I'd work there until evening. That probably hindered my education, but I loved working. They had hundreds of ewes and I used to feed all the sheep. As there were no troughs in any of the sheds, we'd draw buckets of water to them as well. I hauled buckets of water, one on each arm, across the yard. That job alone could take an hour and a half. But it meant I was doing weights before I was doing proper weights, so when it came to rugby, I had farmer's strength rather than gym strength. I was also bedding and feeding cattle. David's mother and father would usually feed me after we were finished working, and then I'd go home, before going to training at 7.30pm.

There was training most nights: Gaelic football or hurling

on Mondays, rugby on Tuesdays, soccer on Wednesdays, football or hurling on Thursdays and rugby again on Fridays. Then it was pure carnage at the weekend. I could be going from a football game to a rugby game or vice versa, and I'd squeeze in a soccer game as well or, if the soccer clashed with one of the others, I'd skip it to play the football or rugby. Generally, rugby was on a Sunday. And I also played basketball between the ages of eleven and thirteen, for Carlow. I played squash as well.

Something had to give. And that's exactly what my body did. I actually ended up in Kilkenny hospital for a night. I was at home on a Thursday or Friday, and I'd done too much. I felt weak and dizzy and I was getting sick. Mam took me to hospital. I was kept in overnight and the doctor who examined me said I was just run-down.

I didn't play anything that weekend. The following week I was back at it, though, and my life remained a juggling act between sports and work and a bit of school. We had a hurling match against Bagenalstown one day, but with the bus ready to pull out from the club car park there was no sign of me. The Nolans drove up to the Leybournes', where I was working on the farm. I asked Mr Leybourne could I go to play the match. I can't remember if we won or lost, but I know I was sent off for turning my hurl on someone out of frustration or something.

One of our best days in hurling was reaching the under-14 B final against Michael Davitts. I played centre-forward and scored an important goal with about fifteen minutes left, and we won. But I just did a job in hurling, whereas I was smart at football and I loved it. I'd like to have seen how far I could have gone in the inter-county set-up with the football. But you can't have everything in life.

3. Home truths

I think I was twelve or thirteen years old when it became clear that not everything was right at home. Stephen was twenty and had already moved to Jersey two years before. Caroline was eighteen and going out with Willie, who is now her husband, so by then I was usually the oldest child in the house.

Looking back, it's now clearer that my parents were going through a break-up. I didn't understand exactly what was happening, but I could hear the constant arguments, at all hours of the day and night. Sometimes I'd just lie in my bed crying. Other times I'd go to their room or the kitchen, where they had most of their rows, and try to calm them down, to be a peacemaker. Not that the rows between them ever became physically violent. They wouldn't necessarily be shouting or roaring either. But they'd be arguing angrily, and emotions would often run high.

More often than not the rows started after Dad had come home from a night out drinking. Mam doesn't drink really at all, but Dad did like a drink when we were young. He was very sociable and known for his storytelling and being generally good craic. He was probably a bit too sociable and liked drinking a little too much. That was most likely the underlying cause of their problems. Also, my parents were married at nineteen. That was the kind of thing to do back then, but that is just too young, in my opinion. They were still kids themselves, and soon were having five kids and all the pressures, financial and otherwise, that come with rearing a family.

Mam says she did try to talk to me about it, to tell me what was going on, but I don't really remember the full conversation. One of the reasons I'm writing about my parents' break-up is because there are probably loads of kids from my area, and in the country generally, who have gone through or are going through this sort of thing. At the time, I didn't deal with it at all, in part because my parents continued to live in the same house even though they had split up, and to this day they still do. Mam cooks Dad meals in the evening and they have a civil relationship now. They put up with each other, there aren't many arguments, and Dad gives Mam money to pay the bills, while Mam keeps the house tidy.

I don't know when they actually agreed to break up, or even if it was ever said. I don't think my dad is the kind of man to sit down and discuss things through like that. Instead, issues would be brushed over and life would just go on.

So the marriage broke up over a period of time as they continued to live under the same roof. And I lived there too, until I moved to Dublin when I was eighteen, so I had six years of living with it. Maybe that's partly why I kept myself so busy: I worked after school every day before going home. There was also a need to bring more money into the house. All through our school years, some days Dad would have lunch money for you, or half of it, and some days not at all. While everyone else in the class was heading downtown for some lunch, I might have been in the canteen having whatever I could afford. That wasn't very often, I have to stress, but I think money used to be an issue between my parents. Mam would spend her last penny to be generous to someone else. Dad, on the other hand, wanted to have enough for his few pints at the weekend.

Some days my parents would be civilized with each other. Other days they'd be cutting at each other. And on some of those days I would blow up myself.

'Will you two please stop fucking shouting at each other!'

Then that would make me feel bad, a fifteen- or sixteen-year-old young fella talking to his parents like that, because normally I was very well-mannered towards my parents. I never disrespected them, but after listening to the rows for three or four years I became very frustrated with them, especially as the rows were usually over the same small little things.

Of course, their frustration with each other were at different levels, and their tolerance for each other had virtually ended, so anything could set off another argument. My dad is a very stubborn man and my mam, although not quite as stubborn, is certainly more animated. Discussing things together is not their strongest point.

It is probably not mine either. I have a short fuse. There were times, particularly when I came home from Dublin in the early years with Leinster, when I'd go out with friends in Carlow and there were lads wanting to have a cut off me.

'Do you know what?' I'd say to myself, fuck this. And I'd let fly!

The one thing I would say is that I've never started anything. I hope all the lads at home would verify that. I never initiated a fight during that period in my life when there were lads looking for a scrap, and it would take a lot to rile me. But if something kicked off, I'd lose my marbles altogether. Stand back, everybody, because the red mist would consume me and that would be it.

There were two big fights in Carlow when I was eighteen. Apart from a few punches being thrown on a rugby or Gaelic pitch, I'd never been in a fight before then. I thought, why are people having a cut off me here? Neither fight was sparked by me, but it was my fault engaging with that shite. I had to learn to walk away, and that's what I did soon after those fights. And I had to, because if I lost my temper, I could hurt somebody. That was also a very real fear.

I did knock a few guys down and I got hit myself. Lads tried to kick me down the stairs one night. But I was never badly hurt, and I never badly hurt anyone else. It's the same with verbal rows. Over the years, away from the rugby pitch, if someone really annoys me, I've learned that I have to walk away for half an hour to think about it, cool the jets and come back to speak to the person.

At the time, however, I didn't realize how much of an effect my parents' break-up had on me. I was an angry young man until I went to Leinster and began to learn some discipline, but even that came only after a few fights in training. It was only around that time that I began to deal with my parents' breaking up and started to understand it a little better. Until then, I always had this anger towards my parents, and wondered why they hadn't fixed their problems. To be honest, that has never completely left me. It still annoys me now when I see them getting on really well because it only reinforces my feeling that they could have worked things out. Like any kid, I never wanted my parents' marriage to break up. If I ever become a dad, I'd never want that to happen to my kids without trying everything imaginable to sort out whatever problems exist.

In those early years, I was a bit distant from them, and even now my relationship with my parents isn't as close as it should be. I don't call them as much as I ought to, although I love them to bits. It scarred me, and perhaps more than my brothers and sisters, although I'm sure it has affected William and Alex too.

Myself and my older brother, Stephen, are quite similar in our desire to get outside of Tullow or Carlow, whereas William will happily stay in the county for the rest of his life, and Alex is the same. Stephen has worked outside Ireland since he was eighteen, and he met his wife in Jersey. He's also lived in Spain and Gibraltar, and he got away from it all at the right time. He didn't really experience our parents' marriage collapsing. Caroline is similar to me emotionally and would have had to deal with it more than Stephen, but she was older and moving on, both with her own life and with her husband-to-be, Willie.

Of the five kids I was, perhaps, the one who was most aware of their problems at the time. I am also the one who tries to fix everything. I felt an obligation to try and fix their marriage, or at any rate manage it. It was too much responsibility at that stage in my life, and I wasn't able to do it. It made all those years from age twelve onwards tough times, right up until I was twenty-six or twenty-seven. At that stage, I finally came to the conclusion: I can't be dealing with this any more.

I went to see a psychologist in Rathgar. He simply said: 'Get to the root of the problem.' The root of the problem was, of course, my lack of trust in my parents. After all, for any young kid, the two people in the world who you are meant to trust the most are your parents. And as a result of this trust being broken, I didn't have too much trust in myself or in many other people. And I probably still don't trust that many people, not least because of various incidents on nights out that have grown legs compared to what actually happened. I only trust a handful of people.

The psychologist gave me some perspective. I realized that all my anger issues and emotional baggage stemmed from my parents' breaking up, and from the way I bottled it up and kept it to myself. I've learned that it is good to talk to someone else. Don't wait for ten or twelve years.

I look back and wonder what might have happened if Mam or Dad had come to me when I was fourteen or fifteen and asked: 'Are you okay? Do you want to talk to someone about this?' As stubborn as I was at that age, I was also upset, and I might have said: 'I think that would be a good idea.' But no one asked and I said nothing. I put up with all the rows and all the shit at home and soldiered on. That instils fear in a young mind. I never want to be in that situation again.

It's been a source of sadness in my life for a long time, and sport was my release. The great thing about sport is that for an hour, or however long you are playing, it takes your mind off all your problems. And the great thing about rugby, in particular, is that it teaches you about respect. If I had continued playing soccer after sixteen or seventeen, I could have gone the opposite way. I could have been an angry man. But from early on, even in under-age rugby, I knew never to talk back to referees. I was also very respectful toward referees in football too, even though not everybody else always was. It was rugby that taught me how to behave better on the pitch from a young age, and maybe rugby was also best equipped to make me more even-tempered.

4. Tullow

Tullow as a town has changed a fair amount over the years. It would have been a big drinking town when I was growing up. I think there were sixteen pubs in the town at one stage, but there are only eight or nine now. The population has grown from around 7,000 or 8,000 to 10,500 now. It still has a strong community spirit. The football club, soccer club and rugby club all support each other and are all, in turn, supported by the town. We try to support each other the best we can. Everyone knows everyone else.

Lidl, Aldi and Tesco have come to Tullow in recent years, but there are also businesses that have been established a long time. Like the Grain Store, where you buy all your feed for your cattle. Connolly's Red Mills was originally Rothwell Grain & Seeds, whose owner was the father-in-law of David Leybourne, the farmer I worked for. They sold it to Connolly's, a Kilkenny company. Dobbs Oil is where we've always bought the diesel for our tractors and cars. It's a family-run business and they're in Tullow as long as I can remember, delivering oil, gas and petrol to farms and businesses. They're a nice family from Fenagh and they're very good at supporting charities and sports clubs. Siobhan Dobbs, who runs it, is a lovely woman.

The River Slaney runs through Tullow. When it's full, the risk of flooding makes it incredibly dangerous. When I was a young barman in the Bridge House, which is right beside the Slaney, I had to go down to the kitchen and the storeroom to get everything off the ground in times of bad weather because of the risk of flooding. There could be two or three feet of water in the storeroom and kitchen.

Whenever there was a spell of good weather, the young people would assemble around Aghade Bridge. I associate swimming there with the Leaving Cert! There wasn't much else to do. But one Friday evening in summertime, when I was twenty or twenty-one years old, myself, James Foley and his brother Darragh were near Aghade Bridge when a girl jumped into the river and was soon in serious trouble. I had just swum across the river when the boys, who were on the top of the bridge, let a roar at me.

'She's after disappearing!' they shouted.

'Where?' I shouted back. I had heard a splash, but I hadn't seen anyone jumping in.

The Slaney is a very fast-flowing river, with rapids and plenty of stones. I was quite a good swimmer at the time and I chanced going down under the water. The water was so dirty that I couldn't see a thing. Real river water. I felt around with my hands and grabbed a piece of cloth. It was the girl's hoodie. I dragged her to the edge of the bank, where Darragh and James pulled her out of the water.

She was lying on her side, on the bank, but not moving. The seconds passed slowly. They seemed like long minutes before, suddenly, she coughed up loads of water. She gave me an awful fright and I was too shook to say anything. With that, she stood up, walked over to her car and drove away as if nothing had happened.

Tullow was where my rugby-playing days started, although my first game was against them, for a combined Ballon/Rathoe under-10 team coached by my dad in the Community Games. As Ballon/Rathoe is my parish, I couldn't play for Tullow.

We trained for it in a grass farm field with a small hill where we marked out a pitch. Seamus Hogan, a neighbour of ours at the top of the Bog Lane and probably one of the best farmers in the country, owned the land. It was beside his out farm, away from his house and sheds. Anything he brought down there had to be drawn with a trailer. He couldn't run it over the fields. He provided the field for the Community Games without a charge. That field, which has about twenty-five acres, grows garden peas now. The Hogans have always been heavily involved in anything that happens in the community, and they still provide a field for cross-country runs.

The match was held on part of the pitch at Tullow RFC, from the 22 to the hedge, at the very front of the club. The Ballon/Rathoe team was basically our Gaelic football team and included James Foley as well as Padraig and Eoin Nolan. John Murphy, who is another really good friend of mine from home, was the best footballer in our age group. He played for Grange, but that day in the Community Games he played for Tullow against Ballon/Rathoe. I remember that game being a case of me against John. Later, we would become teammates at Tullow RFC, with John at number 7 and me at number 8, but we were rivals that day. John is now the captain of the Carlow inter-county football team. He's a full-forward and James Foley's younger brother, Darragh, is their centre-forward.

When we played against each other in that match, my first game of rugby, John was bigger than me and he was very fast for his age. I went into the game thinking, you have to play really well today. And I played well all right, but it's funny, looking back, to see that even at that early age I was talking myself into making sure I had a good game. I didn't want to let anyone get the better of me, even then! I don't know where I get that from. Dad wouldn't be very competitive, and he wouldn't have been that sporty, and Mam doesn't have a clue about sport. Having said that, I would never have become a rugby player without Mam or my sister Caroline. For years Mam, and then Caroline when she learned how to drive, drove me and William to every football, soccer, hurling or rugby game we played.

Ballon/Rathoe lost that game against Tullow by a try, three tries to two. Someone has a video of it somewhere. The Tullow lads were better. They played more rugby. I hadn't been to Tullow RFC before because Dad wasn't playing in the club that much any more. He only went up if they were stuck. But the Tullow lads we were playing had been training from under-8s or whatever. They were handier than we were.

But I loved it. I tried to run through everyone. There could have been six lads hanging off you and you were trying to throw a pass. It was pure carnage, but great fun.

That was the start. That was me genuinely hooked.

Another thing I remember clearly from that day was that some of the Gaelic football lads wore their socks pulled up. I always wore my socks down when I played football. I never wore my socks up. It was only when I started watching and playing rugby more that I began pulling my socks up. But only in rugby – they stayed down for football. Football was a socks-down game. Rugby was socks-up. In football, wearing your socks up is regarded as a little bit posh. If a player came in to mark me at full-forward with his socks up, I'd say to myself, I'm going to fucking hop off this lad now. I'd suspect he'd be a bit soft, or a shaper, so you'd want to give him as much hardship as possible.

There was a bit of controversy after the game around a

fella called John Bolger. He's still in the club now and I get on really well with his dad, John Senior. John lived in Ballon/Rathoe parish but he played with Tullow that day, so there was a bit of ruckus about him playing for them. But I thought, who cares? It's a game at the end of the day.

The following September I went up to Tullow RFC. I was ten years of age.

Most of my memories of Tullow are playing on Sunday mornings, and they're all good. We trained or played among ourselves and then occasionally we had blitzes. I liked the physical part of it, obviously. As a child I loved tackling and I loved running with the ball. The competitive side of it was brilliant as well. Right from the start, in any sport I played, I always wanted to win. Maybe it's a selfish thing. I played from under-10s through to under-20s, the Harry Gale Cup, although I was still only seventeen then. But I don't have many memories of my under-12 and under-14 days. I remember the under-16s and under-18s better.

At Tullow, our games were usually on Sunday mornings. This meant a breakfast roll in Tullow – eggs, sausage, rashers, black and white pudding, and red sauce – and then away to the game at 11am or midday. Lads would be arriving at the club in Tullow still finishing their breakfast rolls and wiping the red sauce from their faces. I'd be the same, even though we'd be playing a match an hour later. I remember one day suggesting to the lads that we get a brown roll rather than a white one, as it would be healthier. Still had the same stuff inside though!

After the games we'd usually hang around and watch the seniors play. Always Sundays. Never Saturdays. Saturday rugby still doesn't suit Tullow. We won promotion to Division 1A a few years ago, which meant Saturday matches, and we fell apart. Our club is drawn mostly from the farming community, construction workers, carpenters – there might be only five lads in the squad who work in offices in Dublin – so the squad members tend to work on Saturdays. Sunday is their day off to play rugby and that's it, so going back down to Division 1B was better for the club.

As long as I have known the club, on Sundays the club-house would be rocking after a Firsts game. Most lads would have their twenty-first-birthday parties there or in Kelly's or in the Tara Arms. It's a real family club. Lots of people would watch games with their kids and then go into the bar. Usually the women would be driving, and the lads would be drinking. A very traditional club.

Vinnie Mahon and Larry Canavan were our coaches the whole way through the Tullow under-age system. Pat O'Keefe and Ger Kavanagh, who had sons playing in that team, helped out as well. I played at full-back initially, and then at 12 for a while. Our basic tactics were to get the ball to John Murphy or to me. If we were in the opposition 22, sometimes I switched back to full-back so that they'd kick the ball to me, and I'd take off again. A few other lads, like William Canavan and Conor Mahon and three or four others, were well able to play, too. Everyone in the area also played Gaelic football or soccer and I'm 100 per cent sure playing Gaelic football helps the development of a young rugby player, particularly hand–eye co-ordination.

With Tullow we won the under-16 South-East, and got to the Leinster semi-final that year, where Navan beat us. Actually, Navan kept beating us in those years. The South-East was generally a handy enough one for us. It was us, New Ross, Enniscorthy, Athy and Carlow. With the under-18s we won the South-East again in 2003/04, beating Athy in the final in Carlow.

One of our best days was in the semi-finals of the Harry Gale Cup (under-20s) in March 2005, when we surprised most people by beating a Navan/Athy selection 10-6 in Cill Dara. Navan seemed nearly unstoppable then. They had four or five on the Leinster Youths team, and they had a cockiness about them. I only knew one of them, Shane Dawson, who had been a number 7 on the Leinster Youths the previous year. Conditions were perfect. I made a couple of good breaks. We had a really good full-back, Niall Byrne from Grange, who had an exceptional game. Larry Canavan's son, Willie, who also went for Leinster trials, was our out-half. He could be hot or cold, but he had a good game that day. And we needed him to play well.

Alongside me in the back-row, John Murphy could read the game brilliantly. A real loose openside. I played 8 and if you made a break, you knew he'd be on your shoulder. It didn't matter where you made it, he'd be there. And he had a big game that day, too.

We had a centre, Gavin Doyle from Tullow, who was stocky and powerful, and he also had a big game that day. And we needed all of these players to perform if we were to have a chance against Navan/Athy.

We were losing 6-3 at half-time and that was the score when the game was stopped for twenty-five minutes in the second half when one of their players suffered a neck injury. The medics had to be careful before he was stretchered off and taken to hospital in an ambulance. Thankfully, he was fine. To begin with, we tried to keep warm in groups of four by doing passing waves, but we gave up on that and went to the other end of the field with our coaches, Larry and Vinnie.

We had been making plenty of line-breaks but couldn't finish them. We'd left a few tries behind, but after the game resumed Vinnie's son, Conor, started a free-flowing move from inside our own half. Pretty much every one of us was involved, phase after phase, and offloading, before John Murphy finished it off with a dummy to score under the posts. That was typical John. He popped up everywhere.

For the last ten minutes they pounded our line, but we were just flying into them. That was one of the best days with Tullow. Maybe the best.

Winning that semi-final earned Tullow its first Gale Cup final since 1983. But a week after the 2005 Four Nations Under-18 Tournament in Wales, which I played in, Tullow lost the Gale Cup final against Portlaoise in Carlow by 15-8. That was a bad one to lose. We never got going. But what I remember most was the physical pain. I got an awful slap in the balls that day. The area around my groin was black within two minutes. Everything was bruised and my balls were up in my stomach. They wouldn't come down. I couldn't play on. Eventually, after ten or twelve minutes, they came back down, but I was in fierce pain.

I was on the ground, roaring with pain. I didn't know what had happened. I thought I'd been cut open. It was possibly as bad as I've ever felt on a rugby pitch. I was on the sideline, heaving, but couldn't throw up. I was struggling to breathe. Dad hadn't jumped over a railing in a long time, but he did that day. Mam was so shocked she didn't move. Anthony Kenny, who owns Kenny's Menswear in Tullow, told her afterwards that every bit of blood drained from her face. She still took me to training, but that was the last game my mother attended until the France game in the Aviva in 2017.

I somehow went back on with six or seven minutes remaining, but I couldn't turn it around. Although the club has won it since, it was a shame that Tullow team didn't win the Harry Gale Cup then. We should have done. We were always there or thereabouts with Tullow. We didn't win many trophies, but overall that team which came up through the ranks together won way more matches than we lost. Some of us developed, and became stronger physically and mentally, while other lads lost that edge and drifted away from the game. And you could tell it would be like that, because on big match days you sensed who might turn up and who wouldn't. And that's what let us down a lot of the time. In the big games, lads went into themselves.

I was also playing with Tullow Community School throughout my teens. The school set up a rugby team when I was in fifth year, and we played our matches in Tullow Rugby Club. Before that, lunchtimes had become rugby matches, with forty or fifty lads in a free-for-all. Lads went back into class with their trousers ripped off.

We won the Shield in our first year, and in the second year we reached the final of Section A. On the back of that I was called into the Leinster A schools squad. We played Munster A and Connacht Schools in Wilson's Hospital. I hardly knew anyone in the Leinster squad, and I remember hardly anything about either game.

I also played one Towns Cup game for Tullow against Rathdrum on the Seconds pitch in Tullow. I was seventeen at the time and Andrew Melville was the coach. My appearance caused a bit of a row in the club, because some people didn't think a player of my age should have been allowed to play with, and against, fully grown adults. It didn't bother me. I was delighted to be playing. I'd been training with them every Tuesday and Thursday and loved it.

The Towns Cup is always a big deal for clubs, bigger than

many lower-division All-Ireland League (AIL) games, and there must have been at least a thousand spectators at that game. It went well and we won. Rathdrum had two Kiwis, at 12 and 8, and I was playing 8. There was a row during the game, after their Kiwi 8 hit me a belt at the side of a break-down. As I landed on my back, I saw this karate-type kick above me. It was Conor Doyle, or Chesty as we call him. He caught the Kiwi under the jaw.

I was still on the ground and looking up as the shemozzle developed. An old prop, Tommy Dwyer, who is in his sixties now and still playing Seconds rugby, came in and leathered yer man with a punch – I can still hear the thump – and the Kiwi hit the ground.

My teammates were protecting me!

No one was sent off, though, and that is the outstanding memory of my one and only Towns Cup game. My Leinster and Irish Youths commitments prevented me from playing any more.

We'd had one Ireland under-19 player before me in Tullow, called Harry Byrne, who was a good bit before my time. Harry went to Newbridge College and was a hooker. I remember watching him play for Tullow and he was a hardy bit of stuff and a good player, but never really got the most out of his ability, and I'd say he'd probably agree with that. He didn't push on as he might have done, although he was a great club player, even if he possibly didn't play enough for Tullow either. He was happy enough to leave it, but he was a fine player.

Another hooker, Bernard Jackman, also had an association with the club. Bernard is from Coolkenno, which is only fif-teen minutes down the road in County Wicklow. His dad and his uncle would have played for Tullow, and Bernard's first coaching role was with the club. He coached me as a sixteen-year-old, when I was training with the Firsts in Tullow.

Being the first player from Tullow, or from the county of Carlow, to play for Ireland and the Lions is not something I'd given a lot of thought to until recently. I'm proud of this, of course, and of everything I've done with my career so far. I hope everyone in the area is proud, too. I have also been very lucky, and I needed to be. It's not like there's a well-trodden or proven pathway from Tullow, or Carlow, to professional rugby and the Leinster and Ireland teams. However, that is not something that motivated me.

Actually, it was the Tullow rivalry with Carlow RFC, or County Carlow as they were known then, that motivated me. They won promotion into Division 4 of the AIL when I was ten years old, and when I was fourteen they won promotion to Division 1 and spent five years there. So they were seen as this brilliant senior rugby club.

It was some climb, in fairness, but it was some fall too. By 2010 they finished last in Division 3 and became a junior club again. Local lads used to play for Carlow when it was a junior club, but when the club climbed the AIL ladder they were replaced by imported foreign players and forgotten about.

It makes me wonder how many people at the time in my own club, Tullow, actually said I'd make it. But putting Tullow Rugby Club on the map motivated me too, because anyone who says that Carlow didn't look down on Tullow years ago is telling some lie. They didn't have any time for us. So they were feisty derbies. Carlow used to beat us up a fair bit, but once we got up the age grades we gave them good games.

When I started, Tullow RFC had two pitches: a First pitch and a training pitch. The First pitch had a rickety old stand.

There was a clubhouse, four tiny changing-rooms, a referees' room and a room for the physio.

The Tullow main pitch is exactly the same now as it was then. It hasn't budged an inch! It's one of the best pitches in the country. As it is slightly elevated, it has always had naturally good drainage. You could play five or six games in a row on that pitch. Its only flaw is that it has never been dug up properly and it's starting to bubble in the middle. We call one of the corners 'coffin corner' because if you pin teams in there, they don't come out of it! The wind generally goes in that direction, so we'd put kicks in there the whole time, and then it's very hard for the opposition to kick their way out of it.

I've often asked why professional players aren't allowed to go back and play with their clubs. All Blacks players are allowed to do this when coming back from injury. I think that's the missing part in the Irish rugby pyramid. We're losing touch with the grass roots of our game. You could imagine the crowd that might turn out for a game if Johnny Sexton went back to play for St Mary's or if I played for Tullow. Opposing lads would love to play against us, too.

When my professional career ends, I'll play a little junior football if I can, and I'll hopefully play a season or two with Tullow RFC as well, regardless of how my body feels. I wouldn't need to be performing at an elite level. That's where it all started and that's where I want it to end. Complete the cycle.

5. The road less travelled

After I played for the Carlow Gaelic football under-16s and hurling under-16s in one-day tournaments, I made the county's minor football panel and played one challenge game against Wexford. But that was it. I couldn't commit to it at the time because I was making strides with rugby. By that stage, I reckoned I had to make a choice: give the rugby a go now or stay with the football. I went with rugby.

The physical part of rugby was more enticing. If I hit someone with my shoulder in a football match it would be a free, even if it was a clean shoulder. I found that very frustrating. If I was coming in hard, referees would just go: 'Ah, that's too hard.' I might well have been going in hard, but that's the way I played, and I was feeling aggrieved with how I was being continually penalized.

So I had no choice really. Rugby chose me as much as I chose rugby.

Making the Leinster South-East under-16 trials, along with a heap of lads from Tullow, and then the team itself was the first step on the ladder. When I first went up to all those Leinster South-East trials, I said to myself, just go hard here now and make sure you make an impression. I'd seen young lads from my club go into their shells when thrown into trials.

That wasn't going to happen to me.

Vinnie Mahon's son, Conor, was a scrum-half on the South-East team, and he drove us down to Enniscorthy twice a week for training with the South-East squad. That took an awful lot of pressure off Mam and Caroline. There must have been 180 players at those South-East trials. We played shortened matches against North-Midlands, Midlands and Metropolitan in one day in Wilson's College, and from those trials the coaches picked sixty players for the Leinster Youths.

I went really well in the first game, had a quieter second game, and then went really well again in the third game. I scored a few tries – two in the first one and one in the third, I think. But I was still only sixteen and I didn't make the Leinster Youths, which were under-18s at the time. I made it the second year.

By then, I was driving my own car. Mam and Dad ensured that myself and my brothers and sisters had provisional licences at sixteen so that we could drive the tractors, and they bought us all our first cars. Mine was a little red Mazda 121. It looked a little like an old Ford Fiesta.

I remember driving to my first session in Dublin with the Leinster Youths in my 121 with James' dad, Jim Foley, leading the way in his car. Jim was working in Dublin with Manor Farm at the time and knew every road in Ireland. My attention wandered at the wheel near the Long Mile Road before I saw Jim had pulled up at a Stop sign. I screeched on the brakes, but couldn't prevent tipping him from behind. I left a nice little dent in his back bumper.

Jim is the loveliest man you could meet off the field, but on the football field he'd have been known for having a hot temperament, very similar to James. When he got out of his car and went around the back to inspect the damage, I said to myself, Jesus, he's going to flip the lid here.

He looked down at the bumper and shook his head. I'd say he was thinking, that stupid fecker. He didn't flip, though.

I sat my Leaving Cert in June 2004, and late that summer I drove to Tullow Community School to collect my results. I had just started an apprenticeship with a local carpenter, David Dermody, and that morning I had driven a nail into my hand with a nail gun.

My day wasn't going to get any better.

I came to a bad bend, near the Fighting Cocks club, and there was oil on the road. I felt the car slide and, not having much experience of driving, I panicked and hit the brakes. The car virtually took off and went straight through a four-rail fence before toppling over at the front door of a house. A timber stake from the fence had come through the bottom of the car and straight across my leg, somehow missing my leg, and went out through the driver's door. Another timber stake came through the windscreen and broke the frame of the driver's-side window. I looked up at all this around me.

I climbed out and rang Mam. She collected me and brought me to the school to get my Leaving results. To my surprise, I'd passed everything. There weren't many Honours, if any, but I was happy out.

We went back to my car and organized to have it towed away. The next day, Willie O'Toole, who is a fencing contractor – and who is now my brother-in-law – helped me repair the fence. The car was nearly a write-off, though, and thereafter became known as 'The Mazda One Too Many'.

That 2004/05 season was taken up with working with Willie in contract fencing at the weekends, plenty of farm work and, combining Tullow with the Leinster Youths, plenty of rugby. Kieran Moloney, or Mush as they called him, made the Leinster Youths the season before me. Back then, he was the New Ross number 8, I was the Tullow number 8, and we used to have cracking games against each other. We were always going at each other, the whole way up the ranks.

Eventually, Mush went into the Leinster Academy as a tighthead prop, and when I followed him a year later we lived together in a house in Booterstown Avenue. We became really good friends, and we still meet up every now and again. A great lad, and his parents as well. Lovely people. He played for Leinster a few times and with Blackrock for a while, and then he went back to New Ross for one or two years, helping out coaching.

There was some attention coming my way at this stage, but I was oblivious to that kind of stuff. Around about then a headline in the Carlow *Nationalist* read: 'The sky's the limit for Tullow lad.' I didn't know a thing about building a profile or anything like that. Thank God there was no social media as such when I was starting off. Even after they were launched, I didn't join Twitter, Facebook or any of those for years. I had no interest in social media. That all passed me by.

I made the Leinster Youths team for the first time in the Interpros in October 2004, when we went to Musgrave Park and beat Munster 20-17. We hardly gave them a look when playing into the wind in the first half, and I carried plenty of ball. Shane Monahan, a winger from Boyne who would make the Leinster Academy and play for Rotherham and Gloucester, and Niall Cummins, from Enniscorthy, scored the tries, and both Munster tries came in injury time. Tommy O'Donnell played for them that day, and we'd become team-mates later that season for the Irish Youths.

The following week we clinched the Interpro title by beating Ulster in Barnhall, and we were presented with the trophy. Again, it went well. It had been built up all that week that Ulster would be a real handful physically and that we'd need to be at our best. We were well up for it. Anything that moved, we hit it. That was an enjoyable game, and a good sunny day as well. I had a load of good carries. I was becoming more physical. My main strength was running with the ball, more over and through people than around them. But once I had a bit of space, I could open up.

It was when I broke into the Leinster South-East set-up that I switched completely to number 8. Until 16s level, I'd moved around between the back-row, full-back and number 12. 'Throw him out there in the centre and give him the ball' type of thing. Or 'Let him run from full-back when they kick the ball to him.' And this could be during matches. But I was never going to be a centre or a full-back. I only ever wanted to be in the forwards. In the thick of it.

The switch to number 8 suited my game, and after Leinster won the Youths Interpros in October 2004, one day in early December I came home from my carpentry apprenticeship to find a letter addressed to me on the kitchen table, with an IRFU crest on the envelope. The address was Ardristan, Tullow. I didn't give the Union 'The Bog Lane' as my home address. The postman would have known where we lived anyway. There's no other Seán O'Brien in the area.

The heading on the letter read: Irish Youths Squad Session. Session 1 – December 17th and 18th

Dear Seán,

You are invited to attend a Youth/U 18 Squad session on the above weekend by the Irish Youth Management . . .

That's how it was done then. The IRFU letters always included train timetables and meeting points, and what gear to bring.

The first camp was a weekend in Clongowes Wood College in County Kildare. We stayed in dorms. I was the only player from Tullow, although I'd come to know some of the players in the Leinster Youths.

The Irish Youths squad was made up of players who came from junior clubs through the youths' interprovincial sides and Exiles players based in England. There was a trial match between the Irish Youths squad and the Irish Schools squad in Wilson's Hospital.

There were a few posh lads from the Schools who were saying things like, 'Where the fuck is Tullow?' I soon got stuck into them. That was my first real introduction to players from the Schools system, what they were about and how they acted.

I did my own thing in that trial game. There were so many players that it was bedlam. Some Schools lads had opinions of themselves. I just tried to get my hands on as much ball as possible and run over tacklers.

I got on well with some of the lads from the Schools. Some were genuinely nice. Some of them didn't give you the time of day. You could see them thinking, this big bogger has been called in here, but he's not going to do much.

That made me think, I'm going to show these boys now.

That was my attitude, because sneaky remarks about where you're from and other little things grew very quickly for me. I had a chip on my shoulder from early on, a desire to prove lads wrong. I tolerated some stuff, but sometimes my temper got me into trouble – grabbing lads or fighting them. I remembered the little remarks all the way through, until I made it as a senior player.

I was picked in the Irish Youths squad for a game against Italy, away, in February 2005. A coach picked up players at Heuston and Connolly stations to take us to Howth, where the squad assembled in the Deer Park Hotel on the Wednesday for a light session, a squad meeting and lights out. Our wake-up call was at 5am for breakfast and we had a 6.15am check-in for our 7.20am flight to Milan. Even on the farm I never got up that early. Cheaper flights – that's all it was. The Youths were run on a tight budget, and probably still are.

After landing we were transported to our hotel, which was very basic, and the food was cat. In fact, of all the hotels I stayed in during my Youths days, I don't remember one seriously nice breakfast. But I was happy out. I hadn't known anything else. I didn't care where we stayed.

After lunch we trained, then had dinner, another team meeting and lights out at 10pm. The next day, 11 February 2005, three days before my eighteenth birthday, was going to be the first time I pulled on a green jersey and represented my country. I was thrilled. I wasn't nervous at all. Just delighted to be there.

Wake-up call was 8am for an 8.30am breakfast and 9.30am departure to the ground, Varese RFC, about an hour north of Milan, for a 12.30pm kick-off. We were relatively used to early kick-offs at Youths level, all the way up through Tullow and Leinster.

Even though it was February, I'd never played in warmer weather. It was an absolute scorcher. The sun was splitting the stones.

All the Italian players had beards and looked like grown men rather than Youths! They were all giants, too. Tall and athletic. It was the first thing Stephen said to me afterwards: 'How big are the second-rows?' Birth certs definitely should have been checked. They were massive. That's my abiding memory of that day, and the heat.

There were a surprising number of Irish fans at the game. As we came out from the dressing-room, they were all to our immediate left. It would have been a first Irish cap of any kind for almost all the players, so plenty of families and friends were over. My brother Stephen flew to the game from Jersey via Dublin, so that he and Dad could travel from home together. Stephen still has my cap, and a poster, from that game.

The gear in those days was always far too big. I'd still be swimming in that jersey even now. I played at 8 and David Whately, a lad from Dundalk, was at openside, with Tommy O'Donnell at 6. There were some good players in that Irish Youths squad. Jamie Hagan was a prop from Balbriggan who went on to play for Leinster and Ireland, and then Connacht, London Irish, the Rebels in Melbourne and Béziers. Shane Monahan was the winger from Boyne who played for Leinster and Connacht, as well as Rotherham and Gloucester. The team was coached by Willie Gribben, a lovely Ulsterman who sadly passed away in November 2019.

We lost 15-3, but I don't remember anything else about that game. In truth, I didn't realize the significance of playing for my country the first time.

The day's official itinerary set aside the afternoon for rest and then 'study time' from 5pm to 7pm. We were mad into our studying, we were! Dinner at 7pm, team meeting at 9pm and lights out at 10pm. There were strict curfews, and we were on an early flight home.

The following month, we played Scotland in another Youths international, in a place called Dalziel, and beat them 21-3.

In Easter 2005, the Irish under-18s competed in the Four Nations Under-18 Tournament in Wales. We were based in Howth for a four-day training camp and then the tournament was run off in a week, three double-headers in Ebbw Vale, Dunvant and Pontypridd. The IRFU letter inviting us into the squad for that tournament told us to bring 'Dark grey trousers, smart black shoes, white shirt and enough training gear for at least three sessions, swimming gear and whatever IRFU kit which was provided previously'.

They were tight on the gear back then.

'All accommodation and travel will be paid for but you should bring some sterling for personal spending money if required. Supervised study time will be made available most days so please remember to bring your books.'

I definitely brought a book. But I definitely didn't do any supervised study. And I can guarantee you no one else did either. Nor would there be any supervised study time nowadays, I'd say. They'd be studying plays and moves maybe, but that's it.

My sister Caroline and her boyfriend Willie, who is now her husband, came over, along with my younger brother, William. So did Peter Sutton and James.

The Ramada Hotel in Swansea, where we were based, was again very basic, although I didn't know any different at that stage. Nor did any of the others, I'd say. We were just a bunch of massively excited young lads.

This time another lovely Ulsterman, Charlie McAleese, was the head coach, Terry Kingston the assistant coach and David Eakin the manager. The squad was a mix of club players, Exiles and any Schools players who hadn't made the Irish Schools team. So Ian Keatley came into the squad, as did Ian Whitten – a lovely fella who's still playing for Exeter and is the same player today as he was then: very hard to stop. We had Kevin Sheen of St Michael's, who played for Cork Con in the 2019 AIL final. Jamie Hagan, Tommy O'Donnell, also exactly the same and a lovely fella, and Shane Monahan were all still there, as well as the other out-half, Michael Skelton, who's from Naas.

We drew our first game on a Saturday against Wales in Ebbw Vale 13-13, but we should have won. Ian Keatley scored our try but our hooker, Ger Slattery from Munster, actually did the kicking. Left peg. Serious goal-kicker. I made a good few breaks in that game, I was defensively sound and I was just hardship for the opposition. I was a little more comfortable in those surroundings by then, and I realized it was an opportunity to make an impression in that kind of environment, whereas maybe other lads were shying away from it. Back home in Tullow, we still have a screen-shot of four pictures in a row of me from that game, framed and hanging in the hallway.

I think that game put me on the radar. Colin McEntee, who was the Leinster Academy manager, and Richie Murphy, who was the squad's video analyst and was also Leinster's Player Development Officer at the time, were at the tournament and I remember chatting to them after the game. That was on the Saturday. The following Tuesday I was made captain for the next game, against Scotland in Dunvant.

The pitch had been soaked by rain beforehand and the steady rainfall during the match did nothing to improve the conditions. It could easily have been called off. Running out onto it, the pitch squelched under your feet. It was just one of those roll-up-your-sleeves-and-get-it-done days.

Scotland were stubborn defensively and just wouldn't go away. We were camped deep in their 22 several times, but couldn't get over the line. It was 0-0 at half-time, but we eventually won 10-0. Our full-back, Dan Lavery, scored the first try. He was an Exile and a handy enough player. I scored the second. Both were pick-and-go drives. Job done.

I was captain again for the final game against England, in Pontypridd, when we got absolutely pumped, 38-19. I was very disappointed after that game. But the England players were absolutely humongous, much bigger than us, and they just kicked lumps out of us. I remember thinking, we're nowhere near these boys.

Back in the Ramada Hotel, we were all presented with our caps. There were a few firsts that week, because that was also the first time I had a few pints after a game. Pints of lager were going around. We had a big sing-song. All of us in one big room. We had blue shirts and big heavy green jumpers, and black trousers. I had a pair of black Wrangler shoes as well. I used to buy Wrangler shoes the whole time!

Playing for the Irish Youths in those games confirmed I'd made the right decision to plump for rugby over any other sport, and it was then that I made another conscious decision: Right, I'm going to have a crack at this. This is the game for me. I'm going to try and make a career out of it.

6. Plan A

I love farming, but would I be a farmer? No, definitely not. There's not enough of a living to be made from it, and certainly not if you want to raise a family. It's very tough financially, and it's a very hard way of life.

In the year after I finished school, I worked for Murray Timber in Ballon. After a few weeks I was made a foreman of one of the sheds, making sure that production was going well. It was hard but handy work, and at the time it was good for me. I also knew a fair bit about carpentry because Dad had been a builder, so I didn't need to learn much.

Jim Kealy, a builder in Tullow who has since passed away, owned the site where I laid the roofs on four houses and did the timber floors. He was one of Dad's best friends and, in many ways, he was like a second father to me. He was a big rugby fan and brought me everywhere with him, giving me a taste for big rugby days. On the week of the Wasps–Leicester Heineken Cup final in Twickenham in 2007, when I was still in the Leinster Academy, he said: 'Do you want to go to the Heineken Cup final?' Leo Cullen and Shane Jennings were on the losing Leicester side and Eoin Reddan scored one of Wasps' tries.

Jim was President of Tullow RFC and had a big influence on the club as well, making it more progressive and ambitious. A lovely relaxed character, he was a very shrewd businessman. He had a big construction company back in the good days, which his son Darryl took over. Jim also helped me secure the carpentry apprenticeship with David Dermody. But one morning in June 2005, at about 10am, David called me over. He told me that the work was slackening off: 'I have to keep on the other two apprentices because they've been with me for two years.' Things were starting to get tight for the builders and as I was the last one in, I was always going to be the first one out, which was fair enough.

That same day, I returned home from work to find an envelope addressed to me on the kitchen table with the Leinster harp on the top right-hand corner. Inside it was a letter on Leinster-headed paper, and signed by Colin McEntee, the Academy manager.

Dear Seán,

I am pleased to inform you that you have been selected for the Leinster Academy programme 05–06 season.

Your selection is subject to a full medical and muscular skeletal examination. Once this has been completed a contract will be sent to you for signing.

I will be in touch with you over the coming days arranging for the medicals to take place. Once again, congratulations on your selection. I look forward to working with you over the coming months.

Yours sincerely,
Colin McEntee

I had had a feeling I might get it. My mam and dad had brought me up to the Old Belvedere clubhouse for the interview a few weeks earlier. That's where Leinster were based and trained at the time, with a Portakabin for their gym. Colin was on the panel, as were Mick Dawson, the Leinster CEO, and Frank Sowman, who was chairman of the

Academy. They did most of the talking. They explained to me and my parents that there would be support for us as a family, but that I'd have to quit Gaelic football and commit totally to Leinster.

They wanted me to go into the Sub-Academy, but we said that it wouldn't be feasible for me to get up and down to Dublin three times a week, or to move to Dublin at my own expense. It would have cost a fortune, and just wasn't going to happen.

So they said they would consider other options. And then the letter arrived confirming that they'd taken me straight into the full Academy.

They took a bit of a chance on me, really. Many kids, unless they've had a standout career in schools rugby, have to serve their time in the Sub-Academy. They could easily have decided not to take the gamble on me.

I was thrilled. This was, literally, a life-changer. UCD also offered me a scholarship, and I did a Diploma in Sports Management over my first two years, while also playing for the college. I wanted to be a professional rugby player, and this was the first step towards that ambition. That was all I wanted at that stage. After my carpentry apprenticeship fell through, I talked to the gardaí about joining them; and sometimes I think I'd have loved to be a vet. But the truth is that at that point I had no real Plan B.

I started with the Leinster Academy in August 2005. I went straight into UCD that semester and moved into the Merville apartments, which are on campus. There were four single bedrooms in the apartment, with two bathrooms, a shared kitchen and a living room. That was different. I was living with people I didn't know – two lads from Kilkenny and a girl, from where I can't remember. The Kilkenny lads were a bit older than me but were sound out. We never saw each other until the evenings, watching *Home and Away* or whatever. The TV only had three or four stations. It was that or the PlayStation, and I wasn't really into the PlayStation.

I was a little homesick and missed the great little routine I had with my mates at home, where most weekends we'd go to a nightclub in Bunclody. It was basically a shed run by a fella called Mick Keogh and it was all seventeen- and eighteen-year-olds. We had some cracking nights there. Yeah, I missed that. In UCD, I was out of my comfort zone, meeting new people and going to college.

There was a Centra shop in Merville and I'd have the same lunch out of there virtually every day: hot chicken fillet rolls with spicy wedges and ketchup. I was training hard, but that would have been my meal after a weights session in the Academy. Little did I know! There was such a lack of information around nutrition then. I look at some of the pictures of me after going into the Academy at eighteen years of age, and it's clear I hadn't a clue what I was doing. I was just a young lad playing rugby, the same as if I was in Tullow on Sunday mornings. I wonder what kind of animal I might have become had I known about weights or prehab or rehab or sports nutrition back then.

Gradually, when we did start to get nutritionists into the Academy and get advice on diet, it was a big eye-opener. I slowly started to adapt. But at the beginning I struggled.

Before going into the Leinster Academy, I was used to training twice a week. Suddenly I was not only training twice a week with UCD, on Tuesday and Thursday evenings, but I was doing two or three times a day with the Academy boys as well. My body was in shock. I had to sleep for around an hour at midday, just to get myself going again.

I had never touched a dumbbell or a weight until I started at the Academy. I remember saying to Colin McEntee: 'I don't know if I'm going to be able to do this.'

He said: 'Just stick with it for another few weeks and you'll be flying.'

Lo and behold, after about five or six weeks I had passed out a load of lads in terms of my strength. Because I was doing weights for the first time, my gains were almost instant. I felt fitter, stronger and more powerful than I'd ever done.

Mondays to Fridays, my days began with a wake-up call at 6.30am and a drive to Old Belvedere to be ready for Academy training by 7am. Michael Cheika had just come in as Leinster's new head coach after Declan Kidney had left, and Brad Harrington, another Aussie, was our Academy coach. Like Checks, he was hard-nosed, but a really good guy to sit down with for a talk. He wanted to toughen us up. Each day started with a weights session, and then we'd do skills sessions. We'd be finished by 9am at the latest, as that's when the seniors came in to train. We'd be pulling out in our cars as they were driving into the Belvedere car park in theirs. I was in awe of some of them, especially Brian O'Driscoll. Initially I wouldn't have recognized half the players, but you'd know the bigger names, and gradually I began to know everyone.

We came back in the afternoon after they had finished their field session to do another skills session or some conditioning or running. That was almost every Monday and Tuesday, and again Thursday and Friday. Wednesdays were a day off, so I'd usually drive back down to Tullow on Tuesday for the night. By then I was driving a blue Audi A4 1.9 diesel.

There were seventeen of us in the Leinster Academy that season, between lads in their first, second or third years. Jamie Hagan and Shane Monahan had also come through the Youths pathway. Devin Toner, Cian Healy, Fergus McFadden, Johnny Sexton, Kevin McLaughlin and Fionn Carr were all there. So were Dermot Laffin, Ron Boucher, Alex Dunlop, Stephen Grissing, Ross McCarron, Gavin O'Meara, Matt Darcy and Kieran Molony, a good friend coming through the Leinster and Irish Youths. He was the New Ross number 8 I'd played against regularly, but by then he'd moved to tighthead.

Myself, Big Dev and Kieran moved in together in my second year at the Academy. Dev is easy to live with – just so relaxed. Never a bother on him. Myself and Kieran would wrestle some evenings for a bit of craic, but we'd never wrestle Dev. He'd just hold you at arm's length. It was hilarious.

Myself and Kieran stay in touch – not as much as I'd like to, but that's the way life is. He's a teacher and a rugby coach in St Mary's College now.

Johnny Sexton was quite pudgy in those days. But you could see how good he was. I always thought he was class because of the way he passed the ball. He wasn't as grumpy as he is now, but he definitely had a big attitude about him, even back then. He was similar to the person and player he is now. He kept everyone on their toes.

Cian Healy was a meathead then. All he wanted to do was lift weights. He was absolutely massive. Twice as big as he is now.

Most of us went into the Leinster under-21s for the Inter-pros in September 2005. Our first game was against Connacht at Donnybrook. I remember it quite well, and that's probably because we lost. We just never got going. I was so frustrated that day. They led 15-3 at half-time and we absolutely pounded their line for most of the second half. Couldn't score. I eventually did score a try late on, but we lost 21-15.

A week later we played Ulster at Donnybrook. There had been a lot of talk about Stevie Ferris in the build-up to that game. I think he'd already been capped by Ulster at that stage and coming up against him in Donnybrook I do remember thinking, this is where you've to make your mark, against these really good players.

I was moved from number 6 to number 8 for that game and we won 37-6. A week later we lost 21-19 against Munster in Rosbrien, but due to other results and bonus points we qualified to meet Munster again in the final in Athlone. This time we beat them well, 21-10. I scored one of our three tries. All of them were converted by Sexto.

Although I was still only eighteen, I'd played for a Leinster under-21 side that had won the Interpros and I was definitely one of the stand-out back-rowers. I'd gone well against Stephen Ferris and there were times during those Interpros when I thought, I can make the Irish team. So I wasn't that surprised when I was picked on the bench for the Ireland under-21s in their first Six Nations game against Italy, at Dubarry Park, in February 2006.

I came on for Ejike Uzoigwe for the last fifteen minutes and we won 34-9. 'Edgy', as we called him, was one of the Exiles players the Ireland Youths were keen on looking at in those days. He was a good hard player who just went around chop-tackling players, and he played for Nigeria.

'Big Bad' Billy Holland was the number 8. Very similar to the player he is now – a workhorse and a real team player. Sound as a bell too. Big Dev and Dan Tuohy were in the second-row, Paul Marshall and Sexto were at half-back, Darren Cave in midfield and Fionn Carr at full-back. Paul Derbyshire played in the Italian back-row that night.

Next we played France in Strasbourg, three days before

my nineteenth birthday. I was on the bench, and again I replaced Edgy for the last fifteen minutes. We lost 29-10. My main thought from that game was simply, how big are these guys? I was still an eighteen-year-old boy and I was coming up against twenty- and 21-year-old French men. They had Loïc Jacquet and Fulgence Ouedraogo up front and their pack did most of the damage, although they also had Lionel Beauxis, Maxime Mermoz and Maxime Médard in the backs.

My first start, just after turning nineteen and at number 8, was against Wales at Dubarry Park a fortnight later, when we lost 14-13. They had some team: Alun Wyn Jones, James Hook, Dominic Day and, opposite me, their captain, Tom Smith of the Ospreys. Jamie Roberts was at 15. Alun Wyn wore a scrum cap then too. I remember Jamie Roberts playing at full-back and again I was struck by how much bigger than us they seemed to be.

There were always big crowds at Dubarry Park and the atmosphere was good, but two weeks later we lost there again, by 24-21, to Scotland. They had John Barclay and John Beattie in the back-row. I was at number 8 and was dope tested for the first time afterwards.

We finished the tournament by flying to Birmingham for a game against the English under-21s in Worcester. They had a serious team. Dylan Hartley at number 2, David Wilson at 3, Tom Croft in the second-row, my future buddy James Haskell and Jordan Crane in the back-row at 6 and at 8, Ben Foden and Toby Flood at half-back, Nick Abendanon at 11 and Mike Brown at 15. They were going for the Grand Slam. They beat us 40-5.

I started at number 8 that day and I was nearly in big trouble for something that happened during the game. We were getting spanked and I was getting frustrated, but we were still trying. It was men-against-boys stuff. They absolutely kicked the fuck out of us for the whole game. I was trying to get through to Toby Flood on a charge-down when David Wilson stuck out his arm and clotheslined me. I got up off the ground, didn't say anything or even look at him. I just caught him with this perfect right hook. He dropped like a stone to the ground, as if he'd fallen from the air.

I broke his jaw in two places. Rob Andrew said afterwards that I should be suspended but, for some reason, I wasn't even cited. I was also dope tested again after the match. I thought that if you were playing well, you had a better chance of being tested. I'm not saying that was the case, but that was what I told myself.

In April 2006, there was an under-19 World Championships in Dubai, but I was picked in the under-21 squad for the World Cup in France. The squad assembled in the Shannon Oaks Hotel in Portumna, County Galway. A lovely spot, great food and we stayed in the holiday chalets on the grounds. I was moving up in the world! It was perfect for our preparation. Mark McDermott was the coach and Niall O'Shea the manager.

The tournament was held in Clermont Auvergne in June, and it was unbelievably warm. Our first game was against France, and even though it was a 7pm kick-off the temperature was near 40 degrees. There were water breaks every ten or fifteen minutes. I remember sitting in an ice bath afterwards – a round, plastic, inflatable ice bath. I was so disorientated, and whoever was examining me was considering hooking me up to a drip because I'd lost four and a half kilos in body weight – the most I've ever lost in one game in my life. Sometimes you might lose two or three kilos from a very hard game, but this was different. We were fit, but not as fit as we are now.

They had a huge home crowd roaring them on and, as with any game in France, the noise was incredible, with the banging, shouting, clapping, chanting. I played okay that day, but the ref was atrocious. He hadn't a clue what he was doing. The French showed us again how far we had to go. They were big and physical, and they beat us 26-8. We had a nice team, with talented rugby players, and we were trying our best, but we didn't have big players.

I started at number 8 that night, with Ross Noonan and David Pollock in the back-row, both of whom retired through injury before they'd finished their stints in the Munster and Ulster academies, respectively. I liked playing alongside Ross. He was a quiet, unassuming fella. He loved the physicality and always played with emotion. I think he was caught a little between being a number 6 and a second-row, but if you wanted someone in the trenches with you to hit people, he'd be there. I played against him in UCD games against Shannon, but he had a bit of an injury profile even at that stage.

David was a huge prospect. He captained the team, was smart, incredibly fit, spoke very well and was just a really good, handy, tough player. Even so, he never wanted to be a rugby player. He always had it in the back of his head that his studies and becoming a doctor were a priority for him. Maybe he was right!

I played again when we met Argentina in our second pool game four days later. This time it was around 35 degrees and we really struggled with the heat. We led for an hour, Fionn Carr scored two tries and Ferg got one, but they outlasted us and Agustín Creevy scored their winning try.

Agustín was moving between flanker and hooker then, and me and him had a bit of a falling-out in that game. We were driving forward at a maul and broke off it, but with him still attached to me, and he caught me with a sweet uppercut. It put my teeth through my top lip. I went off to get my lip stitched and said to myself, I'm going to get him. Not in a bad way, but at a ruck or with a big hit. But after I went back on, the opportunity never really came. Agustín was a tough man as well. I'd say you'd have to be at your best to go toe-to-toe with him.

Our next game was a 47-0 win over Georgia, and their second-rows were the same size as their props, so nothing has changed there. Big, big men. I remember sitting in the stand afterwards, watching France play South Africa. The French were coming alive, but the South Africans were huge and had Pierre Spies at number 8. Although they beat France that night, France would meet them again in the final. France won, but in that final Spies burned the French winger from his own 10-metre line to score under the posts. I remember thinking, what is he on? Really, he was just incredibly fit and incredibly determined and no one could live with him in that form.

In the play-offs we beat Argentina 42-20. When you get an Argentine team that's really up for it and emotionally charged, you've a fight on your hands. But I don't think they were as up for it second time around. We'd also solved a few problems from the first match and we scored some nice tries. Although it was our earliest kick-off, in the middle of the afternoon, we were becoming used to the heat and that was our best performance.

Maybe the heat took its toll, too. In the fifth-place play-off four days later, we met England again. I scored a try early on to put us ahead, but they rolled us over again, 32-8. The Gloucester centre Anthony Allen absolutely ran amok. He couldn't be touched. Danny Care was the same type of player he is now, electric. As in the Youths tournament a year earlier and the Under-20 Six Nations, that was another big beating against England. The IRFU have since put excellent fitness programmes in place, but back then England were way ahead of us in their physical development.

The World Cup was a great experience. But I wasn't happy that we were getting spanked by the bigger and better teams. Although I was still only nineteen, I came away from that tournament knowing that I needed to put in massive work on my strength and conditioning. I also thought I'd have three years at under-21 level, but the following year the under-19s and under-21s were rolled into the under-20s, so I would only have one more shot at it.

After that first year in the Academy, I went out to Jersey to visit my brother Stephen for three weeks. Jersey is a beautiful spot, especially in summer. The circumference of the island is only ten and a half miles but it has lovely beaches, nice restaurants and good nightlife.

It was a holiday, but I decided to train with the Jersey Reds for a couple of weeks, so as to stay fit. I was wet behind the ears about my contract and technicalities like that. I was still a raw nineteen-year-old from Tullow and didn't realize I probably should not have been doing this.

The Seconds team were going for promotion, and I agreed to play with them for one game. Every year they played their main rivals, Guernsey, for the Siam Cup, which is the second-oldest rugby trophy in the world after the Calcutta Cup.

I scored three tries in the game, but it was actually quite a good standard. One of the Guernsey players had the hump with me and swung a punch. He missed, and I dropped him instantly onto the ground with a punch. I grabbed him by the throat to hit him again, but someone pulled me from behind and this meant I hit him straight down on top of his head. The bone went straight out of my hand as I connected with his skull. It's what is known as a boxer's break. I knew straight away.

I went to the hospital, had my hand put in a cast and flew home. Then I had to ring Collie McEntee. I told him I'd broken it after a fall while I was running.

'Right,' he said, 'come on home.'

Collie came with me to the hospital when the cast was opened up. He said: 'That's a boxer's break. You're after hitting someone.'

I admitted it. 'Yeah, I played a game and I hit a player who tried to punch me.'

He just looked at me and said: 'Let this be a lesson to you now. You cannot do that when you're contracted.'

It was definitely a big mistake on my part. I was naive. Thankfully, the hand mended and I was back for pre-season.

I was injured for a lot of my second season in the Academy, but I was still eligible for the Leinster and Irish under-21s as I only turned twenty that February. Eric Elwood was Irish under-21 coach for the 2007 Six Nations and we had an exceptional squad. The pack had Cian Healy, Tommy O'Donnell and myself, and even though Luke Fitzgerald had been ruled out after picking up an injury playing for Leinster, the backline still had Felix Jones, Keith Earls and Darren Cave.

We beat Wales in the Liberty Stadium in Swansea and France in Dubarry Park. But in the third game, against England, I ripped my hamstring for the first time. I'd actually torn it slightly two weeks before against France. But I felt good and I'd made a few breaks against England. I couldn't get over how well I felt. I picked up the ball about twenty metres out, at the base of a ruck, and I was half tackled. I tried to power on and, snap, it went again. I knew then I was fucked because it felt like a proper tear. The lads went on to beat Scotland and Italy away to clinch the Grand Slam. So I wasn't missed.

I was unlucky, too, that there was no under-21 or under-20 World Cup in 2007, and that in 2008 the Six Nations Under-21 Tournament was changed to the Under-20 Tournament, making me over-age. My under-age days were over.

7. Learning my trade

In my first year in the Academy I trained occasionally with the seniors. I'd usually have to wear a 'combat suit' – upper-body padding – for protection, as I was instructed just to go into the breakdown and try to poach everything I could.

In one of those sessions, on the main pitch in Anglesea Road, I remember clearly we were defending on the far right-hand corner from the terracing and clubhouse. I was as keen as mustard, trying to impress Checks and the other coaches. I went in for a poach and I was locked on to it. Nobody was shifting me. A few lads tried but had no joy. Then, I felt studs on my back. Who was it, but only Eric Miller, who came in flying over the ruck and 'shoed' me as quickly as he could. That knocked me onto my back and as I looked up, I saw Drico arriving at speed and punching Eric.

'What the fuck are you playing at?' Drico said to him. 'That's fucking disgraceful what you've done there.'

There was some mouthing between them, but I stayed out of it. It was my first session with the seniors of that kind of intensity, and I was a bit shocked. I'd had a good shoeing, but luckily I had that combat vest on my back. That was my first real encounter with Drico on the training pitch, and from that day on I knew he would stand up for his players, even young Academy players. I never really got to chat with Eric much, and he retired at the end of that season, even though he was still only thirty-one at the time.

The red mist began to fade after I came into the Academy.

Before then, if someone said the wrong thing to me, I'd just snap. The Academy changed that. I quickly realized that I had to be disciplined, and I learned as well from looking at the older lads, like Leo Cullen and Brian O'Driscoll, and even Jamie Heaslip and other players who were only slightly older than me. They were all just very professional and they didn't get involved in fights or anything like that.

At that stage, Leinster was also beginning to change under Cheika. We were starting to get a bit more hard-nosed. We weren't going around like lunatics, but he made us aggressive in a really good way.

Checks was great for us, but he was very hard on that younger group of guys in the Academy, especially myself and Johnny Sexton. Cian got a fair bit of abuse as well, but I remember Checks getting absolutely stuck into me and Johnny the whole time. Sometimes he could give you a compliment, but the next day he could be tearing you to shreds in front of the whole squad. It could be the smallest of things, but I think he was just trying to instil a little mental toughness into us by testing us to the limit.

I suppose he was a little old school in his ways. When I was growing up, I regularly received a clip, at school and at home. That was how it was if you misbehaved, and that's how I saw it with Checks. We were the next generation and he wanted to make sure we had manners and were mentally strong enough to withstand what it takes to be a professional rugby player, and that we had what it takes to bring Leinster to the next level. He had the hardy, experienced men like Drico, Leo and Shane Jennings, who were tough players, but who needed more lads around them with the same mindset to bring it to a new level.

I think that's what Checks was trying to do with us, to

make sure we were prepared for anything that came our way. That's why he was hard on us and, to be honest, I loved it. There were times I thought, well, fuck you, Checks. You'd be training your hardest, but you might drop a ball, or something small might happen, and he'd let loose at you. You'd think, that's the first thing I've done wrong today.

But after a while you'd just say, cop yourself on, and go again. Be better. That's the biggest difference between professionals and amateurs. Amateurs will whinge about it and decide, I'm not playing for him any more. Whereas a professional will say, I'll prove him wrong. I'll get better and I'll make sure he picks me.

That quickly became my mindset.

David Knox was Cheika's assistant coach at the beginning. He was mad. He'd leave his wet socks on the radiator of the office and the room would be stinking. Some days we'd be doing unit work and if he didn't agree with what Checks was saying or was in a bad mood about something, next moment there'd be rugby balls landing in on top of the line-out practices. Knoxy would pepper the forwards with this aerial assault, and he still had an accurate left boot.

Knoxy would be doing a backs session, and he'd tell them he was going to personally destroy the forwards' line-out drills. The backs would come and tell us this. Cheika and Knox had quite a strange relationship.

I was only learning my trade and how to think about the game, and Knoxy would confuse you sometimes. But he could work out the opposition and where to put players through holes. He felt the forwards were there to serve the backs. 'Just give the ball to Johnny and let him fucking play,' he'd say. Knoxy was actually a really, really smart coach and lads liked him when he was switched on, but then he could flip any given second, and that would be him done for the session. He wouldn't want to do anything else.

Mike Brewer, the former All Blacks' number 8, came in as the forwards coach, and they didn't share the same outlook on the game. Brewser also didn't like Knoxy disrupting our line-out sessions. Their relationship quickly deteriorated, although I wouldn't have known the half of it.

Knoxy had us playing a very 'Leinster' brand of rugby, but gradually Brewser's influence grew. We had a big pack and his view was, why not use it? Brewser was straight and hard-nosed. If he liked you, he liked you, and if he didn't, you didn't get a look-in. So you had to continually impress him. If you were training and performing well, he never had a problem with you. I had a good relationship with him.

Ollie le Roux was thirty-four when he joined Leinster in 2007 and was a monster of a man. He could shift as well. Ollie was like a number 10 at training sometimes. He'd show and go and be gone twenty yards. Because he was such a big man, people thought he couldn't move, but he was well able to run. He used to catch out younger lads the whole time. When I was in my third year of the Academy, I vividly remember him once showing and going with me at training. He made an absolute tool of me.

He was quite a funny guy. 'I promise you. I promise you,' he'd say the whole time. But he was a character and very articulate. Whether or not he was bright, he'd certainly let on he was bright. 'Yes, I remember,' he'd say, when he mightn't have a bull's notion. But he could talk until the cows came home. He was big into his meat and his barbecues. It was good business by Leinster to get him at the time and he was great around the environment. He never missed training.

Overall, I look back on my time in the Academy as great

years. Good lads, great craic, a lot of learning and growing up, and also developing an understanding of how the game is played. We had loads of different coaches in with us and I was learning from them all the time. There were skills coaches, line-out coaches, backs coaches – who would sometimes work with the back-rowers as well – and we did plenty of tackle technique with Colin McEntee. Collie was struggling with his hips by then and he wasn't able to do too much hands-on coaching, but he was a great Academy manager. Richie Murphy did all the skills sessions with the Academy and was very good, while Brad Harrington did the conditioning work.

I learned from all of them, but I also learned from the senior players.

One of the guys I watched closely was Leo Cullen. Leo wasn't one of those players that people talked about or who was highlighted on television, but when you watched him close up in training, like in mauling sessions, you realized, fuck me, this lad's a messy bastard. He was tough, no nonsense and hard to play against. He didn't mind the rough and tumble. I looked at him and thought, I want to take a bit of that into my game as well. I don't want to be backing away from anyone.

Another player I always looked at when I was a young fella was Victor Costello, who retired just as I was joining Leinster. He could be unbelievable on his day. Unplayable. But then other days you'd wonder, does he want to be here at all? But the way he played on the good days was incredible. Very hard man to stop.

Shane Jennings was at Leicester along with Leo Cullen for the first two years I was in the Leinster Academy. By the time Jeno came back, for the 2007/08 season, Keith Gleeson had established himself at number 7, and then the two of them played alongside each other in most of the big games that season. So in my Academy years Gleece was the bigger influence on me.

I liked to arrive back early for the afternoon training sessions, and Gleece was always one of the seniors who would still be out on the pitch, doing extras. I thought, feckin' hell, he works hard. He was the first international openside I'd ever got to know, and I thought his professionalism was incredible. I did a few video sessions with him, mostly about lines of running, because I was more of a number 8 who was converting to a 7 at the time. For someone who wasn't overly big, he made good shots, and he knew his detail incredibly well. In that sense he was a little ahead of his time and he had a good head on his shoulders.

During my Academy years I kept busy playing with UCD. In the first season John McLean, the head coach in UCD, wouldn't let me play on the Firsts team or the AIL team, in part because the UCD under-20s were his too and that team was flying. We had a great side. But in my second year in the Academy, 2006/07, he bumped me and a few others up to UCD's AIL team, which was in Division 1. I also started to play a few interprovincial games with the Leinster A team, and they were very good for my development.

The biggest difference in my second year in the Academy was that I was playing against senior, adult players every week with UCD, and travelling all over the country. The away games took us to Dungannon, Shannon, Galwegians and other places. That Dungannon game was my second encounter with Stevie Ferris. It was December 2006. He was twenty-one and I was nineteen. Everyone in the club was talking about the two of us coming up against each other.

Dungannon won that day, but it was a good game. I was still developing and they were the kinds of matches that helped me believe I could play against the big hitters. Fez had already played a few times for Ulster and he was coming back from an injury, so he was definitely undercooked, but it was nice to go toe-to-toe with a player who was tipped to be one of the next back-rowers coming up.

On the last day of the season with UCD we went into our final game at home to Belfast Harlequins second from bottom. If we lost, we would be relegated to Division 2. To this day, I'm still not sure if I've played in worse conditions. It had been raining incessantly for about three days before the game and it was still raining on the day of the match, as well as blowing a gale. There were puddles on the pitch. I'd say the only reason the game went ahead was because all the other matches were kicking off at the same time, including those involving the other sides in the relegation battle. The pitch was not playable. It was dangerous.

Playing into the wind with a 6-3 lead in the second half, we picked and jammed from our own 22 all the way to their 22 and won a penalty. But we couldn't even take a shot at goal with that wind in our faces. We won 6-3. I still remember the final whistle. I think I carried the last ball, and you couldn't recognize who was on each team as everyone was covered in so much muck. Somebody suggested we come into a circle. I just looked at him. 'Absolutely fucking not, lads. Let's get into the changing-room.' Within seconds of the match being stopped, we were almost frozen on the spot. I don't think I've ever known a feeling like it.

We hadn't played well all season. That UCD team had a good few lads in the Academy, like Ross McCarron, Kevin McLaughlin, Jamie Hagan and Kevin Sheen, but so many of

us had under-age and A games and Irish camps that we
weren't all available on a regular basis. That's often the way
with college teams. We struggled big time. But staying up
was massive for the club, and the following season we did
much better.

In my third year in the Academy, I remember a play-off
game against Ballynahinch in the UCD Bowl. The former
Ulster and Irish back-rower Andy Ward was just finishing
up his career then. He was well into his thirties, but even on
videos of them that week we'd clearly seen what a tough
hoor he was. He was still fit. In the first few minutes, with
my first carry, I ran straight at him and sparked him out. I
caught him with my elbow on top of his forehead, and he
had a tennis ball lump on his forehead for the rest of the
game. We won the game to avoid relegation and stayed up in
Division 1.

I had a few injuries in my third year in the Academy. After
recovering from that torn hamstring in the 2007 under-21
Six Nations, I hurt my back at the start of the 2007/08
season.

I came out of that and got going again, working hard in
training to make an impression. Shane Jennings and Leo
Cullen had come back from Leicester in the summer of 2007,
and they were instrumental in helping to change the culture
at Leinster. They'd been in a tough, demanding and success-
ful environment and they brought that back to Leinster.
They did it in their actions. They didn't tolerate any bullshit
when they came back. That's why lads got harder and Leinster became tougher. That's what I think anyway.

Jeno was one of my favourite players to train with and play
alongside. Whatever Jeno said, he did. If he said he was going
to give you a clip, he'd give it to you. He was a good trainer

and hard out. His standards were brilliant, on and off the field.

Drico and Felipe Contepomi were also influential figures, in their desire to win and in their smartness in creating opportunities on the field. There were others, too. It wasn't just four or five lads. But when I first arrived, Leinster may have had around twenty lads who were just happy to be playing for Leinster and around ten lads who wanted to win every weekend. Within a few years that had completely flipped, to the point where Checks had thirty-plus players who really wanted to win and take the club to a different place.

Leinster bombed out of Europe in the pool stages in my last year in the Academy but won the Magners League. Munster also won their second Heineken Cup in three seasons, so the League was very much the secondary prize.

To be honest, that Magners League win in 2008/09 is all a blank to me. I don't even remember the win over Munster, when Felipe kicked six penalties and Sexto landed a drop goal, or the night that the League was sealed by beating the Dragons in the RDS. The club had won something for the first time in six years, but I didn't appreciate the importance it had at the time in the development of the organization. I just didn't see it because I was young. But, looking back, it was hugely important. It was one little box ticked on our journey.

Although Jeno had come back from Leicester and he and Keith Gleeson had either played alongside each other or competed for the number 7 jersey, Keith retired at the end of that 2007/08 season and I was offered my first professional contract for the following two seasons.

In the summer of 2008, I trained with my local Gaelic football team, the Fighting Cocks. That kept me 'running fit'. But I also went to Ibiza that summer, with Lukey Fitz, Cian Healy and a few others. A big crew of us had a villa there. It was my first holiday away with a bunch of lads and it was serious craic. I was twenty-one and we were all young. I drank and ate so much that I came back about five kilos heavier than I should have been for pre-season. I'd never had a holiday like that before and it's like anything in life, with each year and each holiday you become a little cuter. If you have a few beers, you don't eat as much. It's a case of calories in, calories out. But on that summer holiday with the lads in Ibiza, I was drinking more and eating the same, and taking in too much each day.

When I came back from Ibiza, that's when I decided to switch to a staple diet of salmon and vegetables.

I had come through the Academy and although I still hadn't played for the senior team in a competitive match, I knew I had to make a breakthrough in my first season as a professional. It was now, or possibly never.

8. Leinster's breakthrough

I used to drive Checks demented by knocking on his office door in Old Belvedere every week, sometimes every day of the week.

'Well, what do I need to do to be playing this week?'

He got so fed up with me asking that he started locking his door after training. We laughed about it in years to come.

But I really had only one goal starting out in 2008/09: game time, game time, game time.

As well as sticking to my healthy diet of salmon and vegetables, I trained like a dog after coming back from Ibiza. I was still a little overweight, but if you have a big frame, you can hide fat in different places. So, back then, it mightn't have looked like I'd put on that much weight. But when the science came into it and I had my skin folds done – a test to measure the thickness of subcutaneous fat – I was caught rotten and there was no hiding it. I worked hard and got myself into really good shape in pre-season. This was make-or-break time, and I wasn't going to be found wanting.

In a warm-up game against Queensland Reds at Donnybrook, I came on for Jeno for the last twenty minutes. I went well and scored a try from the 22, rounding the full-back. There was a good-sized crowd at the game, one of the biggest I'd played in front of, and I got a little carried away. I threw the ball into the middle of them and gave it a big 'Yeah!' It was just the pure enjoyment of it.

Leinster were starting to build something. After winning

the League the previous May, there were loads of positives going into that season. It was time to kick on.

A week later we were in Cardiff for the first League game of the season as champions. It was 6 September 2008, the Cardiff Arms Park. I was named on the bench and got to play for the last seven minutes: my senior competitive debut for Leinster.

I'd said to Checks the day before: 'I don't mind if it's for one, two or three minutes, I'll make an impact.' But I can't remember if I did or not. A try by Isa Nacewa earned us a 16-16 draw. He had just arrived and that was his debut, too. You could tell straight away that he was an exceptional athlete and had the skills to play anywhere in the backline. He would miss three months with a broken hand that season, but once he came back onto the team his influence was massive. He would become Mr Leinster.

The following week I played the last ten minutes against Edinburgh – my first game at the RDS. These early games were about me going around hitting rucks and getting my hands on the ball as much as I could. Doing the reviews and talking to Checks afterwards, I didn't mind only getting a few minutes on the pitch. I didn't mind at all.

My first start was a week later anyway, at number 7 against Ospreys at home. Steve Tandy was their number 7 and they also had Ryan Jones and Jonathan Thomas in their back-row. Tommy Bowe was with them then, too. They were a tough team in those days. I was a bit nervous before that game. This was my opportunity and I didn't want to fuck it up. They used their wingers a lot off number 9 and I pulled off a few nice hits early on. That helped me settle, and even though Jeno came on for me after fifty minutes, I think I played pretty well that day.

I wasn't involved in the defeat at home to Munster or the first two European games, when we beat Edinburgh away and Wasps at home. That was the day of Drico's 'flick'. I was in the stand, behind the posts at the Simmonscourt end, when Drico came down the blindside, chipped Eoin Reddan, flicked the ball on the volley over Jeremy Staunton and gathered, taking Tom Voyce over the line with him. There aren't many players in the world who could do that. Maybe only Drico.

Although Checks was opting for experience for the big games, I was going well in training. I just had to bide my time.

I scored my first competitive try in our win over the Dragons on a Saturday night in November. Off a wide ruck on the 22, I came flying off Johnny's shoulder with a tight line and he hit me with a short ball to go through the hole. I came to their full-back and I had someone on my inside; I think it was Lukey Fitz. I showed with my two hands and he stayed on Lukey, and then their out-half was on me and I flipped him over with a hand-off in the face and slid in. I was fairly ecstatic, scoring my first try.

I played the full eighty minutes and was awarded Man of the Match. That was the start of it, I think. That's when people began to realize, fuck, he can play.

I needed it, though, if I was to get into the team for the big games. The back-rowers in the squad then were Jeno, Gleece, Cameron Jowitt, Jamie Heaslip, Stephen Keogh and Kevin McLaughlin, and Rocky Elsom had joined that season too. To Checks' credit, if he thought you were good enough, you were old enough. A week later he gave me my European debut at home to Castres, when I started at number 7 alongside Rocky and Jamie. We won well, I made a few breaks, and I was happy with how I played.

The following Friday night, on a heavy pitch in Castres, Checks recalled Jeno and left me and a few others on the bench for eighty minutes. We'd beaten them 33-3 at home and then six nights later lost 18-15 over there. We were still blowing hot and cold.

I was back a week later when we won up in Ravenhill two days after Christmas Day. The crowd was hostile, but you'd expect that. Rocky was on the top of his game that night. I also played the last quarter of the win over Connacht at home.

I played the full eighty in the win over Cardiff at home, when a Nicky Robinson drop goal left us with one play to win the game. We kicked off up the middle and I made the tackle. That was the plan. Someone barged the ruck and they went straight off their feet. Penalty to us. Getting to my feet I thought, thank God. Our kick-off plan, which we'd practised that week, had worked. Felipe kicked his seventh penalty to win it.

Checks went for Jeno again at Twickenham against Wasps, but I came on in the first half for Stan Wright, meaning uncontested scrums with me at prop! That didn't go well for us, but they had a right team then and won 19-12, which earned us a bonus point.

I was left on the bench for the full eighty of the final pool win over Edinburgh, and it was the same again for that 6-5 quarter-final win against Harlequins at the Stoop. For such a low-scoring game, so much happened that you couldn't keep up with it. What stood out for me, though, was how deep the lads dug. I wasn't the only one thinking, this is on now. And that was possibly the game that won us the Cup. That was some game to come through.

Chris Robshaw, Will Skinner and Nick Easter in their

back-row were running amok that season. I would have loved a run-out, but Checks wasn't keen on using his bench in those tight games. It was later proved that during that game Tom Williams had bitten into a blood capsule so as to allow their All Blacks out-half, Nick Evans, to return to the pitch. I vividly remember Ronan O'Donnell going mad on the touchline. He was the Leinster Operations Manager and was saying: 'Where's the doctor? Something is not right here!' He was going absolutely skits. He knew full well what had happened. He was the one who told the Leinster medical director, Dr Arthur Tanner, to go into their dressing-room.

I started away to Edinburgh, in Murrayfield, but we had a horror first half and that ended our chances of holding on to the League.

Going into the Heineken Cup semi-final against Munster at Croke Park, it was the same back-row: Rocky, Jeno and Jamie. I was the rookie and I'd broken into the squad, but it was particularly frustrating not being used much. There were 82,000 at Croke Park and the atmosphere was unreal. Sitting on the bench, I thought, this is what it's all about.

We got stuck into Munster right from the start. I genuinely disliked them at that stage because of what they, but more so the media, had been saying about Leinster. We'd also seen them win the Heineken Cup twice, and we wanted payback for the semi-final three years earlier. They were the title holders. They'd just had nine of their players named in the Lions squad.

We were never losing that game.

We had stuff all around the club, pinned up on the walls in the meeting rooms and around the gym and changing-rooms in Riverview, newspaper articles with everything that everyone had been saying about us. Alongside those, we also had certain other things pinned up. What we were about as people. Words like 'attitude' and others that expressed where we were as a group now, as opposed to how we were perceived. Checks and the leadership group drove that.

Had we lost that game, we genuinely would have been losers in everyone's minds – even our own. One way or another, that game was going to define us for the next ten years. And, as it turned out, maybe Munster as well. Because after that day Leinster took off, and Munster never really recovered.

From loosehead to out-half, Munster were basically the Ireland team that had just won the Grand Slam, minus Jamie Heaslip and Stephen Ferris; while we had Darce, Drico and Lukey Fitz from that team. The intensity from the first minute was unbelievable. Felipe set the tone by charging into Ronan O'Gara a few times and kicking a drop goal to put us ahead before he twisted his knee. That proved to be his last game for us because he moved to Toulon that summer.

My first memory of Felipe was when he initially came to Leinster in 2003 and joined Carlow RFC. I watched him play for them several times, but once I started training and playing with him, I began to really appreciate his ability to play off the cuff. He was just so natural on the ball. The other thing about Felipe is that he was quite a tough player. Whereas a lot of out-halves don't like to tackle, he was the exception, so much so that he could also play at 12 and wouldn't miss a tackle. He won some games for Leinster on his own, flashes of brilliance and then a try. Gordon D'Arcy and Drico got to know him well, and they scored plenty of tries off Felipe's brilliance. He was a phenomenal finisher as well. He'd just run flat and hard. He was a great fella around the club too, great craic. He was always engaging and gave people time.

But what set him apart was his rugby intelligence. He saw stuff that few other players could see, and I'd say Johnny learned plenty from Felipe, about seeing how the opposition are set up and how to exploit them. From what I've heard from the lads, he was exceptional at that, so although he was a qualified doctor, you felt he would go into coaching.

After Felipe went off injured that day, I knew from training and playing with Johnny Sexton at under-age level and at Leinster that he was not going to let a chance like this pass him by easily. He'd been left out of the squad for a few games after being taken off at half-time away to Castres, but he came back with a really good mindset. You could see it in training. Even the way he ran on to replace Felipe. I remember it so clearly. It was as if he was saying, right, this is my time now. It was time for Johnny to set the place alight, and he did.

The backline hummed after he came on. Darce finished off a lovely try in the first half. That gave us the lead, which was crucial. We had talked about not wanting to play catch-up against them. Lukey Fitz scored an incredible try early in the second half to put us in control, stepping off the left wing inside Paul Warwick. Lukey was an unreal talent. He could make something out of absolutely nothing and he'd be gone.

When Drico picked off Rog's skip pass for Paul O'Connell, that was it: game over. I only got the last six minutes. I just kept myself busy, making sure we defended well. That was all. But in that time I managed to barge a ruck and we won the ball back. You're happy to have a moment like that in those games. At least you've done something positive. And at least I'd been involved. Better than staying on the sidelines for eighty minutes in the quarter-final.

But that was what happened in the final when we beat

Leicester in Murrayfield – I was left on the bench again for the full eighty minutes. Back then, that's often how it was. Coaches didn't use all of their replacements like they do nowadays. To be honest, you're half shitting yourself to be brought on in a game of that magnitude, but then you're excited as well and thinking, I'll make a difference here if I go on. I can carry hard.

Leicester's Kiwi flanker, Craig Newby, had talked a big game in the week of the final, saying he was going to bully us. That only served to motivate us. We absolutely melted some of their players. Also, having Leo and Jeno playing against their old club helped us. They knew their psyche, and we knew we had to match that and stay on top of them. And we did.

The boys kept the scoreboard ticking. Drico kicked an early drop goal and Sexto landed a penalty and a monster drop goal. But Leicester were dangerous and made the most of Stan Wright's ten minutes in the bin for taking out Sam Vesty. It was a real physical battle. We just had to man up.

The back-row boys, Rocky Elsom, Jeno and Jamie, were brilliant again. Rocky made some impact in his one year with Leinster. He blew through the club like a tornado and then disappeared off the face of the earth. It was funny, because he'd sit down at the side of the pitch and watch training most days, or maybe train for fifteen minutes. Rocky obviously knew how to mind himself because his performances, week on week on week, were incredible. Some days I could only wish to be like him. He won some of those massive games with strokes of brilliance and his ability to bounce off tackles. He was a big man but he could shift, too. He was a force in the line-out and could make big hits. Rocky had so many strings to his bow. He was incredible to watch.

We trailed 16-9 early in the second half of the final, but then drew level with a try when Jeno latched on to Jamie and drove him over. Sexto kicked us in front with ten minutes left on the clock. For the rest of the game, I can honestly say I wasn't frustrated not to get on because like every Leinster fan watching the game I was thinking, this is brilliant. At the end, I looked at the faces of Drico and Leo and Shaggy and Mal and Darce, and all the boys who had soldiered for ten years and won almost nothing. Shaggy was crying with joy. He had done everything in his power to make Leinster a better place. He would put his body through war for another two years as well.

Shaggy got very fired up when we lost games. He hated losing. He was an out-and-out Leinster man and did all he could for anyone. He was a really good guy to pull you aside, chat to you and give you advice. As he came from Boyne RFC – which was a bit like Tullow RFC – I had a particularly good connection with Shaggy all through my career.

Darce played very well in the final. It had been a long road for him, too. He desperately wanted it by that stage. There were loads of occasions when I thought he played better than Drico, but then he mightn't be in the mind-frame to perform some other days and could be at the opposite end of the spectrum. But on his day he was some player.

In his three years with us, Chris Whitaker had put so much into the club. And what a way to finish his career, lifting the trophy with Leo. That tells you the respect Whits earned in his time with Leinster. He had a good head on his shoulders and was a no-nonsense bloke too in knowing what every player was meant to be doing. He had loads of experience with the Waratahs and Australia, and he brought a sense of calmness to games if they were in the melting pot. A great lad to have a beer with as well. He didn't have a bad word to say about anyone and was very level-headed. Whits always looked after the younger guys and tried to help bring them on.

And Felipe as well. Even though he was in the stands at the end, he couldn't have been happier and he had been a huge part of that journey, too. All the players of that vintage had a huge impact in making Leinster become what they still are to this day. This was their Holy Grail. It had taken so much hard work over so many years to build to this point. I never thought about 'me' during that game, and certainly not in the last few minutes. I just thought how rewarding this was for the lads after all they had put into Leinster.

On the lap of honour, I had a Tullow jersey in my hand and Bernard Jackman posed with me for a picture as we held it between us. He had that connection with the club as well and there was some amount of people from home at that game. Two buses of fifty-four fans took the ferry over and another thirty or forty flew over, although one of the buses broke down on the ferry and they had to get a mechanic to fix it.

The next few days were great craic, starting with the journey home that night from Edinburgh to Dublin and into town. There seemed to be Leinster fans everywhere. We had built a strong bond within the squad, but that win and the celebrations over the next few days made it even stronger. I can't remember all of it, but we were in Kiely's the second day, and the second days are usually the better days. They're called Super Sunday for a reason.

9. Ireland's call

I had a good run of games in September 2009, but against Munster at the RDS, Checks picked Kevin McLaughlin, Jeno and Jamie in the back-row, with me on the bench. I asked Checks why and he said he was 'going for experience'. He didn't seem to think I was quite ready for the big games. I didn't understand it because I had been playing really well. I was still only twenty-two years old and maybe he was trying to look after me a little, but I desperately wanted to play in those bigger games.

Still, it was all about building experience at that stage of my career, getting as many opportunities as I could and making the most of them. So I continued to stay true to my promise, that whether I got four minutes or twenty minutes, I would just make the most of it. Do something good in the game and take it from there. I got the last twenty-six minutes in that Munster game and I couldn't complain too much either because we beat them 30-0.

We were flying. Four wins on the bounce. The following Friday we kicked off our Heineken Cup campaign as champions against London Irish. The RDS was packed. And we lost, 12-9.

Their centre, Seilala Mapusua, caused us awful hassle. They were physical, got stuck into us, messed up our ruck ball and we couldn't get any flow. A bad day at the office. We still had a tendency to underestimate opponents. Every now and then we'd let ourselves down and that was one of those nights.

The changing-room afterwards was an angry place. 'This is bullshit.' 'We can't be this soft.' Everybody was furious because that was a game we should have won, simple as that, given the team we had at the time. That one was a bit of a wake-up call.

Jeno was cited for making contact with the eye area of their lock, Nick Kennedy. It looked like a total accident, and that was his and Leinster's defence at the hearing, so it was a big shock when Jeno was suspended for twelve weeks on the Wednesday night.

The following weekend I started away to Brive at number 7. We had an eight-day turnaround to stew on the defeat by London Irish and knew we had to win or we were goosed.

I remember that game very well because I was so sick going into it. I had a really bad stomach. I was sitting on the toilet before it thinking, fuck me, I don't know if I'm able to play this game or not. I felt devoid of energy. But when I got out on the field I was okay, thanks to the adrenalin. Even so, when someone made a break and I went to take off in support, I had a bit of a spillage in my shorts. I couldn't wait to get in at half-time just to get to the toilet straight away and change my shorts!

I got through the full eighty and we won well, 36-13. Johnny kicked very well and Kevin McLaughlin came off the bench to score two tries. But I was sick afterwards as well. I had definitely picked up food poisoning or something because anything I ate just ran through me. I was terrible for days.

A week later, Ulster beat us in the Kingspan. We had our problems against them sometimes in those days. But we'd always kick the living daylights out of them when it came to knockout rugby.

I'd missed out on Ireland's summer tour. Some of the Ireland back-rows were on the Lions tour in South Africa, and John Muldoon, Niall Ronan and Denis Leamy were picked ahead of me for Ireland's tour of Canada and the USA. But I was called into an extended Ireland squad for the first time in advance of the Guinness Series in November.

I was looking at other lads in the back-row, and while I knew I was kind of catching Leams, David Wallace was on a different level. He was just so powerful and strong. I was a similar player to him and perhaps a better poacher, and by that stage I was confident in my ability. I was thinking, keep pushing and he'll have to pick you at some stage.

I trained with the squad before going home to watch the 20-20 draw with Australia at Croke Park. I went back into camp the next day with the rest of the squad in the Killiney Castle Hotel, before training together on the Monday in Donnybrook.

We were playing Fiji at the RDS the following Saturday and Deccie announced the 22 on the Tuesday. Leams was named at number 7, alongside Fez and Jamie, and four names into the replacements he called out: 'Seán O'Brien. Number 19.' I was delighted. As I knew well from Leinster's Heineken Cup run the previous season, it was no guarantee that I'd get my first cap, but I knew there was a good chance I would. Johnny also made his debut that day, at number 10.

Early in the second half, Leams was carried off injured and I went on. I just thought, this is it now, let's go.

My first involvement was a scrum and the first time one of their players came running at me I thought, I'm going to belt this fella as hard as I can. I put in a good shot and I was into it then. The Fijians are big boys and my thinking beforehand was, this is where you'll either stand up or shrink. I was hellbent on making sure that I left a mark on the game in some shape or form. I had a couple of nice carries after that, but otherwise that whole day is a bit of a blur because I was so hyped up with adrenalin. I just remember feeling ecstatic afterwards.

It remains the only Test match played at the RDS, but that didn't devalue the day in any way for me. It was quite special, in fact, because it was my home ground. Myself and Johnny had talked about that after the Captain's Run the day before, that it was actually quite cool to make your debut in the RDS regardless of who it was against, because that's our home turf. I'd say any Munster lad would love to make his Irish debut in Thomond Park, like Keith Earls had done a year before against Canada. It remains an incredibly proud day for me, one of the proudest of my life, for my family and everyone else who was a part of my journey. Stephen, William, Caroline, Dad and my brother-in-law, Willie O'Toole, were all there, as were James and a few of my other good friends as well.

A week later we played South Africa, who were then the world champions and the Tri Nations champions, at a sold-out Croke Park. Wally was back at number 7, but with Leams injured from the week before I was named on the bench.

I'd been going to Croke Park every year for years, whether it was Carlow making it there the odd time or for All-Ireland semi-finals and finals. If it was Carlow playing there, that would have been a big day out. The day of the South Africa match, it was freezing cold and there was a blanket of thick mist over Croke Park. Afterwards everyone told me it was one of the coldest matches they'd ever attended. For a 22-year-old who had grown up playing Gaelic football and hurling, it was special playing in Croke Park and having all my family and friends there. Although it was freezing, it was such a good atmosphere that night, and I can always say I played there. And I might play there again one day. You never know!

Fez had been troubled with a sore hip all week and just after half-time he went off, so that meant I was on at number 6 with Wally and Jamie for virtually the whole second half. We were 10-6 down at the time, but Deccie had kept faith in Johnny and he kicked five penalties and we won 15-10. There was plenty of discussion around Johnny being picked ahead of Rog and people were questioning his place-kicking. He was under enormous pressure. But Johnny delivered that day, and their rivalry at international level was up and running. Rog had been there, he'd been the king of the castle for so long, and then this young fella, especially from Leinster, came along, so he wasn't going to be happy about it, was he?

The Boks' captain, John Smit, was one of those players I always looked at simply because he was so good. He came through the middle at one stage and I made a good contact with him. You get a bit of confidence from making good hits and grow into a game. I got my hands on a bit of ball that day as well and when you are making half-yards and breaks and having good moments, it gives you so much self-belief.

The Fijians were big men, but the South Africans were monsters, and after putting myself about again physically, I was happy that I could compete at that level. It was a step up. You can't be sure how you're going to cope with a higher level until you experience it, so those two games were huge confidence-boosters. After them, I was sure that I could cope. I thought, well, if I can mix it with these boys, I can mix it with anyone. I was flying, almost literally. It felt like I was on air for weeks.

I also waited until after the South Africa game to celebrate my Test debut. I recall being up on the table after the meal, singing, but after that point the night becomes a bit blurry. Every player had to buy you a drink and whatever it was, you had to drink it. Yeah, I was in good order that night! But I had all the older lads to look after me. You know what's coming, so you just have to suck it up and follow tradition.

I was still floating on air a couple of weeks later away to the Scarlets in the Heineken Cup. I scored our fourth try for the bonus point and was Man of the Match. A week later we scored seven tries against them at home, and then we beat Ulster. But suddenly it was bench duty for me again.

Jeno had completed his twelve-week suspension and straight away he started the European games against Brive and London Irish. When it came to the big ones, Checks still preferred Jeno. He was one of the leaders of the team, so I couldn't complain too much. Also, he was flying in training. The competition was brilliant too. I had to bide my time until I was playing well enough that Checks had to pick me.

I actually got on very well with Jeno. I learned plenty off him because he was a hard, tough player and a no-nonsense type of fella. He didn't tolerate bullshit and he was very honest. He knew all his detail, and he was all about the team getting better as well. He was always one of the guys who drove the big weeks, who made sure standards were good. He never got enough credit, but he did an awful lot of dirty work behind the scenes.

I also enjoyed playing with Jeno, which happened plenty of times as well. He looked after one side of the field and I looked after the other. He was good to be on the pitch with. You knew what you were getting with him.

A draw against London Irish in Twickenham was enough

to earn Leinster a home quarter-final, and then I had to focus on Ireland and my first Six Nations.

For the opening game I was on the bench against Italy in Croke Park, but I didn't come on until the seventy-second minute, when I replaced David Wallace. I was annoyed about that, really, because I thought that was the game to give me more time. I was sitting in the stand and thinking, just bring me on here to change the dynamic of the whole thing, with fresh legs and get a bit of carrying going. It was my Six Nations debut, but I wasn't in the mood for celebrating afterwards.

In Paris a week later, Deccie left me on the bench for the entire eighty minutes, even though we were 17-0 down at half-time, 24-0 down after an hour and 30-0 with ten minutes to go. The game was long gone well before the end, but every other sub except me was used. I wanted to be out there, trying to make some impact.

I spoke with Deccie briefly in the dressing-room afterwards. He didn't go into any great detail and I was still too young to question why I hadn't been brought on, but he said something along the lines of wanting the back-row that started the game to finish it. The way the game had gone, he didn't want to bring me on.

I was frustrated, but I came away thinking that he was looking after me in a way. I was still young, and except for Drico's hat-trick ten years earlier, Paris had been a graveyard for Ireland for decades. Maybe he didn't want me scarred by such an experience. I wasn't overly happy about it, but you roll with the punches and respect what the coach does. You can't sulk.

Going back into Leinster the following Monday, I knew I needed game time. I'd played sixty minutes of rugby in seven weeks. I also needed to remind Deccie, as well as Checks, what I could do because we were playing England at Twickenham a week later.

So I started at number 8 against the Scarlets in the League at the RDS a week after Paris. Less than five minutes into the game we used this move off the back of the line-out where two back-rowers drop off and get the ball off the scrum-half in the front of the line-out. I made half a break and thought I'd gotten away from Deacon Manu, the Scarlets prop, but he just had me by the jersey with his fingertips. As he clung on, his body spun in the air and his legs went either side of my right leg as he came down. I knew straight away my leg was broken. I still remember the feeling as I hit the ground.

In the changing-room I said to Dr Arthur Tanner: 'My leg's broken.' And it was. The fibula and tibia were both broken and I had to have a plate inserted the next day. I was fucked. I knew that was the Six Nations over for me, and possibly the rest of the season. It was a freak accident. I've never seen anyone being tackled like that.

A week later, Ireland beat England in Twickenham. It was a hard watch from back home in Tullow. They beat Wales, too, before saying goodbye to Croker with a defeat by Scotland.

Leinster's season ended disappointingly as well. They beat Clermont at home in the quarters of the Heineken Cup, but Johnny suffered a broken jaw and without him they lost the semi-final away to Toulouse. It's hard to beat Toulouse away without Johnny.

After that, there was a renewed focus on the Magners League. We said we wanted to keep our run of trophies going. I was in the stands in the RDS for the final game of the season, the Magners League final against the Ospreys. Two weeks after beating Munster, that was a tough one to lose, because it meant the club finished without a trophy. We didn't look like winning that day either. It left a sour taste in the mouth for a while.

That made it a nothing season. It was also Checks' last season, so it was the end of an era. He did so much for Leinster. He hardened us up and helped put us in a position to win trophies every season. That was a big step forward for the club. Checks was the one who initially changed the culture. I was sad to see him go, too. You build a relationship with someone who gives you your first opportunities. I really liked Checks and respected him a lot.

I also missed Ireland's summer tour to New Zealand and Australia. It had been my breakthrough season, but it was ended by the first bad injury of my career. I had to deal with it mentally and make sure I came back more determined than ever and better for the experience. I was an Irish international, the first from the county of Carlow. It was a huge achievement, but it had been a shit season, too. More than anything, it had taught me that every single time I played for Leinster or Ireland was precious. From then on, I had to make them all count.

10. Enter Joe Schmidt

When I first heard Joe Schmidt was going to be our new coach at Leinster, starting in the 2010/11 season, I have to admit I'd never heard of him. No one had really heard of him. But by the time he arrived we knew he had been involved with Clermont over the previous four seasons and that they'd gone really well. Then, just before he joined us, they won their first French title.

Even so, this was his first job as a professional head coach, something he himself had brought up with Johnny, Leo and a few of the lads at the start. Joe admitted he didn't know if he could master the role.

They said: 'You give us ideas. We'll drive the rest of it.'

The real connection was probably Isa and Joe, from their time together at the Auckland Blues, when Joe was their backs coach. Isa knew how smart he was. Even so, Joe was coming into a club that had been European champions just over a year before. It was a massive jump.

Joe made an impression immediately. In his first pre-season he began setting new standards as he sought to make us masters of detail. All the basics had to be executed perfectly. It was refreshing that no one was treated differently. Checks wouldn't have pulled up the likes of Drico or Shaggy to the same extent. He tried to harden up the younger guys a lot more than the older guys, whereas Joe didn't let anyone get away with anything.

Whenever a new head coach comes in, it feels like a clean

slate; but this was particularly true with Joe. I immediately became a regular starter. I felt he saw that he could build plays around my carrying and give me a bigger role within the team.

Joe coming in was good timing for me. I felt energized by him straight away. We were playing a power game. 'Seánie, I want you to go in here and get us over the gain line.' It was very easy to follow. Nothing too complicated about it. Once we had our game locked away, it was about playing and running hard. It suited me perfectly.

Whereas Checks saw me more as an out-and-out number 7, I played across the back-row under Joe. The number on my back never really bothered me. It depended on what Joe was doing. So if some plays were developed off number 6, I played at 6. If they were off number 7, I played at 7, and if they were off number 8, I played at 8. I played eighty minutes in each of the three positions in our first three games.

We lost three of our first four Magners League matches, and there was a bit of outside noise about our slow start under Joe, but that's all it was: outside noise. We were adapting to a new style of coaching and a new calling system, trying to master a really high level of detail. As players, we knew it was going to be a bit of a process. It was like going back to school: we had to learn how to do it properly and review it and correct it. This was a different environment from the one we'd been used to.

We were pissed off that after three or four games some of the media were already on our backs, and on Joe's back. But we definitely knew that we were building nicely because, at training and around the place, the standards were getting better and better. That was Joe's way. We knew we were on to something good. We just had to be patient, but the way we were training and the standards we were setting, we knew it was only going to go one way.

Our fifth game was against Munster.

They had won their first four League games, winning in Edinburgh and Glasgow, where they'd scored over forty points. Our meeting would be the first competitive rugby game at the newly redeveloped Aviva Stadium.

That, and the fact that we were playing Munster, were all the motivation we needed.

Early in the match, Alan Quinlan gave me a box. There was a small bit of a scuffle and Quinny punched me in the mouth.

'I'll fucking get you back for that,' I said to him. I wasn't going to back down to those boys, because in those days they still thought they could bully us.

He said he was 'sorry'. He was always great for that. But I kept my word. At a ruck later in the game I got a good shot on him.

It was a proper arm-wrestle. Isa and Rog traded penalties. With almost ten minutes to go they were winning 9-6, but we were getting on top. I went around the corner and took a hard line between two of their players. I made a half-break and then, with 50,000-plus people in the ground, all I could hear was a call on my right from Drico.

'Seánie!'

I just left it on my right-hand shoulder. A blind pass. By then I'd become so used to training with him that if I heard him, I'd just leave it there for him, knowing he'd grab it. He went through and did his normal finish, sliding in on his arse. I actually thought he should have put it down a lot sooner than he did. He kind of ran towards the dead-ball line with it!

Isa converted and that was the game really. That broke them. It had been a big arm-wrestle. Never more than a score in it. But that made it an even bigger statement from us. It showed that we had that bit of character, that fight in us, and that we still weren't anywhere near our potential. In the changing-room, the leaders within the team, like Drico, Leo and Jeno, would say: 'We won this weekend still not playing our best rugby. Once we get it right, the rest of the pack will have to catch us.'

Every win is enjoyable. But the feeling after that win against Munster was better than a lot of Ireland games. The fans of the two teams still hated each other. The atmosphere was electric, better than most international games. Back in those days, the Leinster–Munster rivalry was as big as it got, anywhere. The players had massive respect for each other. Most of us were Ireland teammates. But we weren't going to give each other an inch. That was Leinster's fifth win in a row over them. It was a statement all right.

A week later Jeno was recalled, so Joe shifted me from number 7 to number 6 for our first European game at home to Racing, and I had a serious game that day. I was Man of the Match and scored the first of our five tries in a 38-22 win. I think I won about five clean turnovers, and I offloaded and carried well.

Sébastien Chabal nearly knocked me out when I scored. He caught me with a forearm on the head as I was hitting the ground. I was fairly startled from that. Nowadays, I wouldn't play on.

We went after Chabal and a few of their boys that day. We duffed them up. It was a good all-round performance. They had a big team, with a Fijian at outside-centre, Albert Vuli-vuli. He was a beast of a fella and scored one of their two tries. They had a huge, strong, physical team, but we ran them around the place and made them work. We were comfortable enough, on top throughout. Joe's methods were starting to work.

A week later we were at Wembley, against Saracens. I'm not a big soccer fan but it was a class stadium to play in, and over 45,000 were there to watch us. I was at blindside again, with Jeno at number 7. Johnny was back and he scored all our points in a 25-23 win. We had to defend well at the end, but we were the better team. They had a heavy South African influence and a really good team then, but they couldn't handle the pace we were playing at.

Although our breakdown was a work-in-progress, we were starting to generate really fast ball. Joe wanted two 'barrels', as we called them, into the ruck all the time and he wanted them there extremely quickly. Sometimes we were there so quickly, there was no contest. We wanted two- or three-second rucks but by this stage we were already generating one-second rucks. The second the ball-carrier hit the ground, the ball was gone again. In the early days, teams struggled to live with us. They couldn't work out how we were playing so well. The key was our breakdown. It was so quick and clean.

The November Guinness Series marked the opening of the Aviva Stadium for internationals. In the first of them, against South Africa, it was Fez, Wally and Jamie in the back-row, with Leams on the bench. At that stage I was thinking, why is Declan Kidney holding on to Leams? In one sense, I could understand it. Leams was a skilful player who gave his all, and Declan knew him better than he knew me. Also, I'd missed the last three games of the Six Nations and the tour to New Zealand and Australia because of my broken leg. But

I felt I was playing better for Leinster than Leams was for Munster. I wanted my chance.

The next week against Samoa, I started alongside Leams and Jamie, with Fez on the bench. We all knew that it was going to be a tough one and that we needed to put in a good shift. On your first start for Ireland, you want to make sure that you do the jersey justice and make sure that the coach is picking you the following week.

We won 20-10 without the team or me setting the world alight. It was a real physical game. The next week, against the All Blacks, Deccie went with Fez, Wally and Jamie, and Leams on the bench. Despite the All Blacks winning 38-18, it was the same again for the win over Argentina.

As I had only played one game in five weeks, I was delighted to get the full eighty on a miserable, wet night away to the Scarlets – although I was a little lucky to get the full eighty. This was the game when Nigel Owens pulled all thirty players in, and I was largely the cause of it.

About half an hour into the game, I chased a box-kick by Eoin Reddan and I genuinely didn't hear the whistle go. When their number 9, Tavis Knoyle, caught it, I hit him with one of the nicest shots I've ever put in. I hit him chest-high and I was at full tilt. I stood up, looked around and saw two Scarlets lads absolutely tearing at me. That was that. It all kicked off. Then Nigel called us all in.

'I don't want to make a big issue out of this,' he said. 'It ends here. You're adults, you'll be treated like it, as long as you behave like it.'

Funny when you look back on it now.

In the shemozzle that had followed my hit, our flanker Dominic Ryan was blindsided by Knoyle with a forearm, but it wasn't picked up. Dom, or Dippy as we called him, wasn't sparked out, but he was very rattled by it and went off early in the second half. Watching the review the following week, I didn't say anything aloud but I said to myself, I'm going to get him back for that.

Back in Europe, next up was Clermont away. They had just won the French Championship for the first time in their history, in Joe's last game with them. Although we lost, we did get a bonus point. They were very good back then, but Joe had us well prepared and we knew what areas to attack them in. We were in the game from the off. Shaggy scored an early try and we made plenty of half-breaks and breaks, but didn't convert them. Jeno was unlucky to have a try disallowed for a double movement.

I played at number 6 and probably got knocked out that day. Getting up off the ground, I was caught on the side of the head by Julien Bonnaire's knee. Completely accidental. Going back into the defensive line, I had a bit of a speed wobble. There wasn't anything like the same focus on concussion then as there has been in recent years, but I felt grand afterwards. Thankfully, there haven't been any episodes since then.

That was my first time playing in the Stade Marcel Michelin. The ground was packed and the atmosphere was electrifying. It was a great experience. They were a really tough team, especially at home, and were into a long unbeaten run in the Stade Michelin.

Although we lost, we took plenty of belief from that game, as well as a bonus point.

We had them at the Aviva six days later. We were growing in confidence as a team and learning as we went along. We'd learned from the week before where to open them and we went into that return game knowing we had to do everything at pace. They were a big, physical team. They had some very obviously skilful players, but we wanted to move them around a lot in the Aviva. That's exactly what we did.

The try that I scored was from Jamie's quick thinking after a good kick chase. Their winger went over the touch-line and dropped the ball down. Jamie just picked it up and fired a quick throw to Shaggy. I had turned my back to look for Leo, to see what line-out we were going with, and as I turned to look forward again, I saw Jamie firing it in. It was one of those moments where you're like, oh shit, I'm not ready! But when Shaggy hit me, all I had to do was go over the top of Brock James, their number 10.

We were on a roll that day. They couldn't live with our tempo. It was a brilliant day for the club, a dominant victory in front of a huge home crowd, and we gained even more confidence after knocking over one of the big boys of France so comprehensively.

Physically, we were getting on top of opponents, but we were also becoming a very smart team. We weren't giving away very many penalties. All the things we were doing in training to maintain discipline and all the points that Joe kept reinforcing were starting to become embedded in us.

Cian Healy scored our other two tries that day. He is so hard to stop when he's close to the line or he gets up a head of steam. Church is a big, powerful man, 122 kilos, and able to run like a back. He was playing really well and a lot of the other lads were coming into good form as well.

Like Cian, I was twenty-three then and also on top of my game. Teams weren't able to handle me. They didn't know about me, which was an advantage, and they couldn't deal with my carrying and my poaching ability. Were they doing their homework on me? Maybe not. But this was the year that propelled me onto another level.

Over Christmas, we were away to Ulster. We won well and I scored a couple of tries that night from number 8, both two hard lines from outside the 22. Going in under the posts for the first one, I thought, we're on it today. We were becoming hard to contain then because so many things were going right for us.

Back in Europe, we had Saracens at the RDS. Doing the video research for the first of them, we knew Saracens' threats. Kelly Brown was their number 6, Andy Saull, who had played for the England under-20s and was tipped to be the next big thing, was at number 7 and Ernst Joubert was at 8, an experienced, hardy player. Scouting them, I said to myself, we're going to have a battle this week at the breakdown. I would play against Brown in Ireland–Scotland games and he was a hard competitor with a high work rate. I didn't know as much about the other two, except that Joubert was a big, tough man. Saull was one of those fancy England number 7s. So during that week, I developed a bit of a chip on my shoulder: I am going to sort out these boys as best I can this week.

They couldn't live with our breakdown. Joe's system of two barrels going in quickly every time was becoming second nature. That was where Eoin Reddan's brilliance came in: the very second the ball became available, it was gone again. After every squad training was finished, Reddser did conditioning drills where he'd have five or six balls across the pitch. He'd run from ball to ball as hard as he could, flinging it to someone who'd give him the call. It had honed his skill to perfection.

In the final quarter Saracens were crawling back into the

game a little bit, but we had the ball around the 10-metre line. I picked it up from the base of a ruck and I went straight through the middle of Saull and Brown, and Isa eventually scored off it.

I felt unstoppable by now. The more games I played, the better I played, and that's why I didn't like the 'player management' programme. You're only getting into your groove after two weeks and then you are rested again. Then you come back and you get a stupid injury or something because your body is not battle-hardened enough. I believe the reason I didn't pick up any big knocks that season was that I was playing consistently. I started twenty-seven of my twenty-eight games that season, and I usually played the full eighty minutes.

A week later we played Racing in the Stade Olympique Yves-du-Manoir, knowing a win would earn us a home quarter-final. I started the game well, but I cost us a try early on with a missed tackle down the short side. I was completely flat-footed and got stepped.

'Fuck you, Seán,' I cursed myself as I slapped the ground. Time to roll up the sleeves now, I said to myself going back to the halfway line. Grab this game by the scruff.

And I just carried and carried and carried and ran at holes and caused them all manner of grief. I scored a try about ten or twelve minutes later, running off Isaac Boss. In the second half I even had a chip-and-chase! I stepped back inside, went about thirty yards, put it on my boot and chipped it up the touchline. The linesman said I was out when I regathered the ball, but I was actually in mid-air when I fired it over my shoulder infield. We would have scored one of the best tries ever off it, if he hadn't put up his flag, and to this day I'm still saying, you fecker.

Drico got a try off me that was nearly a carbon copy of the one against Munster. I came around the corner just inside the 22 really hard and, again, who was on my shoulder? Only O'Driscoll. I literally handed it to him and he was under the sticks again.

Racing had signed several internationals, but yet again they couldn't live with our tempo. It was another French scalp, 36-11, a home quarter-final and another Man of the Match award – even though Johnny scored two of our five tries and twenty-one points! He was on fire that night.

I was ready for my first, full, proper Six Nations.

I started against Italy in the Stadio Flaminio, but it was a terrible game. We didn't protect the ball and our plan wasn't great. It was one of those games where you're looking around thinking, where are we meant to be going here? How are we not getting this right? We got out of jail, but it was one of the most frustrating days I've ever known on a rugby pitch. You know when there is so much more in a team, but we were all over the place in every facet of the game.

With five minutes to go they worked the ball out wide to the left for their full-back, Luke McLean, to score. They missed the touchline conversion, but they were 11-10 up and we were five minutes away from becoming the first Irish side to lose to Italy in the Six Nations. We'd also lost Denis Leamy to the sin bin, so we were going to have to do it with four-teen men, but Drico hit it up in the middle to set up a drop-goal play and Rog, who had come on for Johnny, nailed it. As he does.

Playing with Leinster, we had been bossing it for the previous few weeks. We were all playing well and our confidence was high and then . . . well, welcome to international level and welcome to Italy. It was a little bit of a life lesson. No matter where you go, the minute you underestimate a team you're in trouble, and we definitely underestimated Italy that year. We went over to Rome, a lovely sunny day, thinking, first Six Nations game, we'll beat these boys, no problem. But they had a hugely experienced pack, with Sergio Parisse, Leonardo Ghiraldini, Martin Castrogiovanni and all those boys, and they turned it into a really tough battle.

Jamie and Fez were both injured, so I started at number 8, with Leams at 6 and Wally at 7. Leams was one of those play-ers that I really enjoyed watching growing up, and when I first went into the Ireland camp as well. He was hard. He was smart. He was a skilful number 8, but he would get wound up very easily and sometimes in games you'd be wondering, what are you doing, you madman? But, hey, I'm sure team-mates thought the same about me at times. Under Joe's guidance, though, I had adapted and quickly became more disciplined. I made sure I understood what my role was in the team, so that's why I was probably playing so well for Leinster. My discipline was under control and I knew my role inside out. There was very little negativity around my game at that stage.

Had we lost, we never would have heard the end of it, but we just about got away with it.

A week later we had France at the Aviva. Jamie was back, so I switched to number 6. They had a hell of a back-row: Thierry Dusautoir at 6, Julien Bonnaire at 7 and Imanol Harinordoquy at 8. Dusautoir was a machine – I think he put in thirty-one tackles that day.

We started like a train. Ferg, who had made his debut against Italy, scored early on. Tomás O'Leary also scored and we led 15-12 at half-time, but penalties and errors killed us. We actually scored three tries to one, but couldn't save it at the end. The French were big, physical, nasty fellas and it was a very frustrating experience.

At Murrayfield there was a group of Irish supporters in the open stand, opposite the running track. In front of them John Barclay came through a short hole and I short-armed him with a big hit. I also put in a big chest shot on Kelly Brown. When I stood up, the crowd were going ballistic! Physically, I was in a really good place.

I was at number 6 again and we were looking comfortable after tries by Jamie, Reddser and Rog, but our discipline nearly cost us again. Chris Paterson kept nailing his penalties and Dan Parks kicked a drop goal to make it 21-18 with ten minutes to go. As in Italy, we clung on at the end.

Two weeks later we went to Cardiff. Again, we shot out of the blocks. Wally, myself and Earlsy had carries before Tommy put Drico over. Tommy was with the Ospreys at the time and was always up for games against Wales.

Again, we didn't really sustain it and our discipline cost us heavily. We led 13-9 at half-time, but the game turned on that infamous try by Mike Phillips. Johnny, who had just come on for Rog, sliced a kick out on the full. They took the quick throw with a different ball but the touch judge, Peter Allan, told Jonathan Kaplan that it was the correct ball.

I got pinged later for being beyond the 15-metre mark at a line-out and James Hook made it 19-13. We still could have saved the game, but Paddy Wallace cut back inside when he could have put Earlsy over in the corner. I'd say he was thinking of the conversion.

Between their dodgy try and all the chances we'd missed, that was one angry dressing-room. The defeat meant we couldn't win the title, and a week later we had England coming to Dublin looking for a Grand Slam. That was all we needed. We took out all our frustrations on them. Johnny kicked three early penalties and we absolutely creamed their back-row – Tom Wood, James Haskell and Nick Easter. We beat them around the place.

James would later become a buddy and roommate of mine on the Lions tours, and I occasionally remind him how I absolutely annihilated him at a breakdown that day. He was on a poach and I hit him a rib shot but he held on and I actually had to lift him out of it. Nowadays you might get done for a tip tackle. Ben Youngs saw it and ran in to hit me with his shoulder. I just flapped him away with my hand, like I was swatting a fly, and he dropped to the ground.

We were fired up for that, and that was the thing about Ireland then. We could do that one week whereas another week we were average. We had the potential to be brilliant, but that performance against England showed we had underperformed in the previous four games.

Still, it was nice being in the reception at the Aviva Stadium having a few pints with those England boys afterwards, after denying them a Grand Slam! There was a TV screen showing France beating Wales, which confirmed England were champions, but they weren't celebrating. It was bittersweet for us, but at least it was a good way to finish.

11. Let's run at them

A couple of weeks after our final Six Nations match, Leinster went down to Thomond Park for a League game. Munster had been knocked out of Europe, so this was almost their season on the line. Shaggy scored the only try of the game, but Rog kicked his seventh penalty in the last minute to win it 24-23.

Joe was not amused. He was particularly hot on discipline because he knew our lack of it sometimes was the main reason we let teams back into games. To be honest, discipline hadn't been a priority until he arrived. Joe made it a priority. Joe got us believing that if we did everything he told us to do to the best of our ability, we'd win the game.

Munster were very good at bringing teams down to their level. That's Munster all over. If a team play a fast, expansive, unstructured game, when they go to Munster they get pulled into a shitfight of a slow slog. They take you out of your own routine. They make it uncomfortable for you, which is what Thomond Park is about. It's steeped in history and that's the way they've always done it. And the crowd get after the referee as well. Admittedly, almost all crowds do that nowadays and the more experienced referees generally deal with it.

Maybe it was no harm losing that game, because a week later we had Leicester Tigers at the Aviva in the Heineken Cup quarter-finals. That was the day of Isa's wonder try early in the second half. And also my wonder tackle a few minutes before that, when we were leading 9-3. But nobody remembers that! We were on top for long periods, but hadn't managed to put daylight between us, and that tackle is probably one of the proudest things I've ever done on a rugby pitch. If someone were to ask me for an example of what I was like as a player at the time, I'd show them that clip from that game.

I was on our left side of the field, on our 10-metre line, when they flooded through a ruck to force a turnover. I looked up and I saw space on our right-hand side. Lots of space. I scanned their numbers and headed for the corner flag. You can see me passing out the first two lads and then putting the hammer down.

I ran and I ran, watching the ball reach Alesana Tuilagi, Manu's older brother, on our right touchline. And then, bang: he bounced Drico! I was shocked to see that. I said to myself, fuck it, I'm just going to have to lunge at him now. And that's what happened. As Tuilagi dived in by the corner flag, I threw myself at him. I didn't get a good shot at him because he was ahead of me, but I got enough of a shot on him to force his left leg onto the touchline. And I knew instantly he was out because I watched his leg drag the ground before he put the ball down.

Straight away I said to Nigel Owens, 'No try. No try.' He had signalled a try, but then he checked with his TMO.

No try.

Maybe, sometimes, you make your own luck. That was instilled in us then by Joe: never give up.

That's my fondest memory of that game, and the second is Isa's try about five minutes later. Isa fielded a kick and passed infield to Shaggy, who got absolutely boned coming back down the short side as he passed back to Isa. Then Isa just took off, turning Scott Hamilton inside out. Isa was virtually unstoppable when he had the ball in his hands – an absolute force of nature.

Another of their Kiwis, Craig Newby, was their captain and during the week he had given an interview saying that we were soft. I don't know where he got that from. Maybe he'd read too many articles in previous years. He didn't even know some of our names, and that was an insult too. We felt he didn't really respect us.

Talking to some of the Leicester boys about it afterwards, seemingly Newby thought he was the hardest player going and, yes, he did fire himself about, in fairness to him. But he never got a sniff of our back-row that day. We never gave him a moment's peace. We hounded him. I think I had three clean poaches, but everybody was on it that day. We led 17-3 until they scored a try in the last minute.

A couple of weeks later we played Aironi in the Stadio Zaffanella. I was at number 8, up against Nick Williams, a former New Zealand under-21 international and Junior All Black. Ian Madigan was at number 10. He had this play where he used to show a pass from right to left, then turn back the other way, and he just fired a perfect pass to me off his left hand. I was in the hole already and scored.

Later on, we had a trick play with Eoin Reddan just inside their 10-metre line, where I was coming hard off Reddser and the winger was in behind me. I was running at full tilt, bringing two people on to me. The hole opened up for Reddser, exactly as we had trained for it to happen. He had a five-yard walk-in. But Reddser still floated the ball to me and Nick Williams absolutely blindsided me from my right with a forearm. It was high as well. One of those ones with a whiplash effect. I never saw him coming.

For some strange, stupid reason I got up and my immediate reaction was to say to Williams, 'No arms, bro.'

The lads were on to me after the match. 'Did you just talk to Nick Williams like a Kiwi and say *bro* to him?'

'Yeah, I did for some fucking strange reason.'

When Eoin O'Malley and Lukey Fitz see me now, they will still screech 'No arms, bro' in a Kiwi accent.

Joe had brought quite a strong team for the Aironi game because we were playing Toulouse a week later in the Heineken Cup semi-finals at the Aviva – but we were given an early shock nonetheless. Florian Fritz scored a try in the fifth minute, after a penalty by David Skrela rebounded off the post. We were playing pretty well and were on top in lots of areas, but they kept trying to slow the game down and they wanted to scrum all day.

At half-time, leading 16-13, we spoke about how we needed to play at our tempo and make sure we sorted out our breakdown. In fairness to us, they had Yannick Nyanga at 7, Louis Picamoles at 8 and Jean Bouilhou at 6. Bouilhou was coming to the end of his career and he was a bit too light, but he was really, really fit.

We started the second half just as poorly as we'd started the first, and I was lucky not to be sent off, too. They had a scrum five metres out and they were on top of our scrum. Mike Ross wasn't having his best day at the office and we were going backwards. I remember lifting my head on the open side of the scrum and Nyanga grabbed my jersey. I put my hands up and shouted at the referee, Dave Pearson: 'He has me grabbed. He has me grabbed.'

Picamoles picked up and literally fell over Reddan to score a try. Just as he was about to touch down, I pulled on Nyanga with a punch and flattened him onto the ground. I whacked him in his upper chest or stomach. He went down, completely winded, and then went off.

I was furious. Even though I had punched Nyanga and knocked him over, I ran to Pearson. 'He was fucking holding me. That's no try. He was holding me.'

Thank God he didn't go to the TMO. I knew I'd flattened Nyanga, but I was so upset because I was blaming myself for being held in and not preventing Picamoles from scoring. Anyway, I got away with it. Afterwards there was a big hullabaloo in the French media about why I hadn't been sent off.

But from that moment on I was even more fired up, and we started to play much better. Johnny kicked a couple of penalties and Rossy nearly scored his first try. He must have run twenty metres with the ball deep into their 22, and Drico scored off it in the end. Jamie played really well that day. He put in some big shots on lads, ran some really nice lines, scored a try and was just really clever, like Jamie always was.

Jamie captained us the following Friday, when Drico, Johnny, myself and a few others were rested for our League game at home to Glasgow. Ferg took over the kicking and we scored four tries in the last quarter to secure a home semi-final against Ulster.

I was the better for the rest, and after Darce, myself, Drico and Isa combined to put Ferg over, we always had Ulster at arm's length. Joe was rotating and using the bench heavily, but once Luke scored our second try, we knew we'd booked two finals in a row. As I said on TV afterwards, though, we knew we'd won nothing yet. We also knew that to have come that far and not win anything would have undone everything. All the hard work. All the good rugby. All the big wins.

In Heineken Cup weeks, everyone would usually be on high alert and there'd be a bit of aggro around. And this was the final.

Drico had received a yellow card against Munster and another in the semi-final against Toulouse, and on the Monday before the final he was standing behind the posts. He wasn't training for some reason. Must have had a knock. I'd been involved in some little scrap or something and Joe sent me on a lap to calm me down. As I went past Drico, he said: 'For fuck sake, Seánie, will you have some fucking discipline out there?'

I turned around to him as I was running and said: 'You're one to talk, after two yellow cards, you fucking asshole.' As I was jogging away from him, I added: Who do you think you are, Mr fucking Perfect?

I was so fired up that if he'd said anything else to me, I'd say I'd have gone back and started a fight with him.

That night he texted me: *Well that was certainly one way to make me shut up!*

I just sent back 'Peace', or something like that, and that was the end of it. It was funny. Mr Perfect. We still have that ongoing joke to this day.

In the build-up to the Heineken Cup final against Northampton in Cardiff, their Tongan loosehead prop, Soane Tonga'uiha, had been shortlisted for European Player of the Year. He was their go-to carrier and had been running over players, but he wasn't a good scrummager. During the week a few us had a chat about getting Rossy fired up, because Rossy needed that sometimes. And a massive part of winning this final was whether Rossy could do a job on Tonga'uiha.

Joe had certainly said a few things to him, and players

were making comments about Tonga'uiha, like: 'He's a serious bit of stuff. He'll be coming after you, Rossy.'

I definitely remember saying to Rossy: 'I want you to fucking smash this fucker this weekend. I don't want him to get an inch and I want you to destroy him.'

I used to do that a lot with Rossy before games. Saying things like: 'This is your area. You own this now tonight.' And Rossy would react to it because that's his personality. He is such a lovely man, but once you got him going and in the zone, he was devastating at his job.

Match day, and at the very first scrum they did a number on us. I was thinking to myself, this is not what we want here now, for Rossy, for our pack mentally. It couldn't have been a worse start for us, and every time I look back at this game I think, what the fuck were we at?

We started so slowly, and they did a Leinster on us. They started at 100 miles an hour. In the first six minutes we made three errors to give them back possession, and with a penalty advantage off that first scrum they came around the corner so easily. It opened up in front of Calum Clark, and Phil Dowson scored the try. We were 7-0 down in seven minutes. They had done their homework. They knew they were going to have to start fast against us, and that's exactly what they did.

For them it was the perfect start, for us it was the worst start possible. But then Rossy started sorting out the scrum, we settled a little and Johnny kicked a penalty.

We knew Northampton would be coming for me in the tackle. There had been comments from their camp that week about stopping our back-row and our carrying threats. So Joe had me using my hands a lot more than in previous games. He saw that I had the capability to use my hands even though I wasn't known for it. I was known for being physical and direct. So even though this was a final, this is where it started, a further evolution of my game. We had a lot of plays designed around me passing rather than carrying, like one off the tail of the line-out where I drew in their tail gunner and first receiver.

Even though we messed up the line-out, I went through with it and Johnny's inside pass put Shaggy in behind them before I linked with Drico. If Drico had given the ball straight back to me, I don't think Clark would have stopped me from five yards out, even with him on my back, but Drico carried on, then flung the ball and it went to ground.

We had another move off the tail of the line-out where I shifted it on to Kevin McLaughlin and he broke away. Their tighthead, Brian Mujati, was sin-binned for tugging Cian from behind off the ball. But even with fourteen men, they score a try. Their out-half, Stephen Myler – who's now a teammate of mine at London Irish – did a show-and-go between me and Nathan Hines. We were too far apart. Me and Hinesy fucked up. I had waved and called Rossy around, but that part of the game wasn't his strength. Hinesy stayed for the inside pass and Myler beat my tackle. As a consequence of me, Hynes and Rossy not doing what we should have done, Myler was in behind us, and off the ruck Foden beat Drico on the outside to score. Foden was very quick then – the England full-back and full of confidence.

So it was 17-3 after thirty-one minutes; and then Roger Wilson muscled over to make it 22-6. Behind the posts we were looking at each other and saying, what the fuck is going on here? All my family and friends were in the crowd and afterwards they told me that they just started drinking at that point, because they reckoned there wasn't a chance Leinster could come back.

Honestly, though, walking down the tunnel at half-time, not once did that idea come into my head. I can put my hand on my heart and say that. I didn't even think, we are in major trouble here. I just thought to myself, how have we made this so hard on ourselves? How have we made so many mistakes?

There actually wasn't a whole lot said at half-time in the dressing-room. We said we hadn't made as many mistakes in the whole of the Heineken Cup that season as we had in the first half. Just before we went back out, Johnny mentioned Liverpool coming back from 3-0 down against AC Milan in the 2005 Champions League final and that this was our chance to make history as well, but he didn't go on and on about it.

The messages at half-time from Joe were crystal clear: Don't make mistakes. Stick to the process. Keep our discipline. Let's run at them.

And that's what we went out and did.

We had worked on our plays during the week and we started to execute them straight away. Normally the hooker would never throw to me, but I went up in a line-out on half-way and carried hard off second phase. Now we were getting over the gain line. Drico picked and went up the guts before they had set defensively. The ball was so quick that they had to make a decision: What's going on? In that split second, Drico was already gone. Jamie was in support, and we kept hammering at them until Johnny scored.

After we scored, some of the Northampton lads had their hands on their heads or on their hips, and others were giving out to each other. Yet they were still 22-11 up.

We were starting to ramp it up and they were starting to fold. Back on the halfway line, as Johnny was about to add the conversion, we started saying things like:

'Let's keep this going.'

'These boys are out.'

Now we went for them. In the fifty-third minute, Johnny did his wrap with Jamie, and Jamie was very cute to keep running his line and make half a block on Dowson. Johnny just powered over. He had work to do for that finish, but no better man. He had decided he was going to grab the game by the scruff of the neck and he did. That's what Johnny is about. That's why he's so good.

Jeno had come on for Kev at half-time and brought his engine, his voice on the field, his physicality, his tough manner, his breakdown work, his ability to annoy the opposition and his experience. You wouldn't want anyone else to come on in a situation like that.

By now Rossy had Tonga'uiha's number too and we walked their scrum back for Johnny to kick us in front. If you watch the game, you can see the looks on our faces when we came up from that scrum. We're smiling now. We know we have them, even though we're still behind. We know these boys are rattled. They're not living with us now. We're finally playing the rugby we wanted to play. It's a great place, that place where you get into your flow and you know you're going to win. It's only fifty-six minutes on the clock, but we know.

On sixty-five minutes we were still full steam ahead. We'd said that whenever we got into their 22, we would stay in control of every situation, just keep the ball and grind them down. I was nearly in before Drico and Jeno made the clear-out. That's what Jeno does. Then Hinesy, such a cute player, pumped his legs to power over.

Their body language confirmed they were gone. Players with their hands on their knees, or lying on the ground. Calum Clark giving the ground a box. Tonga'uiha on his hands and knees. We were watching all of this and our chests were up. We'd scored twenty-seven unanswered points in twenty-five minutes. They were in shock and exhausted.

That was Hinesy's only try for Leinster. He had some of the most subtle touches for a second-row I'd ever known with his offloading and passing, but he was also one of the hardest players that I've come across. He could break up a ruck on his own. A no-nonsense player and an incredible asset to Leinster over those two seasons.

When the final whistle blew, it marked the greatest come-back in Heineken Cup final history and I think that's what made it so sweet, the way we went about it. I was exhausted after that game, I had five staples above my eye and a cracked arm, but it was an unbelievable feeling. We had some few days after that.

That was the season I also won the European Player of the Year award. As well as Tonga'uiha, Isa, Jamie and Sergio Parisse were on the shortlist. I'd played every minute of the nine games bar the last two minutes against Northampton. I'd been Man of the Match in three of them and scored four tries.

The only pity was being handed the award on the follow-ing Wednesday. I was in a rough state going in to the RDS to receive that award. You'd swear I'd been dragged through a field of thistles. I had a black eye and marks all over my face from the Heineken Cup final, and I'd been out for a couple of days.

The problem about playing and winning a game like that is that you celebrate for a few days and then it's so tough to turn it around. Plus, of all the teams to be waiting for us in the long grass, it had to be Munster in Thomond Park, and them with a chip on their shoulder after our famous comeback. And we'd now won two Heineken Cups in three years, just as they'd done before us.

I actually thought Joe might let me off, because my body was wrecked. I wasn't the only one thinking like that. I started at number 6 and Jeno was at 7, with Jamie at 8. James Coughlan, their number 8, was on fire that season and he had a super game that day.

They scored first, when Lifeimi Mafi put Doug Howlett over. Johnny gradually inched us in front early in the second half with his third penalty, but we couldn't turn our pressure into points. We had plenty of chances, but then we wilted in the final quarter. I was whacked and I'd gone off when Earlsy had a fine finish and then their scrum was awarded a penalty try.

Missing out on the double and losing against Munster hurt, but you move on and tell yourselves, we'll get them again. You remember those days when you play them the next time. That was the one positive about that day.

But Europe was our thing. That was the primary goal. Given the choice, we would definitely have taken beating Northampton over beating Munster. That was one of the best days of my life, winning that final in Cardiff with those boys.

12. Next stop, the world

The 2011 World Cup was my first time in New Zealand. I'd just played my first Six Nations, Leinster were European champions and I was the European Player of the Year. I was twenty-four and I was flying. Yet when the squad flew from Dublin to Auckland, most people at home were down on our chances. That was because we'd lost all four warm-up games: against Scotland and France away, and then against France and England at home.

I played in the two games against France. In the first of them, in Bordeaux, we lost but we played well. Conor Murray made his debut off the bench and straight away he looked the part. When the squad was named, Mur was picked ahead of Tomás O'Leary and Peter Stringer, which was tough on the boys, but it's always good to have fresh energy in a squad.

After losing in Bordeaux, we started well a week later against them in the Aviva Stadium, but the French had a few nasty lads in their pack and they were tough physical games. We were eleven points down when Reddser tapped a penalty to me with the last play of the game and I barrelled Fulgence Ouedraogo and went between Louis Picamoles and Maxime Médard for my first Test try.

I was happy enough with my own form at that stage because those two games had me match fit. Felix Jones was the loser that day. It was his first Test start, but he suffered an ankle ligament injury that put him out of the World Cup.

We made plenty of mistakes again but came away feeling

that if we met them in an important game, we'd know how to manage them. The squad was announced the next day and a week later we lost our final warm-up game, against England.

While it was disappointing to lose those four games, it wasn't the end of the world. What people seem to forget in the outside world is that, as players and a squad, you are aiming to be at your peak at a World Cup final – not even at a quarter-final or a semi-final, but at a final, and that was still eight weeks away. All the leading countries are trying to do the same thing, and to do that takes precision planning.

The warm-up games are primarily about achieving match fitness and giving lads chances. That's all they are. Those results didn't matter to us. It's one thing pundits or supporters thinking, oh Jesus, we are in a bad place because we've lost a warm-up game. If coaches or players are thinking along those lines, that's a different matter. Personally, I thought, well, that's done with now. Thank God I got minutes under my belt. I'm not hurt. We showed glimpses of what we can do. There's loads to work on and the real stuff starts in two weeks' time. And then we'll separate the men from the boys. That's the attitude I always had.

Honestly, though, I didn't think we'd win the World Cup. There's no point in saying differently. I didn't think we had a strong enough squad. I thought we had a really good starting XV, but I felt there was a little bit of a gap to the bench or the next eight or ten players. That's where Ireland became much stronger in the following years: strength in depth. In 2011 I didn't think we had a big enough or a strong enough squad to reach that level at that stage. Other teams were just performing too well.

As a country, I thought New Zealand was class. Declan

Kidney and our manager, Paul McNaughton, had arranged for us to be based initially in Queenstown, which is a lovely spot, and the people there embraced us. We stayed right beside Lake Wakatipu and after the first day's training a few of us decided to do some recovery in the water. Some fella who owned a yacht said: 'You can jump in off the top of the boat if you want.' But on that first day we had no idea the water would be so cold. It was worse than an ice bath. Some lads were hyperventilating and scrambling to get out as quickly as they could. We became used to it over time, but seemingly at that time of year no one gets into the water. People stared in disbelief at all these Irish fellas, white as ghosts, swimming in the coldest lake in New Zealand!

There was a lovely bar across the road from our hotel that always played live music. Myself, Fez and Ferg would sit in the corner drinking 7UPs like eejits. There was always a good buzz around Queenstown, too, with a few backpackers about, and people were so open to having a conversation that an hour or two in there would slip by in no time.

On the first day we landed in Queenstown we went on a Skyline Luge, which is a bit like a go-kart. As we were going up onto the top of a hill and looking down on a winding go-kart track, I was thinking it could get out of hand because we were so competitive.

The luge things didn't have engines and you started by pulling back two handles and you slowed yourself down by dropping the handles forward. At the start I said to myself, I'm going to beat a good few of these boys.

We were bumping each other and knocking each other over while going thirty or forty kilometres an hour. I came around the bend and Jerry Flannery was lying face down in the middle of the track and I swear to God someone's kart, I think it was Jamie Heaslip, missed his feet by an inch. Otherwise he would have broken his ankles.

We were ducking and dodging, and lads were flipped out of karts. At the very last bend, and I still remember it vividly to this day, I was right behind Jamie and he missed the turn, mounted the kerb and went airborne like a flying carpet. He flew through the air for about four or five yards and buried himself in the fence. We were lucky no one ended up in hospital. It was the worst idea ever, and I think the coaches got wind of what had happened when they saw so many lads with scrapes and cuts.

Great craic, though.

A lot of the boys did the bungee jumping, but I didn't. When the boys went to Nevis and a couple of them jumped off it naked, I did the famous Nevis Swing instead. I hadn't the gonads to do those big bungees. I'm not a massive fan of heights anyway.

We also went white-water rafting and did a few other things. I loved Queenstown just because of the fun factor and it has a really nice atmosphere. There was always something to do, and the training facilities, with a backdrop of mountains half covered in snow, were unforgettable. I'd love to go back one day.

I was single at the time and I received a text one day saying: *Hey, met you yesterday evening at that bar.*

I remembered talking to people, but I didn't remember giving anyone my number.

We exchanged a few more texts before I wrote: *I don't remember giving you my number.*

One of your teammates gave it to me. Do you fancy meeting for a drink?

I replied: *No actually I'm not drinking, we're in the middle of training and playing.*

What about some food?

I said: *Yeah, I'll grab some food with you.*

I headed down to this spot we used to go to where there were a few pool tables, but as I was walking down I got a feeling: This is a wind-up here now. So I went a different way, around the back of the place, and found about twelve of the lads tucked in behind this big white van.

I walked up to them, grinning. 'All right, lads?'

They just burst out laughing. One of them had set up a New Zealand mobile phone. I wasn't the only one to get caught out on that trip either.

After that first trip to Queenstown, we were in great spirits when we went to New Plymouth for our first pool game, against the USA, who were coached by Eddie O'Sullivan. I was rested, but the rain bucketed down and it wasn't the most handsome of wins. We had our third try after sixty minutes, but we couldn't get the bonus point and they had the final say when their centre, Paul Emerick, scored and gave it the old military salute.

Even before we set off from Dublin, we knew that our second game, against Australia in Eden Park, was going to be make or break for us. Win that game and not only were we probably in the quarter-finals – we were likely to be in the half of the draw that avoided South Africa and New Zealand.

We had targeted the Wallabies game for a long time, and we decided to choke-tackle them from the word go. We had perfected the tactic with Les Kiss on the training ground. In the first minute, from the first line-out of the game, I was stationed beside Johnny. They sent Pat McCabe charging down the out-half channel and we choke-tackled him straight away. The second I got underneath McCabe, bang, bang, bang, there were about three lads around me and I thought, this fella ain't going anywhere now. We had him, and after Bryce Lawrence awarded us the scrum I wanted to make a point and didn't let go of the ball. Myself and McCabe had a bit of a shoving match and Lawrence awarded us a penalty. When something like that happens you think, we are fucking on it today. And they saw that. They saw we were properly fired up. It was the first minute of the game, but from that moment on I believed we were going to win.

Before that, you have doubts. It's Australia after all. You're a young lad in your first World Cup and you're wondering, Jesus, how good are these Wallabies?

They had a good team. Rocky was at number 6. Will Genia and Quade Cooper were at half-back. They had Adam Ashley-Cooper and James O'Connor on the wings, and Kurtley Beale at full-back, but they had lost Stephen Moore just before kick-off and it was a wet night in Auckland.

Our scrum and our defence were well on top, and coming up to half-time, with the score 6-6, their scrum was under huge pressure when Fez picked up Genia and frogmarched him back about fifteen yards. I was behind Fez, and Paulie came in like a rocket and drove everything in front of him. Every other forward piled in over the top and Lawrence gave us the scrum.

It was brilliant to see that kind of intent and the intensity. We had emotion in our performance, and you need a little bit of emotion. We skipped off down the tunnel at half-time before any of the Wallabies.

I know the game is different now and you want to play with a little more control, but being Irish we need to have a bit of madness in us. You ask Jason Leonard or Martin Johnson, and they'll admit that's one of the things they admire most about us. Haskell openly admitted to me once that he was sometimes afraid of me.

Johnny landed a penalty to put us ahead, but he missed a couple of kicks that night – one hit the post – and Rog came on and landed two penalties to see us over the line.

Johnny had been picked ahead of Rog for both of the opening two games, and I thought Rog was sulking a bit. When you know the Ronan O'Gara who can be the match-winner and you know the Ronan O'Gara who could have his head down, they're two different people. But when he came on and kicked those two, he was on top of the world again. He was probably thinking, well, I am the fucking man still. That's the Rog you want to see.

Our third game was Russia in Rotorua, an old-style, open stadium with grass banks on three sides of the ground. It was like playing a game of club rugby at home, which was quite cool. And the crowd were mental. Green everywhere.

It was a lovely sunny day when we arrived at the ground, but that didn't last. By 6pm, when the game kicked off, the rain was absolutely pissing down, for our third game in a row. On top of that, in that World Cup they were using new balls which we only got during the Captain's Run the day before. And they were terrible. They had a different end to them or something, and you were trying to handle them brand new out of a packet the day before the game. Knowing you were playing with them the next day was unnerving.

But the Russians couldn't handle our lines of running. I scored our second try early on. Jamie always used to get on to me after that game, saying that I took his meat pie that day. Three of us were running virtually the same line, it just happened that Reddser picked the right option, which was me in the middle. The defenders didn't know who to go to and I skated in.

Their full-back, Vas Artemyev, had been a Schools star with Blackrock and played for UCD as well as being in the Leinster Academy. He had just agreed to join Northampton and was their danger man. Their number 9 ran wide off a scrum and I got caught following him. I went a bit too wide and the 9 hit Vas on a little switch. I got my hand to him, but he was straight through. I was fucking fuming, because we had prepped for it during the week, filling up the seam between the scrum and our first defender.

It's funny when you make a mistake like that in a game. It's not that you try harder afterwards, but I think you start to hit harder and you start to carry harder. You want to make up for it in a positive way. And I did. I got my skates on after that in my carrying.

Although we scored nine tries, it was a sloppy enough game and we knew what we were getting with the Russians as well. Their whole pack was over 115 kilos, apart from one of their back-rowers. Their second-rowers were built like props but were about 6 foot 4 inches tall, so there were a lot of big men that we had to move at the breakdown. It's actually very hard work and they were so physical and so pumped. It was like their World Cup final. You invariably feel really sore after those games.

We had a full seven-day turnaround before our final pool game. It seemed like the Kiwis loved the Irish and hated the English, and beating Australia had made us even more popular. When we went back to Queenstown, en route to Dunedin for our final pool game against Italy, the whole squad went out for dinner one night. We were allowed one glass of wine each, so it was a tame enough night, but the manager came over to our table and told us: 'Two weekends ago, when you played here, every pub was out of beer! No beer left in the place! Every bar had to close up early.'

A new, enclosed stadium had been built in Dunedin for the World Cup. At least it meant it would be our first dry game.

The attendance was given as 28,027, and I'd say 28,000 of them were Irish fans. It was an absolutely incredible atmosphere. It was noisy for the warm-up, but when we walked back out for the kick-off I looked around and thought, what is going on here? It was like a home game, and they were all absolutely on it. The whole lot of them were drunk, every one of them, and it was absolutely brilliant to see. It's one of those games where you say to yourself, fuck it, someone else can go and play today and let me into the middle of the crowd for the craic. It was class, though, properly class.

Our confidence was high, we'd prepared well and we wanted to put in a shift. It took us a while to put them away, and Jonathan Kaplan disallowed a try by Tommy on the basis that my pass was forward, but it looked fine to me. We dominated the second half, though, and after Drico scored a lovely try following good work by Tommy, Earlsy added a couple more on what was his twenty-fourth birthday. I carried well and was named Man of the Match.

So we topped the pool and earned a quarter-final against Wales. No one remembered us losing those four warm-up games now.

I was told that the New Zealand TV commentators regularly referred to me as 'The Tullow Tank'. When the New Zealanders are talking about you, you know you are doing something right because normally they don't talk about anyone but themselves! I knew I had to take it with a pinch of salt, though, because the New Zealand media could flip it around on you fairly quickly.

I'd gone out to the World Cup not believing we could win it, but by the quarter-final against Wales we were so confident that I was thinking, this is the time now. We'll beat these boys. But the problem was that we really had only one plan. We had bits and pieces within that game plan, but it all hinged on me, Fez and Jamie getting over the gain line. So Wales just chopped us three down. Like felling trees.

Dan Lydiate had perfected the chop-tackle technique, in fairness to him. Sam Warburton was a fantastic player as well: brilliant over the ball, tough and fast. Their lock, Luke Charteris, was like another loose forward for them. He made sixteen tackles in the first half. Little had been known about him before that World Cup, but he seemed to become a different player when he pulled on that red jersey.

It was a windy day in Wellington, but it wasn't blowing a gale. Craig Joubert penalized us a lot, especially at the scrum. Some of his decisions were curious, but that's just referees in general, I think. We didn't have a good day with our set-piece. It felt like one of those games where we weren't really in it, and yet we weren't far away at times. But their back-row was stopping our back-row and we didn't get a sniff of anything. Gethin Jenkins is a hard man to deal with as well. One of the concerns going into that week was how much of an angle he was scrummaging at, and I think the referee was made aware of this before the game, but he didn't do much about it. Our line-out creaked, too.

We had plenty of ball, territory and continuity, but their defence was excellent. We did put together some good rugby, and we drew level early in the second half when Earlsy finished again in the corner. But five minutes later Mike Phillips sneaked down the blindside to score their second, and that was the one that killed us. Darce got done. He just literally wasn't paying attention and Phillips spotted that gap down the short side, fended off Darce and scored in the corner. At that level, you can't make those mistakes. When Jonathan Davies' try made it 22-10, there was no way back. Our World Cup was over.

It was a very, very bad day and one that stung for a long time. We would have got France in the semi-finals – and they were at war with themselves, all over the place. And maybe a nervy New Zealand in the final! We'll never know.

That was one of the most disappointing defeats I've ever known because we never fired a shot really. Not too many teams had multiple game plans, I'd say. But we could have been a bit cuter. We should have changed our tactics during the game when we saw how hard they were coming off the line. We were still trying to run over them a little bit when maybe we should have picked and jammed, put the ball in behind them or in the air, and turned them around. Their defence was in the ascendancy because they were getting us on the ground quickly and were flopping down on our ruck. I think that day left me with a bit of a chip on my shoulder about Wales.

Afterwards, we went back to the hotel and met up with our families and friends. Caroline and Willie and my other sister, Alex, and my brother William were there, as were James Foley, Diarmuid O'Toole and Seamus Corcoran, another really good friend of mine. They had been travelling around in campers. We met them for a while, but then stuck together as a squad and had a few beers in the hotel.

The following morning at 9am, I rang Ferg to see where

he was. Ferg said: 'I'm in the D4 Bar here with Paulie.' When I walked in, there was Ferg and Paulie and a bottle of champagne at their table. They were sipping away, just telling stories. They hadn't gone to bed at all and I hadn't either. I went up to the room, showered, changed and came back down again.

Paulie looked like he had died and come back to life. He hadn't eaten anything since the match. He was barely speaking and disappeared after an hour, or maybe a couple of hours.

Then the owner of the D4 Bar, who was from Ringsend in Dublin, came over to me and handed me a card which he said had three grand on it. 'Work away on that,' he said. 'That should get you through the day.'

By midday the bar was rammed full with Irish people. I had texted all the Tullow lads – there were at least eight of them if my foggy memory serves. They drank the whole day away for nothing – bottles of Heineken after bottles of Heineken. They must have had four in each hand at one stage.

I was still there the following morning, at 3.30am, and there was a video put up of me which said: 'Seán O'Brien dancing in the D4 Bar'. I love jiving and waltzing. I was teaching a Kiwi girl how to jive, and I was amazed at how good my dancing was at 3.30 in the morning! There was just me, Besty and a few other lads left at that stage.

We went home the next day, but that day in the D4 Bar was brilliant. Everyone had been so down the day before and the night before. But what else can you do, after months and months of hard work, and knowing it was all over, but only enjoy each other's company? All our friends and family were there as well in that bar. It was perfect.

I don't remember watching either of the semi-finals or the final. I was back at home, licking my wounds. When you're put out of a World Cup, you lose all interest. In fact, you want to block it out. And given that I was only twenty-four, I reckoned I was going to get two more cracks at the World Cup – definitely.

13. The longest season

After the World Cup, myself, Rory Best, Fergus McFadden, Seán Cronin, Denis Leamy and Paul Duffin, a friend of mine from home, went to Dubai for a week. It was exactly what we needed. We chilled out by the hotel pool, sat around, drank a few beers, ate some food and got a bit of sun on our backs. There was only one night when we gave it a good kick, and that was at a beach party.

There was a fair amount of criticism coming the team's way after the defeat to Wales, and that was one reason why we didn't go straight home. Ireland is a great little place, but it can also be a very negative place when things aren't going well. So we avoided all that. On our second week off I came home, caught up with people and met a few mates for a beer or two.

Physically I felt fine after the World Cup, and after the two weeks off I was itching to get back on the horse. Returning to the Leinster environment was refreshing. Jono Gibbes had arrived as Leinster's forwards coach in 2008, so this was my fourth season working with him. Jono was excellent, a good motivator, and there was no bullshit with him. He was a very good fella and very good technically. Like Joe, he was a stickler for detail. You could bounce ideas off him and he was always very good at reviewing your game and giving you feedback, whether it was critical or positive.

He was a good man to have a pint with, too, although there was one occasion when a Leinster player took that too far.

This player had been out sick for a few days but was having a few pints one Wednesday evening and Jono was also there, with some mates of his who were over from New Zealand. This player began to drink Jägerbombs and was eventually so drunk that he went over to Jono and started nagging him to get on the Jägerbombs, too. We had a right laugh in the changing-room when all that came out. Needless to say, the player didn't play much for Leinster again that season!

Our first game back was a handy one: Munster in front of 48,000 at the Aviva. I was pretty pumped up for it. I can't remember what exactly had been said beforehand, but they were cocky enough coming into it and they'd beaten us the last two times we'd met, including in the League final the previous May.

We had a bunch of players back playing for the first time since the World Cup, and so had they. It was a bit strange, because we had been training together and playing alongside each other for four months. Their pack had Paulie, Donncha O'Callaghan, Donnacha Ryan and Leams, my drinking buddy from Dubai. We were still mates, but you soon flick the switch back to Leinster versus everyone else, be it Munster, Ulster, Connacht or whoever. While you have respect for the Munster players, you don't want to give them an inch, and you especially don't like losing to them.

I always had a massive bee in my bonnet about that rivalry. Some of the things they said about us never left my mind. Deep down, I can only imagine what they thought of us for years before then, and, in truth, they might have had a point. We probably were a little soft in the Leinster set-up once upon a time, and I don't think Leinster had any respect from them as a rugby team. We had to earn it, and we did, by beating them consistently.

Each player motivates himself in his own way, but for me it was always that Munster thought we were a bunch of wussies from Dublin, that we were soft and we could be bullied. Even when we began to beat them, I felt that they might still have been thinking that way, and that was my motivation. So I'd think back to stuff in the past, and of course I only had to think back to that League final in Thomond Park the previous May.

The focus for us in the Aviva that day, as it usually was when we played Munster, was the breakdown, because they always tried to spoil our ruck ball. They'd flop down on our ruck and referees would allow them to do so. In this game, we wanted to play quickly and present Pascal Gaüzère with a picture that showed what they were doing was illegal. We didn't want an arm-wrestle, because that's what they wanted. They defended well and kept us tryless, but when Leams was penalized for killing our ruck ball and yellow-carded, Johnny's seventh penalty made it 24-12. After all the discussion about Johnny's place-kicking at the World Cup, he wanted to make a point that night. He didn't miss once. And Rob kicked a drop goal from halfway, just for good measure.

When you beat Munster that convincingly, in front of nearly 50,000 mostly Leinster fans, it's very sweet.

That had us nicely prepped for Europe, but our first game was Montpellier away, and it was an absolute dogfight. It was their first game in the Heineken Cup, we were the prized scalps and the ground was packed. The pitch was in horrendous condition, one of the worst I've ever played on. It was heavy, chopped up, there were lumps everywhere and they had watered the surface to make it even heavier, which tells you everything about what kind of game they wanted. Coached by Fabien Galthié, they were a big, well-organized outfit that wanted to scrum and maul all day, and they were heavy blokes to shift at the breakdown.

Fulgence Ouedraogo, their captain and driving force, scored a slightly lucky try for them. He is one of the best athletes I've ever come across. He'd run all day long. Never missed a tackle either. He's also a one-club man, and I don't know why he has seemed out of favour so often in the French set-up.

He was superb that day and we were without three big players: Drico, Church and Shaggy. Drico had to undergo surgery on a trapped nerve in his shoulder after the World Cup and the speculation was that he would be out for at least six months, and maybe the rest of the season.

We were 16-6 down and in trouble until Nugget – Seán Cronin – scored a try. Johnny converted from the touchline and his penalty salvaged a draw with the last kick of the game. As well as being a physical game it had been a draining one. There are bad draws and there are good draws, and that was a good one.

A double over Bath then set us up nicely in Europe. Bath is a beautiful place and whenever I go there, I make a point of going for a coffee and having a gander around. The game at the Rec was a tricky one on a choppy pitch, and I nearly threw that one away. I had a four-on-one and I don't know what happened. I just had a brain fart and tried to show-and-go. It was a sitter and I fucked it up.

We ran them around a lot and it wasn't the only chance we blew that day – Rob should have put Isa over in the first half. But my mistake came in the second half, at a time when it would have put the game beyond reach and we might have gone on to win by twenty. Instead, we were scrapping for our lives.

Ian McGeechan was their coach and they were starting to spend big. Francois Louw had arrived after the World Cup and was a big threat, but he finished the game in the bin after giving away a couple of penalties. Johnny kicked six penalties to get us over the line.

I played well otherwise that day, but blowing that four-on-one was all I and my teammates remembered. Joe wasn't amused, which was fair enough. If we'd lost, it would have been down to that moment. I've rarely been so relieved to win a match.

I was embarrassed at the review, knowing I was going to be pulled up. I knuckled down and trained hard that week and made sure I had a clear head when we played them six days later.

We took our chances that day. We put fifty on them.

In front of a full Aviva in the European Cup you'd nearly feel invincible, especially if it's buzzing when you get there and you've put in the work during the week. For those back-to-back games, if you've struggled away in the first one, you know that the Aviva will help.

Conditions were perfect and we even scored two tries with Leo in the bin. We'd come up with a system to control the game if we were down to fourteen men. We'd trained for it regularly. Joe would send someone to the bin during a session so that if it ever happened in a match, we'd all know exactly what to do – how we'd play, what areas of the field we'd play in, how we'd slow things down to eat up the clock.

Our kicking game was a big part of that. There were good contestables or, if we were deep in our own half, we kicked long to find grass and raced to the halfway line, or at least get to our own 10-metre line, to set a good defensive line.

If we had a player yellow-carded, we also had a dead call at the breakdown. No one was allowed to compete for the ball, regardless if it was on, because we were trying to play with thirteen in a line and if one player dipped in, we'd be short somewhere else.

If we had possession with fourteen men in the killer zone inside the 22, then we just worked and worked to keep the ball. That meant we had to go up a few gears at the breakdown because the closer you get to their line, the harder they will come at the ball. In those years under Joe, we perfected all of that in training.

Every box was ticked with that man at some stage.

When we had fifteen men, teams couldn't live with us when we got into their 22. They'd either give us a penalty or we'd score a try, because we were so clear in what we had to do. We also had good carriers.

But the two tries we scored with fourteen men against Bath that day, one by Lukey and one by Johnny, were actually clinical, long-range efforts. Lukey was on fire and when he scored his second try early in the second half, it sealed the bonus point. He took a flat ball off Isa and he was gone like a train. Lukey was a serious operator.

Joe gave me Christmas off. I think it was my first Christmas to switch off completely. I could enjoy my Christmas dinner. I returned and scored a try in the win away to Cardiff in the League, and a week later we played Glasgow in the Heineken Cup.

Glasgow had become a little bit of a bogey side for us and to go to Firhill on a Sunday lunchtime, on another tight, gluey pitch, and beat them was a good result. Johnny was hobbling from about halfway through the first half, after turning his ankle. Ferg, who was playing instead of Drico at 13, took over the kicking. Rob scored our first try from

Johnny's cross-kick and I made a couple of good poaches, one of which led to Bossy squirming over for the match-winner. I went for one poach too many near the end, though, and Nigel Owens binned me for not rolling away.

That put us into the quarter-finals, but we needed to beat Montpellier at the RDS to get a home quarter-final. They were out of it, but they didn't roll over. They picked a strong side, but we blitzed them early on. I scored the first try, when Damien Browne latched on to me. Browntown, as we used to call him, was an animal to hit the breakdown. Rob, who was flying then, added the second. Cian scored the third early in the second half. Joe took a few of us off before the end and not getting the bonus point didn't matter. We'd done enough.

The 2012 Six Nations gave us the chance to avenge our World Cup quarter-final defeat by Wales, but instead that tournament started as our last one ended, and this time at home.

The lead changed hands five times. We were digging in and we weren't going to give them an inch, until Wayne Barnes pulled a penalty out of his arse, basically, pinging Fez for a tip tackle that wasn't a tip tackle. The penalty was in front of the posts and Leigh Halfpenny doesn't miss those. I was two inside of Fez and it was such a good, hard hit. We were in control in defence, we were comfortable at that stage. Bradley Davies had been lucky to receive only a yellow card when he lifted and tipped Donnacha Ryan head-first into the ground with about fifteen minutes to go. Fez's yellow card would be overturned by a disciplinary panel, but that didn't matter a damn.

We did want revenge, and everything was set up for us, but Wales were a tough team in those days and had us figured out. We scored a couple of nice tries that day, but they saw a chink in our backline defence and they exposed it with their big carriers: Jamie Roberts, George North and Jonathan Davies.

One of their tries was off first phase, when George North fended off our midfielders. They just breached us too many times off set-piece stuff and you're chasing your tail then. The opening game of the Six Nations is always the most important one, and especially at home. But our 'D' just wasn't on point that day.

Somebody up there wasn't looking down on us for that Six Nations. In Paris, a week later, it was a freezing-cold night and we had agreed with the French to do our warm-ups and see if the pitch would soften up. The in-goal areas were rock hard, but the rest of the pitch was playable enough. However, the referee, Dave Pearson, deemed it to be unfit to play five minutes before kick-off.

Player safety is key, but we had prepared all week and travelled over, gone to the ground and completed our warm-up for a Test match that didn't go ahead. And then we went out to do fitness work on the field. So you kind of say to yourself, well, why wouldn't we be able to play a game of rugby if we're able to run on it? The French Federation, or groundstaff, or match officials, between them should have done more to prevent it coming to that.

We were on a bit of a downer after that, and it meant we had to play on four successive weekends after the first break. We beat Italy 42-10 at home in the first of those before doing our Paris week all over again. And all for a result neither team wanted, a draw.

We let that one get away, too. Tommy had scored three tries in the first two games and had another two in the first half, to leave us 17-6 ahead at the break. But then it rained, they came hard off number 9 or used pick-and-jam, and by the end we were hanging on.

Conor Murray was on crutches in the airport and both he and Paul O'Connell were ruled out of the rest of the tournament with knee injuries. We were already without Drico, so Besty took over as captain for the last two games.

I was ruled out of the Scotland game due to a skin infection on my foot, but Pete O'Mahony made his first start and we won well. I had suffered a cut because the strapping was too tight the week before the French game. The cut became infected and I had to go to hospital to have the cellulitis treated.

I was brought back for the last game, against England at Twickenham. People didn't realize, and probably still don't, how important Mike Ross was to that Irish team in all the years he played for us. That day in Twickenham showed it. Rossy was injured from early on with a nerve problem in his shoulder – not ideal for a prop. He lasted until nearly half-time. Rossy would be the first to tell you that he was in reverse gear until then.

It was the same for Tom Court when he came on. We didn't have another big, heavy tighthead and in those days you were only allowed one prop on the bench. Tom was covering both sides, but he was an out-and-out loosehead. We lost 30-9, and all but three of England's points came from their scrum dominance.

Earlier that day, Wales had clinched the Grand Slam by beating France, which just shows how fine the margins are in the Six Nations. So much of it is about a bit of luck on the day. It's the same with every bloody rugby game really, but to win the Six Nations you really do need a bit of luck.

As was the case after the World Cup, two weeks after the Six Nations we resumed our Pro12 season with Leinster against Munster, this time down in Thomond Park.

Joe decided to leave Cian, Leo and myself on the bench and brought us on at 9-9, about fifteen minutes into the second half. We controlled the last quarter. After Johnny kicked us back in front, Ian Madigan replaced him. Ferg landed a penalty and Mads kicked a drop goal. No tries against them again, but another win. We'd lost there twice the previous season and it was only Leinster's second win there since 1985.

Basically, we couldn't beat them enough, and if you went down to Limerick and won, you left with some smile on your face. You'd be smug enough after that because it's such a hard place to win.

A week later Munster were beaten at home again when they lost their Heineken Cup quarter-final against Ulster. We beat Cardiff 34-3, probably the handiest quarter-final we ever had. Isa got the first try and Rob had another two. He was scoring for fun that season, and Drico was on the mark too, which sent a full Aviva home happy. We won pulling up, not scoring in the last half-hour.

After we beat Ulster in Belfast, we had to face Clermont in Bordeaux in the Heineken Cup semi-finals, whereas Ulster had Edinburgh at the Aviva.

Clermont's yellow army made it like a proper home game for them, with the hot sun on their backs. It was one of the best atmospheres I've ever played in. Hinesy had joined them and they disrupted our line-out and our scrum. They went after us at the breakdown, too, and we clung on at times in the first half. We were 12-6 down at half-time but we hadn't used any of our trick plays. We hadn't been able to use them.

But early in the second half it just so happened that we had the perfect place to play one, on their 10-metre line.

We called it 'a Latham' back then, after the Australian full-back Chris Latham, but it's been called many different things.

We launched Drico up the middle and at the ruck we tried to hold people in. Whoever goes into the ruck has to stay in the ruck. I went in a little late because their number 3 went off his feet, to stay on top of him. So I was showing a picture to the referee that we're in the breakdown. That gave us a penalty advantage, so even better. It was a free play.

From the ruck, Bossy hit Straussy going back left. Straussy could have trucked it up, passed inside or outside, or given it back to Bossy on the wrap. But instead he skip-passed inside, almost blind, for Rob to go through the hole we'd created. The defence was watching the ball and they didn't see Rob hiding behind the ruck. It looked like he was doing nothing and then, next second, he was taking off into space, with Cian in support for the try.

It's a good move when it's executed properly, especially against a team that folds hard or comes around the corner hard. We knew Clermont were going to do that and we caught them with it. It worked a treat. Straussy could have hit Jeno as well. That was one of the great things with those moves: we always had options. If someone was going to hunt down Rob, Joe always had something else, a good line somewhere.

Even Hinesy hadn't read it, and we had played these moves with him. That was sweet, too.

Rob landed a monster drop goal a few minutes later but we still had to defend our line for our lives, and I could have prevented all of that happening. Near the end we had a line-out and all we had to do was secure the ball and the game was over. It was thrown to me at the front and as I was coming down one of their players slapped it from my hands and it bounced on the ground.

They got a scrum and a scrum penalty from that, and Brock James wellied it to within about fifteen metres of our line for a line-out. They just kept launching one-off runners and, compared to us, those Clermont boys were monsters.

When Morgan Parra popped it to Wesley Fofana on a hard line to dive over, Fofana, some of his teammates and the crowd all celebrated like they'd just won. But I knew straight away, and so did the rest of us, that it was no try. Darce had done just enough to make Fofana twist onto his back when he landed and he couldn't control the touchdown.

We were awarded the scrum. The crowd went mental. We smashed the first scrum but it was reset, and then Wayne Barnes gave them a penalty. Then he pinged Brad Thorn for not rolling away. Another penalty.

They tapped and I flew off the line with Johnny to hit their second-row, Julien Pierre – a big, filthy player. I got up and made another tackle.

Nugget and Rossy each saved a try on our line and then their replacement prop, Vincent Debaty, picked off the base. He had been causing havoc. But Thorny hit Debaty so hard that his head went towards his boots. Brad nearly folded him in two, and he hit the ground so hard that he twisted onto his back.

I latched on to the ball for dear life and just said to myself, I am not letting go of this. I don't care if it's a penalty or a yellow card, I'm not letting go. Barnes blew his whistle and gave a penalty to us. I was a relieved man, and a happy man.

It was one of the most intense endgames I'd say any of us

have ever experienced. They threw everything at us. No other team in Europe would have beaten Clermont in Bordeaux that day. It was an absolute belter of a game. Everyone was battered afterwards.

We weren't going to be beaten by Ulster in the final if we got our stuff right. We knew they were going to be fired up, because it was their first one in so long and it was an Irish derby, but the quality we had and the way we were playing gave us great belief.

They had signed some seriously good players. Ruan Pienaar had been brilliant for them all season. Craig Gilroy had scored a wonder try when they beat Munster at Thomond Park. But I knew that if we focused on our game that week, we'd be fine.

In 2011/12 some pundits said my form wasn't as good as the previous season. While my form at the start of the season probably wasn't at the height of the previous season, that was at least partly because I was a marked man: when you've two or three lads throwing themselves at you, you're not going to make as much ground. Then leading into that final in Twickenham against Ulster, there was shit written about me during the week saying I hadn't reached the heights that I'd reached the previous season. I said to myself, we'll always see on the big day who comes alive. And I say that to younger lads now, that the big players will always play well on the big days. That's just the way it is.

I went into that final so focused. I'd had a slight medial ligament tweak in my knee for the previous few games, but in all other aspects I was flying. I made a vow: now is the day to shut these fuckers up.

Twickenham was packed with 82,000 people. It was a cold day for May, but the atmosphere was brilliant.

Pienaar kicked them in front early on, but we were behind for only five minutes. They had a scrum on their 22 and when Jamie held up Pedrie Wannenburg off the base, I won a clean poach. Darce put us on the front foot. That was great to see. He was on it. So strong, so hard to stop. Rob was the same. We hammered at them and when Reddser popped it to me, I saw Tom Court, dummied slightly to beat Wannenburg, and reached through Court's tackle for the line.

Nigel Owens went to the TMO, but I knew it was a try straight away.

Leo asked: 'Did you get it?'

I said: 'Yeah, I got it. I was on the line.'

I didn't have any doubt about it. The boys behind me knew I'd scored it as well. It was close. They deliberated over it for quite a while, but then we heard the cheer from the Leinster supporters and we knew before Nigel eventually confirmed the try.

For our second try, Drico gave me a 'giddly', as we call it, a backhander, just inside their half. We stole a scrum, Johnny ran hard and from the ruck Drico stepped inside a couple of their players. Any time he was on the ball and straightened the line like that, you just had to be awake for anything. He regularly did it in training. It's not just something he pulled out during a game. Like Johnny, Drico would show a ball out the back but would actually put you through a hole without his eyes going there. And even in training, if you dropped it, you looked like a gobshite. Over the years you learned that you had to be ready and watch the ball, because these boys could do this stuff. That's the only reason I caught that 'giddly'. The minute he got through the gap, I knew something was going to come.

Then I took off, away from Pienaar, and stepped Craig

Gilroy, and I probably would have scored again except Besty actually caught me. It was only when I looked back on the video that I saw Brad Thorn clearing out two players all by himself: Besty and Stefan Terblanche. He broke that ruck in half, and that's what made the score. Reddser, as usual, was there immediately and hit Cian on a hard line. Andrew Trimble, at the time, was one of the toughest and most hard-hitting players, pound for pound, in the game, and he absolutely whacked Cian Healy. Never moved him an inch! Cian rolled over and scored.

We were only 14-6 up at half-time but we felt in control. We had a big line-out maul from the 22, which peeled off, stayed tight and when they pulled it down Nigel ran in under the posts. A fair call. We weren't going to be stopped two metres from their line.

That left us in cruising mode and at the end the lads on the bench came on and started firing the ball around. We stretched them twice for Nugget to put Heinke van der Merwe over, and then Nugget himself ran in our fifth try when I gave him the final pass. It just applied the gloss to it: 42-10.

There wasn't quite the same immediate elation at the full-time whistle as against Northampton because we were comfy and in control. But that was a good Ulster team and it was every bit as satisfying, especially when you thought of how we'd won that battle in Bordeaux. We were only the second team to win the Heineken Cup back-to-back and we had our third, which put us one past Munster, and I was chosen as Man of the Match.

I had to undergo a scope on my knee to be ready for the first Test against the All Blacks three weeks later, so I missed the Pro12 final against the Ospreys. That was a hugely frustrating day to be sitting in the stand. Being denied the double was worse than losing to Munster in Thomond Park in the Pro12 final a year before. This time we'd topped the table and were at home. But it just got away from us. Even with the eight-day turnaround I thought we were a bit flat that week and we ran out of steam near the end. Shane Williams was the match-winner in his final game, scoring his second try in the seventy-eighth minute, and Dan Biggar converted from the touchline.

Winning it would have topped off the season perfectly. But, then, no team had won a double since Wasps in 2004. It's a bloody hard thing to do, with the finals coming back-to-back. Maybe it would have helped not to have celebrated the Heineken Cup final wins over Northampton and Ulster, and instead have gone straight into recovery mode. They weren't two- and three-day benders, but going out for one night, and then maybe meeting for dinner the next day or whatever, might have had an effect. Then again, if you can't celebrate winning the European Cup, what's the point?

The European finals should always be the last game of any season.

At the end of a tough World Cup season, we went back to where it had started, Queenstown, to prepare for Ireland's first ever three-Test tour of New Zealand. In the All Blacks' last Test they had won the World Cup to end all those years of hurt.

It had been a long and demanding season – about fifty-two weeks by the time we went back to New Zealand – but I was looking forward to it so much. It would be my first time to play against the All Blacks. I would be coming up against some of the best back-rowers in the game: Victor Vito, Richie McCaw and Kieran Read.

Read was an outrageous player – very physical, athletic as well, but incredibly smart and he ran really good lines. He always seemed to come onto the ball at the right time. He wasn't a big talker on the field but was able to manage referees really well. Chatting to referees has always been something the All Blacks have been pretty good at. But he was a class player to watch.

The first Test was in Eden Park. The ground was packed. Brodie Retallick, Aaron Smith and Julian Savea all made their Test debuts that night, and Savea scored a hat-trick.

Dan Carter kicked everything. As he does. He always looked so comfortable on a rugby pitch, never looked like he was panicked or anything, just directed the troops around and pulled the strings. He never looked like he was under pressure at all during his career. As a number 7, you couldn't really get to him. He was one of these players who made you ask, how does he have so much space? And time. Loads of time.

We were pissed off at how they'd run us off the park in the first Test and we gave them a serious game in the second Test. It was the first rugby international in Christchurch since the earthquake there in February 2011, and on our first day we visited some of the worst-affected areas in the city centre.

Match night was wet and cold. We got our maul going, Conor Murray scored early on, and Johnny kicked a penalty to make it 10-0. They came back at us, but we were always in it. After Aaron Smith scored early in the second half, Johnny kicked us level at 19-19, and with eight minutes left they were reduced to fourteen men when Israel Dagg took out Rob late. We had scrummaged well all night and with five minutes to go we went after their put-in and shunted them back.

I heard the whistle and looked up, expecting Nigel Owens to give us the penalty. It was well within Johnny's range. But Nigel penalized us for deliberately wheeling. It should have never been a penalty, or, if anything, it should have given Johnny the chance to win the game. Instead, they went down the pitch and Carter kicked the winning drop goal.

We were all over them in that second Test. We were hurting from the first one. But it was the day that showed me that Richie McCaw was just a machine. You'd want to see the state of him afterwards. Physically, we tried to go after him and stop him. We didn't just target him – we went after all of them – but he was in the thick of everything. More than anyone I'd ever come across, I looked at McCaw after that game and thought, this fella just does not go away at any stage.

I looked through the game afterwards and I was on him. I was all over him. But he just wasn't going away. I learned a lot about him that day. He was absolutely relentless.

The disappointment of that game knocked us mentally, whereas it probably poked them into life. Maybe being at the end of a long season caught up with us too. Certainly, the third Test was a Test too far.

Darce was injured. Deccie called up Paddy Wallace from his summer holidays for his first game since the Twickenham final, and he went straight in against Sonny Bill Williams.

We lost 60-0. Our squad was stretched and some of the lads who played that night just weren't at that level. We all have to take the blame for that night, but some people didn't turn up at all, didn't do their jobs. Also, because we put so much into the second game, physically we just weren't able to reach those heights again a week later. And we didn't have the squad to bring in other players and freshen things up. We needed to build a squad of thirty good players, so we could back up performances week to week against the All Blacks. We were nowhere near it.

Aaron Cruden had come in for Carter, but he and Sonny Bill had developed a brilliant mutual understanding, like telepathy, through playing together with the Chiefs. Cruden limped off after the first quarter, but Sonny Bill had already scored two tries by that stage, and then Beauden Barrett came on for his debut. When you think of it!

Sam Cane was another Chiefs boy on home soil that night, and he scored two tries as well. Sam is a tough lad, but a real nice fella. I've chatted to him after games, and he's big into his hunting as well. He is easy-going and quiet off the pitch, but I knew he'd succeed Read as the All Blacks' captain one day.

Afterwards, you'd swear they'd just done a training session. They started at 100 miles an hour and we fell off tackles early on. We got sat down a few times in the midfield. They made clean line breaks and when they do that, goodbye. They're just gone. A lot of it was individual errors, which led to them pulling away quickly.

It was an embarrassing experience. The most embarrassing, I can safely say, in my career.

14. The pinnacle

I don't write down goals, but in the summer of 2012 I made an exception: the British & Irish Lions tour to Australia in 2013. First and foremost, I had to play well for Ireland. Then I wanted to be on that tour at all costs.

I had never really thought of playing for the Lions until then – there's no point in looking too far forward – but I'd watched the DVDs and knew about the great coaches, the great speeches and the history.

My hip had been at me towards the end of the 2011/12 season, and straight after the New Zealand tour the medics decided I would need keyhole surgery to remove some cartilage damage. That meant I missed almost the first three months of the season and Ireland's November games against South Africa and Argentina.

I came back on 23 November, against Glasgow on a horrible night in Scotstoun when Joe played me at number 8 even though I hadn't been back training that long. We won 6-0 thanks to two penalties by Ian Madigan. My season had to start somewhere, I suppose.

A week later I played the first half of the win at home to Zebre and then we were into the Heineken Cup and back-to-back games with Clermont. They wanted revenge for that Bordeaux semi-final and apparently the game was sold out in an hour. Clermont were unbeaten in fifty matches at the Stade Michelin, which is one of the most atmospheric grounds in the world.

Our scrum went well but our line-out didn't. We created chances but didn't take them. Drico was out for a couple of months with an ankle injury, and a recently signed Kiwi, Andrew Goodman, made his European debut at centre. They led 15-9 at half-time, so to keep them to a 15-12 win and come away with a bonus point looked like a good result.

The thinking after that game was, we'll get these lads at home. We had won all previous seven Heineken Cup games at the Aviva. Maybe we felt a little too invincible. The return game at home six days later was proof that you can't just rock up. You have to make it happen every time.

Clermont came to town and they played rugby. They went after us and schooled us in our own backyard. That dented our confidence in a way that didn't happen in any other defeat under Joe.

Wayne Barnes was the referee again, and I came in for a bit of criticism afterwards for not leaving him alone. You can hear me a lot on the ref mic, shouting, 'Release, release?' if they were holding on to the ball on the ground. I was really frustrated with the way he refereed around the breakdown, and I didn't exactly hide it.

During one break in play I said to Barnes: 'Sir, how long do we have to hold on?'

He said: 'Well, you have to survive it.'

'Survive for how long though?' I asked him. 'Four, five, six seconds? You tell me.'

If someone is holding on to the ball, they are holding on to the ball. If it's one or two seconds, that should be our penalty. Barnes sin-binned me in the second half for an early hit on Sitiveni Sivivatu, and I'd say my chats with him might have been a factor.

I think I've always had a good relationship with referees. I don't think referees ever thought I did anything out of malice or was rude or ignorant to them, but I always felt that they were so inconsistent. It was very frustrating for a player of my type because one week you were getting rewarded for what you were doing and the next week, doing the same thing, you weren't.

After that game my mate James replied to some fella who tweeted: *Could someone please tell Seán O'Brien to shut up on the field.*

I said to James: 'Do not fucking respond to any pothole on social media about anything that's going on with me.'

He went off on a big rant, but I said: 'Just don't do it, please.'

Even so, I realized I had to control my emotional side on the pitch better. Take Richie McCaw. He says what he says to the ref, but he says it at the right time – when he has an opportunity. The All Blacks were cute in having their openside as captain. It meant he could legitimately have dialogue with referees. Five times out of ten he was offside and seven times out of ten he was illegal at the breakdown, but because he was captain of the All Blacks and had a good way with referees, he got away with it.

Now, I got away with plenty as well, partly because some referees liked what I was about, and I enjoyed having conversations with some of them beforehand or afterwards. But not that night against Clermont. The front-row boys and Joe weren't too happy with how Barnes refereed the scrums either. Parra kicked seven penalties and although we scored two late tries for a bonus point, that defeat put us in a really bad place. We needed a miracle to qualify from our pool.

A week later we were up in Belfast against the team we had beaten in the final at Twickenham the previous May. We were a prized scalp again and they beat us 27-19. Morale wasn't great, we had a long list of injuries and Ulster were flying – top of the table. They got stuck into us as well.

I still wasn't hitting it off with the referees. For one of their tries I was blocked by George Clancy. I was possibly a yard behind where I should have been, but I saw Iain Henderson coming like a train. He used to run those blind lines really nicely, but when I went to tackle him, I just hit the referee.

'You're in my way,' I said. 'You've blocked me from tackling him.'

'No,' he said, shaking his head. 'Try.'

George Clancy is a nice fella off the field, but on the field he's a panicker. He is a good referee, I'll give him that, and he's probably one of the ones I got on best with, but referees can be very jittery. He panicked in that situation and didn't review it. I was seething after that.

For another of their tries, I tried to hold up Nick Williams when he scored, but I might as well have been trying to hold up a hippo! He's one of the strongest human beings I've ever come across. I would like to have seen him with Leinster. I think Leinster would have helped him take off some of his weight and turned him into more of an athlete. He had good hands, he was strong and he was a phenomenal player. A hard man to stop, a bit like Billy Vunipola. You had to send two fellas at him the whole time.

In the New Year we managed bonus-point wins over Scarlets at the RDS and Exeter away, but it wasn't enough to make the quarter-finals. Still, that win in Exeter was one of my most enjoyable games. Our pride was on the line that day. We went there and we did what we said we were going to do. They were very, very hard to beat at Sandy Park and although it wasn't enough to get us through, it restored that bit of confidence we'd lost.

Leinster were back on track and, to begin with, it looked like Ireland were, too. We went to Wales for our first Six Nations game and had a dream start. It was a combination of hurt pride and lessons learned from the three previous defeats. We knew what way to go about beating them and we did a lot of good things in that game. We tried to play away from their shooters, who were flying out of their defence. We used our hands a little more. Drico was on fire, setting up one try for Simon Zebo and scoring another himself. We led 30-3 early in the second half, but were hanging on to win 30-22 in the end.

It was a shit show from then on. England came after us in the rain at the Aviva. They flew off the line and we were standing still, receiving the ball. We were like sitting ducks. They were so up for it. At the side of one scrum, Tom Wood was looking across at me, going: 'O'Brien, I'm going to fucking kill you. I'm going to fucking kill you if you come off the back of the scrum.' All this shite.

Afterwards I thought, never again am I going to let an Englishman come into our home and dictate to us like they did today. They dictated everything – physically, emotionally. And we were playing in front of 50,000 people at home!

My mindset as a rugby player is if we win more collisions than we lose, nine times out of ten we win. You can have all the talk and all the game plans and all the bullshit, but if you keep knocking people over and hurting them, it's very hard for them to get any momentum going. That was one of those games where they just knocked us over on our arse time after time. For some reason they were more up for it than we were.

When Ireland are at home to England that shouldn't

happen, but it did. And that's rugby, too. You need to bring a level of emotion to every game. If five or six players drop below it, you've no chance. We lost Zeebs after ten minutes and Johnny after half an hour, and they won 12-6 with four Owen Farrell penalties.

Johnny was ruled out for the rest of the tournament, so Deccie brought in Paddy Jackson for his debut in Murray-field and left Rog on the bench again. Luke Marshall made loads of breaks, but we didn't finish them off. We created plenty but lost again.

It would be Rog's last game for Ireland.

During that Six Nations I used to call him Barry on the training field. When Knoxy and Checks were at Leinster, they had introduced an award for the worst trainer of the day, named after the Australian singer and actor Barry Crocker. In other words, he'd had a Shocker!

Drico and Rog used to have a bit of banter, calling each other Barry, and it became a running joke between me and Rog as well. Even if he'd trained really well, I'd say: 'Well, Barry?' I'd do the same with Drico if he dropped the ball. I'd always get stuck into the senior lads by going: 'Well, Barry?'

Rog laughed his head off every time, but at that stage he knew things were changing and it was probably a tough place for him, being such an iconic player for Ireland for so long and sensing his time was coming to an end. I can understand why he was down. He could possibly have added more value in that last little period of his career, but I think it was hard for him, not being 'The Man' any more.

He was a truly brilliant rugby player, though – above all, always a really good decision-maker and with such a good skill set. I knew he couldn't tackle, because I ran over him loads of times, but his game management was class and he knew how to put teams under pressure by turning them around. Rog was the man who controlled things and his kicking game was phenomenal.

When Leinster played Munster and he put a ball over your head, you'd be running back thinking, fuck you anyway, Rog. Because invariably the kick was on the money. He was mentally tough, too. Need a clutch kick to win the game? No better man. And with a lead, he was the master at closing out games. As a senior pro and as a person, he was brilliant to me. He was always very respectful. I'd class him now as a good friend I could turn to if I needed advice on anything.

Next up, France. We led 13-3 at half-time but about five minutes from the end they drew level when Louis Picamoles tapped and muscled over, and Freddie Michalak kicked a handy conversion.

On his day, Picamoles was very hard to handle, and then on other days he was the easiest man on the field to get into. He was so hot and cold early on in his career especially, and if you got stuck into him quickly it was going to be a good day at the office for you. But if you gave him any bit of momentum at all or let him build a head of steam, he could destroy you on his own with his carrying.

We had injuries all over the place. We were dropping like flies. Johnny was set to play against Italy, but he tore a tendon in his foot in training. In Rome, it became ridiculous. We lost Earlsy and Luke Marshall in the first half. Luke Fitzgerald came on, and went off ten minutes or so later, and Pete played more than half the game on the wing. Wayne Barnes also binned Drico, Donnacha Ryan and Conor Murray. We weren't going to win with injuries like that, three yellow cards and ill-discipline. And that was the nail in Deccie's coffin.

Declan Kidney is an incredibly smart man. He's probably one of the best man managers I've ever come across. His 'hands on' coaching obviously isn't his strong point, but in everything else he's incredible. He'd led Ireland to a Grand Slam in 2009 and this was 2013. All coaches have a certain shelf life, be it a club or an international team, because it's so hard to maintain that drive within players, to keep challenging players and to keep developing as a coach and create new tactics and moves year after year.

The best coaches are the ones who stay ahead of the curve all the time, who have a Plan B and a Plan C fine-tuned and ready to use if they're needed. That's what the All Blacks' coaches do better than anyone. They'll have a Plan C that they'll have worked on for months in training, just in case. A coach has to have a few plans nowadays because defences are brilliant and the opposition generally have you figured out pretty quickly. They have analysts looking at every single aspect of your game. So you have to have a varied attack and a varied way of going about things and you have to do it exceptionally well when you do go with whatever plan you've devised.

Deccie had his time in the sun and did extremely well with that group of players, and it was tough because he didn't have thirty-plus international-standard players. He probably had twenty at most, whereas nowadays Ireland actually does have thirty international-standard players.

But when results go badly, the buck stops with the head coach. We knew Deccie was out of contract, and winning only one match and losing to Italy for the first time in the Six Nations was only going to lead to one outcome. The IRFU were not going to go to him and say: 'Here you go, here's another contract. You're after having a cracker of a Six Nations there, winning one game.' Coaching is a tough place.

We knew Joe was the obvious successor, but as the speculation mounted we had to play Wasps away in the Challenge Cup quarter-finals.

I was really fit and strong going into that one. I had a good block of training under my belt. I was back to that place where I was thinking, they're not going to be able to handle me here now. I made a few half-breaks and set up a try for Rob. I went around the corner, handed off their second-row, got to five metres out and popped it off the ground to him.

Mads came in for Johnny and had a blinder. There was never a doubt about Ian Madigan's skill or his quality. It was only a question of whether he stuck to the script, which can be a hard thing for some players to do. Sometimes he just did his own thing and it wouldn't be what the team needed, it would be what he wanted to do. I'd say he'd openly admit that now, looking back on some of his career, that he should have stuck to the plan a bit more.

The following week we went down to Thomond Park and I ran amok. It pissed rain and we had to dig deep. They threw everything at us, but with about ten minutes to go we put together over twenty phases and Drico did his thing. Another win in Thomond, and another double. They'd just had a big Heineken Cup quarter-final win away to Harlequins six days beforehand. But they couldn't beat us at that stage, and we were loving it.

I missed the Challenge Cup semi-final win over Biarritz. My calf and my knee were at me. Johnny was back, and tries by him, Jamie, Isa and Drico put us in the final. We were rampant now.

The following Monday, Joe addressed the squad in UCD and told us he'd accepted the IRFU's offer to be Ireland's new head coach. We were expecting it. The Chinese whispers had been going around since the IRFU's announcement that Deccie was moving on. I had mixed feelings, as I'd say was true of most of us. We were losing a great head coach at Leinster, but we were gaining one with Ireland.

The next day, the Lions squad was announced. Joe re-arranged training so that the entire Leinster squad was assembled in the kitchen in UCD to watch the announcement on Sky Sports on a big screen. It was one of the most nerve-racking days of my life, but it was very nice to have my teammates there. There was a big cheer each time when Cian, myself, Jamie, Johnny, Drico and Rob were named. I'd put in so much work, so I knew I had a chance. But you just never know what another coach, or coaches, are thinking. It was quite a nice feeling to have it confirmed. My overriding feeling was relief: fuck, I'm in. Thank God. I didn't hear most of the other names being read out. I rang my family straight away. It was definitely one of the proudest days of my life. To be named a Lion is the pinnacle.

I was back for the home win over the Ospreys, which gave us a home semi-final and knocked Ospreys out of contention. We'd had a look back at the final the previous May, when they beat us at the RDS. That was a big motivation.

Joe gave me every chance to be right for the Pro12 semi-final against Glasgow, but my calf was too tight. Drico's back seized up early on, and so did Darce's calf near the end.

Mark Bennett's try brought them to within two, but Stuart Hogg missed a conversion to take the game into extra time, which was just as well as we had a six-day turnaround for the Challenge Cup final against Stade Français.

Then we had two finals in a row at the RDS to send Isa, Johnny and Joe off into the sunset, but we were hobbling to the finishing line a little, me included. I was in one week and out the next. My body just wasn't right, but the staff managed me well and it was good to even get an hour in that final against Stade.

Darce's season was over and Drico was ruled out of that final too, meaning Mads and Ferg were in midfield. The perception might have been that Drico being out would weaken the team, but it was over in no time. Mads, Nugget and Rob scored tries in the first half-hour. Joe had done his homework again. We had some good set-plays and our breakdown was everything.

I was hurt by a clash of knees with one of their players, which left me with some bruising for the remainder of the week. The Lions had their pre-tour get-together and medical check-up that Monday, and Warren Gatland actually ruled me out of the Pro12 final against Ulster. I was a little nervous about making the tour as well.

Had there been no Lions tour, I might have insisted on risking it for that final. It was a big day for the club and I wanted to play so badly. But there was too much at stake. Stephen Ferris, my buddy, contemporary and rival all the way up, didn't play in that final either. He hadn't played since the previous November thanks to the ankle injury that would force him to retire in 2014 at the age of twenty-eight.

Fez rang me two or three hours before the game.

'Where are you?' he asked.

'I'm on the way to the game,' I said.

'Can you come and pick me up?'

'Where are you?'

'We're at the Barge pub,' he said.

I went to the Barge and there were at least seven or eight, maybe even ten, of the Ulster players who weren't involved in the final. Fez didn't sound too bad on the phone, but when

I arrived they were hammered! I wasn't there five minutes before I said to myself, I am getting out of these boys' way! Off to the RDS I went, straight away.

I doubt the Ulster boys missed me, and Leinster didn't either. Jeno scored the first try in the fourth minute and Jamie got the other. We had loads of options in those days. Kevin McLaughlin started at number 6 and Rhys Ruddock was on the bench. We didn't need everyone fit all the time.

It wasn't the double we wanted, but we did want that Pro12 trophy after losing the previous three finals and we also wanted Joe, Johnny and Isa to go out on a winning note. We had two nights to send them off in style before myself, Cian, Jamie, Johnny, Drico and Rob headed to Dublin airport on the Monday morning. We were linking up with the rest of the Lions squad in Heathrow en route to Australia, via Hong Kong. I was about to achieve my goal.

15. Time to roar

As well as my calf and knee issues on the double-winning run-in to the 2012/13 season, I had one other problem bothering me that I simply had to keep a secret. I had a broken thumb.

I suffered it in the first half of the win against Munster at Thomond Park. I came off and said to Jim McShane, the team doctor at Leinster: 'Jim, I'm after breaking my thumb.'

He said: 'No, no. It couldn't be broken.'

I said: 'Jim, it's broke. I know when it's broke. It's broke down low. It's not broke up high.'

He said: 'Right, are you able to play?'

I said: 'I am.'

He strapped it up and I went back on and finished the game.

The following week, myself and Carol Denver, the physio, made a cast out of plaster of Paris. I had a 'Bennett fracture' at the base of my thumb and I was in excruciating pain. But I was able to play in the games against Biarritz and Stade Français.

When I went in for the first Lions get-together and medical check-up, I told Dr Eanna Falvey, the Lions' team doctor, that I had a sore thumb but that it wasn't affecting me that badly. I was still able to pass and do everything else, so, while I was in a bit of pain, it was fine. I played the Lions tour in 2013 with a broken thumb and then had an operation to remove the ligament when I came home.

The night before we flew to London to link up with the rest of the Lions squad, some lads went home early. Needless to say, I didn't. I left Coppers at whatever time and had about an hour's sleep before Jamie and his future wife, Sheena, picked me up in his Land Rover. Drico and Johnny made their own way to the airport, and when we got there they just started laughing at me because I was still giddy from the night before.

Two weeks before the squad set off for Hong Kong, all thirty-seven players assembled in the Syon Park Hotel in London, which was a cool experience. You walked into a big function room and all your gear was there in three bags with your initials on them. There were two other rooms to have your shoes and suits fitted. Getting the Lions blazer, with all the history that's attached to that crest, and meeting all the other players made it a very exciting day.

I tried to chat with as many of the players and backroom staff as I could, especially those I'd never met before. You grab some food here and there, and you're pulled and dragged everywhere. It's a busy day, but also a buzzy day. From that day on you're thinking of the Lions constantly. And when the tour starts, you know you must be ready to rock.

By the time we boarded the plane from Heathrow to Hong Kong I was pretty confident that if I played to my ability, I'd make the Test team. But there was one thing working against me. Our captain, Sam Warburton, was a number 7. Plus Gats didn't really know me as a person at the time. But when we started training, I was in good form. I didn't miss any training sessions and I put my best foot forward. Although I went out there with calf and knee problems, and a fractured thumb, I could rehab both the calf and knee together and I worked hard with one of the physios, Bob Stewart, particularly in the nine days before my first game.

The coaches knew what the story was and there was no pressure on me to play in the first game of the tour, against the Barbarians, as they had enough fit back-rowers. I didn't envy the boys who played in the heat and humidity of that opening game in Hong Kong.

My tour started against the Force in Perth, playing at number 7. Cian, Besty, Jamie, Mur, Johnny, Drico and Tommy all started, too. Drico scored a couple of tries and Johnny, Jamie and Tommy got one apiece as well. But it was a sad start. Cian went off with an injury before half-time and it was a nasty one – ankle ligaments. His Lions tour was over, but no better man than Cian to come back from something like that an even better player, which he did in the long run.

As the tour progressed, I felt I performed really well in all the midweek games leading up to the first Test selection. I played some of my best rugby, using my hands and running ability, and I felt I was in a really good place. But maybe I should have read the tea leaves. I wasn't involved in the Saturday games against the two Super Rugby sides, the Reds and the Waratahs. Instead, I played at number 6 against a Combined New South Wales/Queensland Country team. Shaun McCarthy, who had played for Wicklow and for St Mary's, was on the bench for them. He hadn't been on the pitch long when I went around him for a try. Alun Wyn Jones was pretty pissed off that I didn't pass him the ball, and that's very clear in the footage of the game. He doesn't hide it. I've often asked him since if he still throws his toys out of the pram!

Then I was picked for the game against the Brumbies the Tuesday before the first Test, which probably should have been a clue that I wouldn't be in the Test XV.

For the announcement of the team for the first Test, it wasn't like in Ireland or in Leinster where the coach comes up to you beforehand and says: 'Look it, we're not going with you this week. We're going to start someone else' and maybe gives you a reason. Instead, Gats just announced the team and I wasn't named. Then he announced the bench, and when I wasn't in that either, it was like a box between the two eyes.

Straight away I went to Wig, Graham Rowntree, for a one-on-one meeting and I asked him: 'Wig, what's the story?' He could see I was upset. I definitely had watery eyes. Being picked for the Lions is the high point of a rugby career and I wanted it so badly. I needed to know immediately what I had to do.

'Wig, what do I need to do to start on this team in the second Test?'

He said: 'Kid, I don't really have an answer for you because you've done everything we've asked of you. Just keep your head down and prepare the boys as best as possible.'

I chatted with him for about five or ten minutes and that helped me take the emotion out of it. Right, Seán, I said to myself, get back to preparing these boys. You're a part of the bigger picture.

I'd like to think I've always tried to do that throughout my career whenever I haven't been involved. I know I've no divine right to be picked all the time, least of all for the Lions. So, that's what I did. I trained really well that week. But to make matters worse, Gats came to me and said: 'Would you be the twenty-fourth man?' So I had to get togged out in full kit for the day of the game, do the full warm-up, the works, while knowing I hadn't a hope of getting on unless one of the subs went down in the warm-up.

It was a strange day in my career, because for the previous three seasons I had always been a starter for Leinster or Ireland. I'd played over seventy games in those seasons and only been on the bench twice. It was like being dropped, but it taught me something about myself as well. A little adversity is no harm. I was being selfish and just wanted to play. But it was a tough day all the same.

For that Brumbies game they brought in Billy Twelvetrees, Brad Barritt, Christian Wade and Shane Williams, who was playing club rugby in Japan and was coming to Australia to do some commentating. We had one training session. No disrespect to any of those lads, but they were thrown in at the deep end against a Brumbies team who were top of Super Rugby and had just qualified for the play-offs.

I was at number 6, with Justin Tipuric at 7 and Taulupe Faletau at 8, and Lydiate on the bench. Opposite me at 6 that day was my future Leinster teammate Scott Fardy. I still have Fards' jersey from that game, and he has mine.

The Brumbies double-podded at us at the front and middle of the line-out and made it so hard for Besty to throw anywhere. They had a really good line-out operation and killed us at the breakdown as well.

In the first Test, Tom Croft, Sam and Jamie were the backrow, with Dan Lydiate on the bench. I felt I brought a bit more to a game than Tom and Dan, but I couldn't begrudge them being picked. I got on very well with Dan on that tour. Like me, he's a farmer and I couldn't be jealous of someone who is a good lad and who works his bollocks off. As does Crofty. And they're obviously class players. They're Lions, after all!

The Wallabies took the lead in that first Test in Brisbane when Mike Phillips was turned inside out by Genia. Phillsy is great craic and a character, but he's so cocky that I was almost glad to have something to slag him over that night.

Then George North scored one of the best tries I've ever seen from inside halfway. I wasn't a big fan of the way he pointed at Genia before he slid over the line, but it was an incredible piece of play.

Then Folau scored his second try, stepping Johnny and then Leigh Halfpenny at full tilt. Folau's personal views are not nice, but he's a freak of nature in the way he's able to run at full speed and change direction. There are very few players I know who are able to do that. One was Luke Fitzgerald. Another is Jordan Larmour. A few of the Kiwis could do it: Doug Howlett and Christian Cullen. Drico, too, but not too many others.

Sitting in the stand I just thought: fuck me, this fella!

Alex Cuthbert had a serious finish, too. He was one of the class lads on tour. I roomed with him an awful lot. Brilliant to have around the place.

But we couldn't shake them off. Kurtley Beale had a long-range penalty to win it but slipped as he kicked it. So we won that one by the skin of our teeth.

Tom Croft played very well. He was hanging out on the wing and he was so fast for a back-rower. He made a few good gallops that night. Still, I didn't think my ship had sailed or that I wouldn't get a look-in. Not at all. The one thing I did think was, the minute I get an opportunity in training to hurt someone, I'm going to do it, whether it be rucking or tackling or carrying.

At the end of training we used to do a carrying and a rucking drill, and it was fairly heavy going. At the start of that second Test week, I was in a tackling suit and Mako Vunipola got me with a massive shot. All the starters said:

'What a shot!' and gave him a tap on the back. But I was still locked on to the ball. He hadn't shifted me.

I trained well that week. I made a huge effort to make sure I had all the boxes ticked, that I knew my shit and that I was in match mode if needed. I was putting my best foot forward in other drills as well. The coaches could only see me doing the right thing rather than sulking.

On the Tuesday of that second Test week we played the Melbourne Rebels. It was the last midweek game. After that it was just the second and third Tests. It was now or never for a lot of us. Mur scored early on from close in and I scored one from Dan Lydiate's pass when we peeled around the front of a line-out. We won 35-0. After that game I felt the coaches had to sit up and take notice of me.

The second Test was also in Melbourne, and, the day after we beat the Rebels, Gats read out the team in our hotel. Dan at 6, Sam at 7 and Jamie at 8, with both Crofty and me on the bench. I was relieved, and at the same time I was sorry for Paulie, who had been ruled out of the rest of the tour with a fractured arm. As well as his performances, his words and his presence around the place were incredible. Mike Phillips had a knee problem, so Ben Youngs started and Mur was on the bench. Mur deserved it.

In the second Test we wanted to go after Beale because we felt his confidence was down. We started well. Drico smashed Adam Ashley-Cooper. But, as in the first Test, we couldn't shake them off. I came on for the last eighteen minutes and tried my best to fit in with our systems. I made a few good hits and carried well off the back of a line-out, but six minutes from the end Adam Ashley-Cooper got the game's only try. He celebrated big time, understandably, and so did they when Leigh Halfpenny missed a long-range penalty at the end. They had fought for their lives to level the series, but we felt we'd let it slip.

It set up a series decider in Sydney.

As Sam had suffered a torn hamstring, I expected to start the third Test. And I did. But the way Gats was going with team selection, reputations didn't matter. He was moving everything around. No one was safe. And Drico and Jamie were dropped.

I think Drico might have had a bit of an idea from training, because Gats kept moving him and Foxy, Jonathan Davies, around, and Gats spoke to him before he named the team.

I went to Drico's room after that and he'd just ordered room service. I remember sitting on his bed and asking him, was he okay? He was my Irish captain and one of the legends of the game. To play in that third Test and finally be part of a Lions Test series win would have been the high point of his four Lions tours. So to go out that way, after everything he'd given, was cruel. To his credit, he dusted himself off after an hour or two.

He was very disappointed, but the way he trained the following day was like he was playing a Test series decider himself. He prepared the boys as well as anybody could have done. It just showed his true colours and what he was about as a person. No one would have begrudged him being disappointed, but he showed his proper professionalism. He was phenomenal, even when he didn't need to be. Apart from injuries, it must have been the worst week of his career. But he never let it show, which was classy.

It was strange not having him or Jamie in the match-day squad. Drico being dropped meant there was little attention on Jamie, but I felt sorry for him as well. Things just didn't flow for him in the second Test. He didn't get on much ball, whereas the third Test was made for a number 8.

Our scrum got on top of them straight away. Phillsy tapped and away we went until Alex Corbisiero scored. All week we had said that when we got inside the 22 we just had to get off the ground quickly and go, because the Wallabies were a big old team and we knew we were fitter. Gats had consistently drummed it into us: 'We're fitter, bigger and stronger.'

I had one of those early carries as well and it was good to get into the game early on, for me and everyone else. A few minutes later we had a good kick chase. Dan got a good shot on Joe Tomane and I won a penalty for Leigh to make it 10-0 from halfway.

I won the penalty because I just hung on. I've looked back at the clip, and Michael Hooper absolutely tried to break my back with his shoulder. I never budged and Romain Poite awarded us a penalty.

A lot of people don't like Poite, for whatever reason. I absolutely love Romain as a referee because you know what you're getting with him. If you are a dominant team, he will always reward that team. He's also quite fair around the breakdown. If he thinks you're legal at all, he will reward you. If he thinks you're illegal, he actually tells you: 'Let go.' He's very good around that area.

Poite was also rewarding our scrum and we were in total control, but coming up to half-time James O'Connor got Johnny with a step, and then he got me because I was going too hard. Johnny was pissed off because he knew he'd missed that one. I wasn't overly pissed off because that happens.

At half-time we just said that we had to keep the scoreboard ticking over and make sure we kept doing what we were doing because we had them under a lot of pressure. But we needed to keep the ball a bit more and keep our discipline.

They got it back to within three at one point, but Johnny came up with the power play that led to his try. That was the key score. The game was done then.

Foxy and Leigh created that try. Foxy had a savage game and was ridiculously good on that tour as well, and I was delighted for Johnny to get the try because he'd worked so hard on everything during that week, on our game plan and making sure everything was right, as he always does. He was happy with that one. Everyone was happy and we pulled away then. A handy one in the end really.

Winning that early penalty had set a benchmark for me for the rest of the game. I wanted to leave my mark. There was a lot of talk about the jersey on that tour and what it means and leaving it in a better place. That was always a favourite saying of Jamie's. I wanted to leave that Lions number 7 jersey in a better place than I got it from the week before. But that was going to be a tough ask because I was replacing our captain, and he had been playing extremely well.

That's why I was so pleased at the end of that last Test, because I had played well. I had a few massive moments in that game that no one ever talked about. The Wallabies had come back to within three points of us when Will Genia sniped. As he came around the corner running, I was about the fourth defender and I completely read the situation. I came out of the defensive line and got a superb chop on him. There were a few moments like that which I was delighted with afterwards because I don't think some other players would have read it and got there, but I saw it before it happened. For almost everyone else it probably seemed like a normal tackle, but Genia was gone otherwise. He was under the sticks.

That night we went back to the hotel to see our families and friends. Some of the Aussies were with us and we had a pretty big night. I'd say I went to bed about 5.45am, and got up at 8am. When I walked to the team room to get some breakfast, Leigh was still sitting at the table in his suit, drinking. I thought, this fella is a fucking legend! So I joined him for a beer with my scrambled eggs and toast.

Then most of us went to a bar in Bondi Beach for the day. The round was fifty bottles of Corona on ice in an old galvanized bath. The minute they landed, the shout went out: 'Fifty more!' Loads of Aussies were jumping in with us and having the craic.

That was an all-dayer before we finally began to head back to the hotel. Some lads went to bed. They'd had enough. I had friends and family over and at around 9.30pm my brother William rang me.

'Where are you?'

'I'm in the hotel. I'm going to bed.'

William said: 'Well, come to the Cock and Bull. The place is heaving.'

'Right, I will so,' I said.

My father and my sister Caroline were also there and when I walked into the Cock and Bull, it was a sea of red. People went bananas when they saw me coming in. I was the only player there! A couple of bouncers walked me into a little area where they could make sure things didn't get out of hand, but everyone was just so happy and giddy. I sang with Mumford & Sons on stage, and when I got back down, everyone was coming over with shots.

'No, don't give him shots,' said my dad. 'No, Jesus, don't give him shots, it will drive him overboard.'

But when I looked around, I saw that my father was nicking the shots himself!

After a couple of hours it was carnage. Everybody wanted to buy me shots and take selfies. The bouncers brought me out via the back entrance and I went back to the hotel.

On day three we had to be up at 9am to get showered, changed and packed. Everything was run like clockwork. No one was late. Whoever you roomed with, the code was that you were responsible for each other. If you had to pack his bag, you packed his bag, and made sure he had his passport with him.

What a few days we had in the aftermath of that series. Great, great, great, great craic.

Looking back, I'd say a lot of the Irish boys took lessons from that tour. I've never known a feeling like I had before the first Test when I wasn't named in the 23. I can only imagine what Drico and Jamie felt in the week of the third Test, when they were sitting in the stands in their suits, as was Paulie.

Being the 24th man for the first Test didn't seem so bad after all. At least I wasn't in my Lions suit, and then I was on the bench for the second Test and I started the third. It was also in the right order. Better than having it the other way around. I was quite fortunate that the tour finished the way it did for me.

I couldn't have scripted it better.

16. The void

Leinster were a little all over the place at the start of the 2013/14 season. We had lost a lot of leaders, and that void was only going to grow bigger.

The previous January, it had been announced that Johnny was joining Racing in Paris. No one wanted Johnny to go, but we felt the Union were playing a game with him about his contract and he'd called their bluff. In February, Isa had confirmed that he was retiring, that his family wanted to go home to New Zealand. And, of course, Joe was leaving Leinster for Ireland. We had lost two of our main on-field leaders and the head coach who had brought Leinster, and me personally, to a different level. Joe had set new standards and kept everyone accountable, both the playing squad and the backroom staff.

Things couldn't be the same, although with that there was a chance to bring in new ideas.

Matt O'Connor had been announced as Joe's successor in early May and he looked like a good appointment. I didn't know much about Mattie when he came in, but he had a good track record with Leicester as a head coach and they had just won the Premiership.

A few of us spoke with him before he was appointed and I suppose when you see somebody in an interview you're always going to be impressed. Mattie ticked all the boxes. He had experience, game knowledge and he'd been with a big club that expected big things. It was also exciting for us knowing we had a fella who had run a big club with very good players. But you never know what a coach is going to be like until you start working with him.

Those of us who'd been on the Lions tour were later starting back and then, in September, Drico announced that it would be his last season, prompting the 'one more year' campaign, and Leo announced that he would also be retiring. Losing Joe, Johnny, Isa, Drico and Leo from the club in a twelve-month period had to result in a lot of change. They were five of our key drivers. To be honest, it was too big a gap to fill in such a relatively short period of time.

Mattie also had a different coaching philosophy from Joe. He was relatively lenient with everybody. It just wasn't his way to be overly demanding. Every coach has their own style and he was being true to himself and the way things had worked for him. It was a combination of things. Mattie wasn't very strict about time-keeping or standards in training, whereas Joe was always so meticulous about our meetings starting on time, about players not making mistakes in training and knowing their detail. It wasn't Mattie's way to pull people up. His approach probably didn't suit Leinster, because we needed standards to be set quite high, and that had to be driven by the head coach. Joe had made everyone accountable.

Of course, we have to take some of the blame, too. Our leadership group wasn't strong enough to say that to Mattie early on. I include myself in that. I didn't do enough. I was twenty-six years old. I'd played over eighty games for Leinster. I'd been a Test player for four seasons. I was a British & Irish Lion. So I'd have to take responsibility for that, along with the rest of the players. I didn't appreciate then the extent of the void the boys were leaving behind and I took it for granted that Leinster would be fine. But we weren't fine, although it didn't show initially.

My first game back was against Munster in Thomond Park. Rog had retired as well, so the game was built up as a head-to-head between Ian Keatley and Ian Madigan at out-half. We struggled for a lot of the game. We didn't play in the right areas and Munster brought us down to their level. We just weren't smart enough. Keats kicked his goals, cross-kicked for Earlsy's try and was named Man of the Match

Our first European game was against the Ospreys and some of my Lions buddies – Adam Jones, Alun Wyn Jones and Justin Tipuric. Tips is a really nice fella and has so much skill and talent. He has a bit of everything. Alun Wyn is simply an unreal player, as well as being a top bloke. Drico was injured, the Ospreys were a bogey side and they had a good European record at the Liberty Stadium. People thought we were vulnerable, but it didn't pan out that way.

Rossy went off injured very early and so Marty Moore came on for his European debut. They were 6-3 up and turned down a penalty for a 5-metre scrum. But we knew Marty's ability to scrum. Marty locked it and then we shoved them back to win a penalty. That gave us huge confidence for the rest of the game. Within five minutes Jamie wrestled the ball from Tips and away he went. From the recycle I gave Nugget the shout, he offloaded blind and I caught it just ahead of one of their players and finished.

Given that we were without Drico, Jeno and Leo, it was a good win, 19-9. Jimmy Gopperth had been preferred to Mads and he kicked the rest of our points. He'd arrived from Newcastle and brought plenty of experience from his time with the Hurricanes and the Blues in New Zealand. He was a great fella and a very positive influence around the club. He

1. With my older brother Stephen and sister Caroline.

2. My Communion Day, with my sister Alex, brother William and godfather Sean Fleming.

3. Us five siblings and Mam (back row, right) and Dad (holding Alex) on Caroline's Confirmation Day. I'm in front of Caroline with my arms crossed.

4. Playing for Tullow Rugby Club when we beat Athy 20–10 in Carlow RFC, 2004.

5. With Stephen and William after an Irish Youths game against Scotland.

6. Celebrating with the Leinster Youths team after winning the inter-provincial championship

My debut Test match against Fiji at the RDS in November 2009.
(Dan Sheridan/Inpho)

After breaking my leg during a Leinster match against Scarlets in 2010.
(Dan Sheridan/Inpho)

9. One of the best days of my life: celebrating winning the 2011 Heineken Cup final against Northampton. (*Billy Stickland/Inpho*)

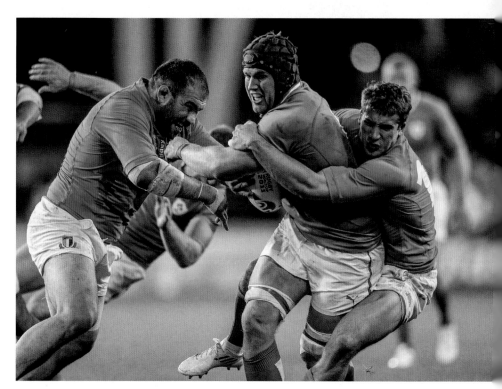

10. Man of the Match: playing against Italy in the 2011 World Cup. (*Dan Sheridan/Inpho*)

11. Holding up a Tullow jersey after the 2012 Heineken Cup final win against Ulster. (*Colm O'Neill/Inpho*)

2. Celebrating the series win on my first British and Irish Lions tour in 2013. (*Dan Sheridan/Inpho*)

13. I like this photo of my second try in the 2015 Six Nations win against Scotland, because it was after two surgeries on my left shoulder and I had to reach out to get it on the line. (*Billy Stickland/Inpho*)

14. I got Man of the Match in this game against France in the 2015 World Cup, but the win was overshadowed for me by the citation the next day for the Pascal Papé incident. (*James Crombie/Inpho*)

5. Scoring 'one of the great Lions Test tries', as Stuart Barnes put it, in the first Test of the 2017 British and Irish Lions tour. (*James Crombie/Inpho*)

6. Leading the team out for a match against South Africa, my fiftieth cap, in 2017 – one of my favourite days in an Ireland jersey. (*Dan Sheridan/Inpho*)

17. With Rob Kearney after my last Leinster game at home in the Aviva, a win in the European Cup semi-final against Toulouse, April 2019. (*Billy Stickland/Inpho*)

18. Lifting the trophy after the Guinness Pro14 final in Glasgow, May 2019. (*James Crombie/Inpho*)

was good at engaging with and talking to people. He was also a reliable out-half for us, nice and steady. We needed a bit of experience in that department and he provided it.

Jimmy was at number 10 again a week later against Castres at the RDS. They were French champions with a huge pack, including a couple of big South Africans in their back-row, Antonie Claassen at number 8 and Pedrie Wannenburg, who had joined them from Ulster, at number 7. It was always likely to be a tricky one for us because they were big and physical. We wanted to run them around the place and for the most part we did. There were a few big performances that day. Jack McGrath came on and scored a vital try. But they were hard to break down. We had to keep playing for the eighty minutes to get the win.

After that, we went into our first November Guinness Series with Ireland under Joe, which must have been very interesting for those players who hadn't worked with him before. There was a lot of emphasis on the Leinster boys bringing the rest of the squad up to speed in terms of the way Joe wanted things done. Joe said as much at meetings, to make sure we were all on the same page.

It soon became clear what was expected from everybody, but as Leinster boys we were way more comfortable because we'd known Joe for three years. The others had to adapt quickly to his demanding ways, but just as we'd done three years before, they soon learned that once you did what Joe asked of you, then nine times out of ten you'd be in a winning position. As I've always said, you don't get a Joe too often. It's like signing a player of a certain standard, like Isa. That kind of quality is rare.

I suppose I wanted the best of both worlds as a player. I wanted Joe at both Leinster and Ireland, even though that doesn't happen. But it was comforting and exciting returning to the familiarity of Joe's ways. I wouldn't say it was easy. Nothing was 'easy' under Joe. But I knew what we were getting and I could just rock in and do my thing.

Les Kiss had stayed on as defence coach and John Plumtree came in as forwards coach. Plum is a real people person. He was very easy to get on with and was one of the lads, as such. A typical Kiwi, Plum is easy-going and likes a beer. He coached us in a really nice manner as well and was very approachable. You could talk to him about anything. I suppose there was an element of good cop/bad cop in him working with Joe!

I was surprised and a little disappointed that Plum stayed for only a year with us before going back to New Zealand to work with the Hurricanes. I'm not surprised to see he is the All Blacks' forwards coach now.

Joe's first game was against Samoa. Cian, Paulie and myself were on the bench, presumably with the Wallabies and the All Blacks to come. Johnny was rested after playing a rake of games for Racing virtually without a break after the Lions.

Samoa had always been difficult for us. My first Test start had been that 20-10 win over them three years before. You always knew you were going into an absolute battle. The Samoans are absolutely huge, strong men and athletic. They also had dangerous runners and flair, and the first game of a new coach's era added to the apprehension. A big focus was our set-piece because, by rights, we should have been more organized there.

We were 14-6 up at half-time, by which stage I'd come on in unfortunate circumstances when Chris Henry suffered a torn hamstring. About five minutes into the second half

Drico passed between his legs, Jamie made the clear-out and Mur passed to me. As I scored, I was accidentally hit with a forearm in the mouth as I scrambled to the line.

Cian, Paulie, myself and Johnny all started against the Wallabies. Reddser was picked ahead of Mur and Luke Marshall ahead of Darce. And we were beaten in every facet, even by the Wallabies' scrum! Were we thinking too much about the detail? We were in the early stages of a transition and we wanted to get everybody up to speed. But maybe we lost that bit of emotion and madness, that hard edge, because we were focusing too much on the detail.

That's the way I felt about it afterwards. It was as if we weren't fired up enough. We'd placed too much emphasis on being disciplined, on being too 'moment by moment'. Our defence was too passive. There were lots of misreads. Quade Cooper and Michael Hooper ran amok. They scored four tries to one and came after some of us very well, me included. It was just a shit day at the office.

It wasn't what anybody had expected and next up we had the All Blacks. They were looking to complete a perfect calendar year after thirteen wins from thirteen, and we'd never beaten them.

The disappointment from the Aussie game fed into that week's preparation. All those areas where we'd let ourselves down, mentally and physically, we put right. And bad as we'd been against the Wallabies we actually had created a good few opportunities during the game, but we'd only finished off one of them. So our big focus now was: when we get opportunities against the All Blacks, let's take them.

It was the big game of the year and a big week. It always is when the All Blacks come to Ireland. You want to be ready for action and I thought things felt really good that week.

We'd done our homework. We had a good plan. We knew we had to be disciplined.

We'd also been humiliated the last time we'd played the All Blacks, so we had plenty of motivation. But to some degree we had to take that out of it and focus on ourselves and our performance. While we were again going moment by moment, we also had to be physically there for the full eighty. We had to be competitive at the breakdown. We had to slow up their ball. Regardless of the motivation – history, previous meetings – once the game starts, you don't think about any of that any more.

Even though it was a Sunday 2pm kick-off, the atmosphere was better than for many a Saturday-night game. Even going out for the warm-up you could feel it building. Of course, the world champions were coming to town and the haka gets an Irish crowd in their seats early. The haka is a big part of the match-day experience, for the players and the fans.

I like the haka. They're setting you a challenge and, to be honest, I'd be licking my lips, thinking, let's go, boys. It's on now in a couple of minutes and we'll see who's dancing around then. That was my mindset towards the haka. I enjoyed it, I respected it and loved that I was about to go to war with them.

Mur started ahead of Reddser and he scored the first try in the fourth minute. Big carries by Jamie and Pete had given us front-foot ball, but it was still a very strong finish. Not many Irish scrum-halves over the years could have scored that try.

Five minutes later we hit them with one of Joe's spot moves. Mur shaped to do a wraparound with Besty, but instead Rory fed Cian straightening through. Rory then took an offload back from Cian before being tackled.

I saw they'd left the fringe unguarded, picked off the base and was nearly away. I heard the shout from Mur, passed blind to him. Our ruck ball took a nanosecond and I was nearly in before Besty sold a bit of a dummy to Brodie Retallick and finished well.

Then Rob scored his intercept try to make it 19-0 in nineteen minutes.

Johnny's third conversion hit the post after Kieran Read had corner-flagged Rob to stop him narrowing the angle. When I looked back on the game I thought Rob might have cut in a little more, but looking back on that clip of Read tracking Rob showed the importance of never giving up. And how significant that moment was ultimately.

But there were so many moments.

We had so much focus on winning every minute, but the start was nearly too good to be true. We started at 100 miles an hour. No one had seen us play at that tempo before. It was down to the quality of the carries and the speed and efficiency at the breakdown. No other team had done that to the All Blacks. Our breakdown was exceptional. But it was quite difficult to maintain, and to beat those boys you have to be there for eighty minutes. Well, eighty-two as it turned out.

They pulled a try back when Ben Smith broke our defensive line and Julian Savea scored their first try off Aaron Cruden's grubber in behind, before Johnny's penalty had us 22-7 up at half-time.

We were in a good place. We were in control. But we knew we needed to keep doing what we'd been doing, stay moment by moment and we'd get there. We possibly didn't quite have the strength in depth either to kill off the All Blacks. When I looked back on the game, I saw the pace and skill their bench added. In comparison to us, their bench was on a different level.

They brought on five replacements in the third quarter and when they went very direct at us one of them, Ben Franks, scored to make it 22-17. We'd lost Drico by then.

We all remember that Johnny had a penalty to make it a two-score game but missed it. Like the rest of us, kickers are human. And sometimes they miss kicks.

Even then, we were still less than thirty seconds away, in possession and running down the clock when Nigel Owens pinged Jack McGrath for going off his feet. Looking at the tape, it was a fifty-fifty call, but at the end of a game, if it's in the melting pot, Nigel will usually go against the team that has the ball.

The last two and a half minutes are sickening to watch.

I've put myself through it loads of times. It just goes to show how far the game has come, how much we grew afterwards, how much smarter we became. Looking back through the two minutes it took them to score that try, lads were jumping into rucks, we weren't coming off the line together. We were just on edge. No one had that sense of confidence in our defence to come and meet them. We just sat and let them run at us. That's why they made so much ground.

Then, for the end part, Mads should have trusted me to make the tackle on Dane Coles, but he came into no-man's-land. He didn't make the hit or make a good read, and left Ryan Crotty to touch down. And that was it. Except for Cruden's twice-taken conversion, the game was over. Coles and Crotty were both replacements, and all the All Blacks' subs were running hard at the end. They brought a lot of energy.

I was so angry, and I let it show in the mixed zone with the media afterwards.

That was the most disappointing defeat of my career. I'd emptied myself. I'd thrown everything into that game. I desperately wanted to win. We weren't perfect. None of us had a perfect game. But we were in a position where we should have won. We needed to trust each other and we didn't. We needed to have confidence in each other to come off the line. They got that penalty on their 10-metre line and we never made one impact hit in the next two minutes. We never pushed them back at all. We soaked up everything and invited them onto us. When the shit hits the fan, you get back to your basics. You get set quickly, come off the line and you hit people. You don't sit and wait like we did for that final play.

Going back to work with Leinster after that wasn't easy at first, but pretty soon you're glad to be playing and getting that disappointment out of your system.

We went to Northampton and won 40-7 in Franklin's Gardens, but I came off with a dead leg after thirty-three minutes and it was actually one of the sorest experiences I've ever had. Mike McCarthy was holding on to one of their players' jerseys, and as he spun around his heel caught me just above the knee, on my quad. Instantly I knew there was bleeding inside. I knew it was a bad dead leg.

I missed the game against Northampton at the Aviva, when they won 18-9. Their pride was hurt. We'd spoken about that during the week, but sometimes it doesn't click. We were off the mark by a yard all day. Our energy wasn't good either for some reason. Sitting in the stands, I was thinking, what the hell are we after doing? That effectively cost us a home quarter-final, too.

I didn't play again for three weeks and then started against Ulster over Christmas. That was a bad night. I remember it so well.

Their number 12, Luke Marshall, carried and I just had a little peep at the ruck. I hadn't gone in for a poach. I was about to do so when someone hit me as I was getting into position, holding my arms in front of me. It was just a freakish incident. But I knew instantly that my shoulder had popped. The pain was horrendous and I knew that was the end of that.

Sitting in the doctor's room with Professor Arthur Tanner, God love him, I said to him: 'I'm fucked, aren't I? I have to get this done, don't I?'

He said: 'Yeah, that's it. Your season is done.'

I admit I teared up a little.

That injury was a reminder of how fragile a rugby player's career can be and how you have to take your chances when they come. My three-year contract was coming to an end that season, and when the Union didn't meet what I thought was my value, within a month I had agreed to join Toulon.

Back in 2010, myself and my agent, Fintan Drury, had met Michael Cheika in Paris. Checks had taken over as head coach at Stade Français and wanted me to join. They made a very, very good offer.

We flew to Paris and went to Checks' apartment, where we met him and his wife, Stephanie. We had a good chat. Checks told me how he saw me fitting in with Stade and what I could bring to the team.

Fintan suggested I go for a wander around Paris for an hour or so. I think maybe he wanted me to get some idea of what a massive, bustling, daunting city Paris was in comparison to Dublin. It was about five days before Christmas and there'd been a massive snowstorm across Europe. Thousands of flights, trains and buses had been cancelled and the forecast for the week was bad, too.

We were desperate to get home and went to Charles de Gaulle airport, but it was virtually in lockdown. We couldn't get a flight out of Paris. There were guys mooching around who weren't taxi drivers but were offering to drive people to other airports. So Fintan paid for a lift to Amsterdam with a scary guy in a red van. It was a long drive, over five hours, and the roads were pretty treacherous. But even more worrying was the driver. We genuinely thought he might take us down a side road and shoot us or something. It was quite surreal.

Our fears were unfounded, thankfully, and when we got to Amsterdam we slept on the floor in the airport. The next morning we couldn't get a flight to Dublin but we did get one to Belfast, where Fintan arranged for a friend of his to have a car and a driver waiting to take us back to Dublin.

I was only twenty-three years old at the time. It would have been quite a jump for a young lad from Tullow to move to Paris without a word of French and play in the Top 14 for a club like Stade, with all their razzmatazz. All in all, I wasn't sold on the idea. So when the IRFU improved their offer, I happily agreed a three-year provincial contract to stay with Leinster.

But this time was different.

I was out of contract at the end of the 2013/14 season and not long after the shoulder operation Fintan told me that Toulon wanted to sign me. The two of us flew over to Nice to meet their owner, Mourad Boudjellal, as Toulon were playing a Heineken Cup game there the next day against Cardiff. We met Boudjellal and their coach at the time, Bernard Laporte, in a really nice hotel where the Toulon squad were staying. This was on Friday, 10 January 2014.

Toulon had won the Heineken Cup for the first time the

previous season and Boudjellal explained to us that he wanted them to have two teams, one for the French Championship and one for Europe. Their offer was very, very, very good – potentially more than half a million per year – and I agreed with Boudjellal that I was going to sign for Toulon.

They asked me to stay on and watch the match, but Fintan didn't think that would be a good idea. We flew home that day. I drove down to Carlow on the Monday evening and I called all my family over to my sister Caroline's house in Kilbride. Fintan came with me and we explained everything to them. I told them I'd made a decision and that I was leaving Leinster and Ireland to join Toulon. That was a tough evening for me because I was emotional about making that decision. Deep down, I didn't really want to go, but the IRFU had given me a very poor offer at the time, way below what I thought was my value.

I'd made up my mind. I was going.

On the Wednesday morning, Boudjellal was due to fly over on his private jet with the contract for me to sign, but there was fog at the airport, or something like that, and he couldn't make it over that day. That evening the IRFU contacted Fintan and made me a much better offer, upping me to an Irish central contract. And that was it. I accepted and told them I'd stay.

I think Jamie had his contract sorted a day before me. Maybe the Union realized that Leinster had already lost Joe, Johnny and Isa, and with Drico and Leo set to retire, to lose myself and Jamie as well would have torn the guts out of the team.

Toulon had a really, really good squad and they went on to retain the Heineken Cup for two more years, meaning that if

I had gone over and then come back to Leinster, I might have ended up with a haul of six European winners' medals! But I didn't really want to go at that stage of my career. I was about to turn twenty-six and I suppose it was like Johnny's situation – in order to make the most out of my career financially, to get my value as a player, it looked like my only option was to leave.

But I've never had any regrets about staying.

You get a feeling when good things are about to happen and I knew Ireland were going to be in a good place under Joe, especially after that game against the All Blacks. I had really been looking forward to the Six Nations but I missed it all, right up to the championship victory in Paris in Drico's last Test. I watched that game on my own in my cottage in Tullow, wishing I was there. But it wasn't to be. I was disappointed, but as a rugby player and as a teammate, when you know what everyone puts into the sport, I could only be absolutely delighted for the boys, especially Drico.

I also missed Leinster being well beaten in the Heineken Cup quarter-finals by Toulon. There'd be no three-in-a-row.

I made it back on Saturday, 10 May, almost four and a half months since dislocating my shoulder against Ulster, and I played the first fifty-two minutes in a 15-13 win over Edinburgh at the RDS. I'd worked incredibly hard to get back to match fitness, with the goal of being involved in the semifinal against Ulster at the RDS.

We were 9-0 down, Drico had just gone off, Leo had come on, and then I was brought on. We didn't look like we were where we were meant to be. I tried to bring some energy and hit rucks to speed up our ball. We did turn it on for the last twenty-five minutes. When Leinster played like that, we could blow teams away, and that's the way it went down.

Mads finished well, Jimmy kicked the rest and we scored thirteen unanswered points.

I was pretty happy to be on the bench again for the final. Rhys Ruddock was at number 6, Jeno at 7 and Jamie at 8.

Jeno was very good in that final against Glasgow, scoring one of our two tries in the first half. Zane Kirchner set it up for him and scored the first. Zane was a flyer and that was his best game for us. It was a battle, though. Glasgow had become a tough team to break down. Drico was gone even earlier in this one, so I never did get to play with him again after that game in Franklin's Gardens the previous December.

When I came on in the fifty-fifth minute, Jimmy kicked a couple of penalties before Darce and Zane set each other up for tries. So this time it was twenty unanswered points. It happens very often that a dominant team doesn't reap its rewards until the last quarter. But we had a strong bench, and I know from starting games that when you see a sub coming on who you know is going to lift things, it can give the team a boost. And as with the All Blacks the previous November, we had good energy off the bench in those two games.

It was a nice way to send Drico and Leo off into the sunset, although Leo was going to become our forwards coach. It wasn't spoken about much, but it was definitely there in the back of our minds.

As a player, Leo invariably delivered. He just did what he said he was going to do. He never let you down. He always spoke so well. Every word counted. He never talked bullshit. I'd say Leo was a constant nuisance to play against, because he was a nuisance to train against. He was a tough, hard, nononsense character.

Drico was simply one of the best I played with because he could pull off anything at any time, but on the other side of it he was as hard as nails, too. If we needed someone to put in a big hit, he was often the man. He wasn't the biggest player in the world, but he fired himself at anything. Very, very few players have it all, but Drico had it all.

There was a right bit of craic over the next few nights and days. Back then it was different for all of us. Unlike nowadays, we weren't looking over our shoulder on nights out. And as for Drico and Leo, two better lads you wouldn't get to have fun with either. They had a bit of everything.

17. A dark place

In the summer of 2014 I only took one week's holidays, and that was to Jersey to see my brother Stephen. For the rest of it, I stayed at home and trained with the Fighting Cocks so as to maintain running fitness. Naturally I couldn't say no when they asked me to play in a junior championship match. Joe was not amused when he found out.

I told him it was a charity game and that I only stood in for the first while, even though I had played most of the game. I told him it had been good for my conditioning because I had played in midfield and so I'd been up and down the pitch. But, looking back, it was a silly decision.

When I woke up the morning after the game, everything was sore. My hamstrings and my calves were aching from doing things you don't do in a rugby match, like solo-ing and jumping for high balls. A completely different type of fitness is required for Gaelic football.

Earlier in my career, when I was combining both sports and I trained with the Carlow panel, it took me about three weeks to adapt. In short running I was beating everyone, but I struggled with the longer runs. There's also less rest in GAA because you need to repeat efforts much more quickly, and you're always moving, even between bursts. In rugby you have more breaks in play. There's possibly the odd fella who is over ninety kilos playing inter-county football, but no more than a few. So put twenty kilos on any of those foot-ballers and see how well they are able to move! Also, we were playing Fenagh, and a few of them were trying to go hard at me. That was funny. But you're going to have that.

It was enjoyable, but I shouldn't have played. Joe had rested me from the Argentina tour in order for me to get myself right, so although I had trained hard and had tried to mind myself in that match, it wasn't the right thing to do.

In September I played in Leinster's first game, a defeat away to Glasgow, when Stuart Hogg kicked a late, long-range penalty. But I was never right. Going into that game I was absolutely massive up top – probably too big – from going hard at the weights and rehab. But after that game my shoulder was hanging off me. I thought, there's something definitely not right here.

I'd had complications after the surgery the previous December. Hannan Mullett, a shoulder specialist at the Sports Surgery Clinic in Santry, had been away that week, so I'd gone to another shoulder specialist, Lennard Funk, in England. The operation went well, but afterwards I suffered a shoulder infection.

The risk in going away is that you're in hospital recuperating for a day or two, but then you're out of hospital and travelling. And I'd had open surgery as well. I went to the hotel next door to spend the night before catching a flight home the next morning. I was sleeping like a baby in my room when the bloody fire alarm went off at 3am. It was winter, and I sat outside in the cold with a sling over my shoulder, and a hoodie, trying to keep as warm as I could, with my body under stress. All the guests were sitting outside the hotel in the middle of the night for two hours.

Looking back, I think that's where I got the infection. It had been a massive operation. They did a lot of stuff in there. My body had been through the mill that morning, and then

I was sitting in the cold for hours in the middle of the night. When we were allowed back inside, I went to bed and slept for another while, but I was uncomfortable – hot and cold.

I flew back to Dublin the next morning, and the following day I drove an automatic car back to Tullow. On the third night I woke up absolutely soaking wet. I got in the shower, felt great, lit the stove, sat in front of the fire for a while and went back to bed at around 3am or 4am.

I woke up two hours later, absolutely drowned – bed, sheets, pillows, the whole works. I rang John Ryan, our doctor in Leinster, and he said to see how I went over the next day or two. I might have had the sweats from all the tablets I was taking. Two days later I was at a wedding in Cork and just after the meal I left and went to bed early. I hadn't been drinking, but I wasn't feeling great. The next morning I got up early and my shoulder was bleeding through the protective plastering. The blood was spewing out of the wound.

The Doc told me to come straight up to Santry. They checked my blood and, sure enough, I had an infection, but they couldn't identify what it was. They had to keep trying different intravenous antibiotics until they found the right one to treat the infection.

I was in Santry for six weeks while they searched for the cause of the infection. I lost ten or eleven kilos of body weight. That was definitely one of the worst times of my life. I was sitting on a bed in Santry for six weeks, not even allowed to go for a walk, and my body was being eaten apart by a mystery infection.

My appetite wasn't that bad, surprisingly. The chef in Santry, a South African, was so good to me. The nurse would ask me what I needed to eat every day and he cooked whatever I asked for. I was trying to get as much protein and vegetables into me as I could, but I was still fading away. The infection was just eating away at me.

My mind was all over the place. I was thinking about all sorts of dire eventualities. I was in a very bad place mentally.

They couldn't keep me in there for ever, so I was sent home. A day nurse visited me at home in Tullow every second morning for two weeks to give me IV antibiotics. I had a team of doctors testing to see what bug was in the joint. In fairness to the Leinster doctor, Professor John Ryan, and his department in St Vincent's, they eventually found the source of the infection and put me on the right IV antibiotics to kill it. That worked within a week and then I was on oral antibiotics for another six weeks.

I started feeling better. I wasn't sweating at night-time. I was sleeping well and putting on a bit of weight. But it was a scary time. There had been millions of parasites eating away at my system. I didn't realize how bad it was until afterwards, when I spoke to Professor Ryan, Jim McShane and Arthur Tanner, and did some reading into it. Something like that can kill you if the infection gets into the bone. It was actually life-threatening. Not that I knew it at the time, which was probably just as well.

I only started one game at the end of the season as well as playing the last twenty minutes or so in the semi-final and final. I didn't really get in over a ball properly or get bashed on the shoulder. But in that Glasgow game at the start of the new season, when I hit a few rucks or tried to go for a poach, I felt vulnerable. While I was big and strong and had been feeling great in the gym, it felt like I had lost all power in the shoulder. The medics and physios could push it around and do what they wanted with it. We knew it wasn't right and so I went for a scan.

The scan showed what looked like a broken screw, with a jagged edge on it. But it's very hard to see metal in a joint from a scan, so they said they'd have to take a look inside. When they opened me up, they discovered that the head of one of the screws used in the original operation had broken off. It had probably happened when I was lifting weights. The joint was hanging on by one screw, and that screw wasn't at the right angle.

Hannan Mullett did the second operation, in Santry. He took out the broken screw-heads and took a piece off my hip to finish the job.

It was a dark enough time, though. I had worked incredibly hard to make it back for the end of the 2013/14 season and again over the summer when I'd skipped holidays and didn't let loose. I wanted to have a big year. Then to discover that my shoulder still wasn't right and that I had to face another four or five months of rehab was demoralizing. 'Ah for fuck's sake, here we go again' – that was what I was thinking.

In the twelve months of 2014 I started just two games and played two more off the bench. I missed all of the November window, when Ireland beat South Africa, Georgia and Australia, and all of Leinster's pool campaign in Europe. My third comeback of 2014 was for the Ireland Wolfhounds against the England Saxons at Musgrave Park in January, a week before the Six Nations started. Dan McFarland and Axel Foley were the coaches.

As an ambassador with the sponsor, Guinness, I had to face the media in Cork that week and I told them: 'I want to come back and show people that I can still rock on. I'm not going to go out like Tarzan and run around the place like a headless chicken!'

Training was typical, I suppose, of Ireland A or Wolfhounds – short and sharp, and we had a bit of craic with each other as well. There was a good atmosphere that week. Stepping out of Joe's environment into something like that, with coaches like Axel and Dan, was less pressurized, too.

I had always got on well with Axel, and speaking to Paulie and other boys, I learned that as a player he was very smart. So anything Axel said, I tried to take it in as best as I could. He provided little bits of advice but never overloaded you with information. He was also direct and straight to the point – some people would say borderline rude, but I got it. He was dead straight, and I liked that about him. Axel and Dan complemented each other, because Dan sided more towards the detail.

Musgrave Park had been redeveloped and there was a good atmosphere for the match, and two strong sides as well. I was with Dom Ryan and Jack Conan in the back-row. Their back-row was Dave Ewers, Matt Kvesic and Thomas the Tank Engine – Tom Waldrom.

I was way off the pace. It was my first game in five months and my third start in over a year. After twenty minutes I thought, I am chucking like a train here. I have nothing in the tank and my lungs are on fire. It was as if I was playing a pre-season game in mid-season, whereas everyone else was at full tilt. I wanted to run, but I just wasn't able. My mind was telling me to keep going, but my legs were like lead. I managed to get through fifty minutes, though. I was relieved. My shoulder was perfect. I had been a little bit apprehensive beforehand, but it had held up good and strong.

I was back in the Ireland squad for the Six Nations.

Simon Easterby had come in as our new forwards coach. I used to love watching Si when he played, and I'd heard from Paulie and a few others how much he'd been a stickler on detail when assessing line-outs. He's been great for me because he's played so many Tests in the back-row. I really enjoyed playing under him and I really enjoyed him coaching us. As well as the line-out, he's good around the breakdown and in other bits and pieces.

Despite only having that fifty minutes for the Wolfhounds under my belt, Joe named me in the team to play Italy a week later in our opening Six Nations game in Rome. I felt good all week and did the Captain's Run in the Stadio Olimpico, but in the warm-up, as I went to carry the ball, the TV cameras were on me and you could actually see me grimace. When you're coming back from something like a shoulder operation, you tend to forget about the rest of your body. Possibly I hadn't loaded enough, but my hamstring had flared up and we didn't risk it. Tommy O'Donnell was promoted from the bench and scored a great try. He slotted in seamlessly. Sitting in the stands, I was gutted. That's when my tendonitis issues started, and they remain with me to this day. Well, I don't have tendonitis in my left leg any more, but I have it in my right.

A week later I started against France in Dublin. There was more attention on Johnny's comeback. He'd been laid off by a French doctor for twelve weeks due to concussion issues. Jamie came back from injury for that match as well.

It was my first international in over fourteen months. I'd played fifty minutes of rugby in five months, and just two games in nine months. And it was my twenty-eighth birthday. But I wasn't worried. I've always had a knack of coming straight back in and being able to play at that level. I've needed to, and I've done it.

Johnny kicked five out of five despite having a clash of

heads with Mathieu Bastareaud. Both of them went off for an HIA and returned.

We were 18-6 up and cruising when Besty was binned for playing the ball at a ruck with his feet, despite being flat on the ground. There was a general air of, fucking hell, Besty, what have you done?

I had to make way for five minutes too when Seán Cronin replaced Besty in the front-row. They brought on a massive bench and their big lock, Romain Taofifénua, scored a try to set up an edgy last ten minutes. Apart from that five minutes when Nugget replaced Rory, I played the full eighty.

As the clock hit eighty, they were attacking on our left touchline. The ball reached their sub, Rémi Lamerat, with Simon Zebo in front of him. Zeebs tried to make a tackle, and I had to go in and finish him off. And that was that. I was fairly pumped.

In the end, it's all about winning.

A fortnight later we beat England at home by 19-9, but I went off with a bang on the head after twenty-five minutes and didn't return. I carried off the back of the line-out and was tackled by Billy Vunipola and someone else. I was going to the ground when an arm caught my head and neck. It was only a glancing blow. Looking at it on the video, it seemed innocuous. But whatever way it caught me I was properly rattled and half sparked. I just wasn't right after it. Sitting on the bench I felt sick. I was disappointed because that was the first time I'd played against England in two years, and it was at home, but it was definitely the right thing to do to come off.

The plan was to go after them in the air that day. Johnny kicked us into a 9-3 lead at half-time and Robbie Henshaw's try sealed it when Mur used an advantage play with a chip

into the corner. Robbie beat Alex Goode in the air and finished well. It looked like an off-the-cuff play, but that was
actually a set-up we had practised during the week. Joe's idea
again – one of those trick plays that he always had.

I'd say that was one of only two times, maybe three, when
I was concussed, and I was lucky in that at least I had another
two weeks before we played Wales in Cardiff. You want to be
in the whole of your health going over there.

That was the day Paul O'Connell became the fourth player
to play 100 Tests for Ireland. He was a phenomenal leader, a
phenomenal player and great person and drove standards in
that Irish set-up for years. He helped bring through a lot of
young lads and gave players great advice on the way up, me
included. An absolute legend and tough as teak. He was one
of those players who just did what he said he was going to do.
He led that way, too – he didn't talk too much.

Johnny and Cian also earned their fiftieth caps and we
were looking to make it four from four. But Wayne Barnes
was an absolute nightmare for us that day. As I've said, I
actually like Wayne as a referee, but that day he drove me
bananas. Typical of the Welsh at the time, they were cheating
like mad on the ground, but his interpretation of a poach, or
of someone holding on, was out the window.

When you look back on that game, there were three-/
four-/five-second rucks where I'm holding on to a ball and
he just did not give us the penalty.

I never stopped talking during the game at the
breakdown.

'Release.'

'Let go.'

'He's holding on.'

As I normally do.

I'll never forget that game because it was a disaster at the breakdown and, in my view, he didn't ref according to the laws. I just think he didn't have any control over the breakdown at all.

He penalized Ireland four times at the breakdown in the first fifteen minutes, and bang, bang, bang, bang, Leigh Halfpenny made it 12-0. Then he started pinging Wales at the breakdown and even sent Sam Warburton to the sin bin. Johnny kicked us back into the game and we were 15-9 down at half-time, but then they held us out for over thirty rucks.

That Welsh defence knew that if they kept knocking us back, we'd just keep trying the same thing. We were normally a hard team to stop when we did get into the 22, but they dealt with us fairly well. And that wasn't the only day they did that.

We were 20-9 down and went to the corner coming up to the last ten minutes. I was at the back of the maul as we were going over the Welsh line when Barnes gave a penalty try – the one time he did catch them cheating that day!

Another penalty by Halfpenny meant the best we could hope for was a draw. In the last play I was at the back of a maul when he was quick to give them a turnover scrum. Mur let rip at Barnes for that one, too.

When you review games, you have to take most decisions on the chin as a player, but sometimes you look back on games and say: 'What are referees seeing here?' They pull decisions out of the air. I know they have an awful job to do. I wouldn't do it for diamonds. But for the referees at the elite level, they're doing it so often that they really should be more consistent. When you scout referees in the build-up to a game, you look for where they are consistent. That's all players look for, but we definitely didn't get it that day.

I still had a beer with Wayne afterwards. I went up to him

because I had been at him a lot during the match. We agreed to differ on his interpretations at the breakdown.

I was so frustrated during and after that game, but it did finally teach me to just get on with it, that there is no real point in letting a referee frustrate you. Looking back, I'd love to have played that game a bit smarter as well. In some respects, we can't have too many complaints. You have to play what's in front of you and we didn't that day.

That ended our shot at the Grand Slam. When you have England and France at home and you beat them both, you have to make the most of it. Instead, that ballbreaker of a game set up 'Super Saturday', when the championship was going to come down to points difference.

Wales were first up. When they put sixty on Italy, we knew we had to win at Murrayfield by a minimum of twenty-one to get our noses in front of Wales. And ideally we wanted to win by more, to set England a difficult target in their game against France at Twickenham, which was last up. Knowing that, we did go out with a slightly different mindset, or a sense of excitement. It wasn't that Joe took the shackles off. Joe never took the shackles off. But the plan all week was to go all-out attack. We still had to play field position, but when we got opportunities, we were going to take them. In one of the huddles at training, Johnny had said: 'We are going to score four tries in this game and then we're going to keep going.'

However, when you're targeting winning margins or bonus points, you can't think about that too much either because you know it will affect your game. You might try too hard. We still had to treat Scotland with respect. We still had to do what we'd said we were going to do during the week. If we did that, then we knew the game would open up, and that's what happened.

Joe, the coaches and the video analysts had done their homework and we'd scouted Scotland very well that week. We came up with a really good plan and used some trick plays we'd practised during the week. We still had to play territory, put them under pressure and then, when it was time to play, we played. We had the perfect start when Paulie dived over in the fifth minute. I got a good shot on Jim Hamilton at a ruck close to their line. It opened up for Paulie because no one could come through the ruck the way I hit it. I remember thinking at the time, bury this fella here and we'll get a try. So the Big Red owes me for that one.

I scored the second try off a trick play at the back of a line-out. The move was called 'Aoife'. The ball was thrown over the number 7 to Devin Toner, and we knew that their 7, Blair Cowan, who is playing with me now at London Irish, was an eager beaver. He used to shoot off the tail to try and get at the opposition 10. I was Dev's back lift. Dev pretended to land and give, but instead he slipped it to me. When I was bringing Dev down, I could see Cowan going already. I took it, ran straight, rounded their winger Dougie Fife and scored. It worked perfectly.

Still, we only led 20-10 at half-time and we'd left chances behind. But it was a calm dressing-room. We were happy with what we'd done. We just needed to go through the gears and ramp it up when we got inside the 22.

Jared Payne scored our third with a nice line off Johnny's switch pass. Jared was a seriously good player. He wasn't big, but he was very strong and defensively excellent. He made consistently good reads. It was a pity that his injuries forced him to retire early. Jared was a player that Ireland could have done with for a little longer.

Johnny kicked a couple of penalties but also missed a

couple before Mads came on for him. We pounded their line, and when the ball came to me I dummied a little hit ball to Tommy Bowe, beat Fife on his inside and went through Alasdair Dickinson's tackle and reached out to score again.

I have that picture enlarged and framed and on my wall at home in the cottage in Tullow. Peter O'Mahony is in the background with his shirt raised and you can see his gut hanging out. I like that picture myself because it was after the two surgeries on my left shoulder and I had to reach out to get it on the line. If I had hit Tommy Bowe, he would have walked in as well. But that's what Joe had said at half-time, that when we got inside the 22 we should beat them around the corner, and we did.

But there was a bigger moment: Jamie's tackle on Stuart Hogg just when he was about to touch down. That was typical of Jamie, not giving up and staying true to his values. Hogg celebrated as if he'd scored, but that's Stuart Hogg for you. The moment I saw it on the big screen I thought, no try.

If they had scored there, and converted, England would have had to beat France by 19 points. Instead, they had to win by 26.

We said that we'd done what we'd gone there to do and that it was now out of our control. While we were pleased, we were anxious about what was going to happen. We showered, put on our suits and went upstairs to a function, and then there was that madness of the England v France game. England went after it and France, who had been boring until then, suddenly started playing crazy rugby.

I pulled up a chair and put my feet up on another chair in front of one of the two big screens in the room. I was fairly wrecked after our game. We got stuck into the beers in the second half, but it was unbearable. As the clock went into the red, England were ahead 55-35. They still needed a converted try to steal the championship from us. Then France, on their own line, tapped a penalty. We all screamed, 'What are you doing?' Then we remembered they weren't playing for us. They didn't care who won the title. They were just thinking of trying to get another seven points, before eventually Rory Kockott kicked the ball dead.

We got another beer into us and went around the room congratulating and high-fiving and hugging each other, but soon we were brought down to the pitch where they were setting up the stand to award us the trophy.

Even when the England v France game was on you could hear the cheers from the bars around Murrayfield, and the atmosphere was still buzzing in the stadium. Credit to the Scottish Union, they did a brilliant job allowing thousands of Irish fans to stay. To have them there when we did actually lift the trophy made the day. The trophy presentation was class, too, though it was a little surreal at first because we were in complete darkness. Then lights lit up the stage as we were lifting the trophy.

That was a powerful day, and it was a powerful thirty-six hours after that! It was probably the best three days I've ever put in, in my life. It was serious craic.

We stayed up all night in the Balmoral Hotel. I had to go up to my room and change my shirt because it was soaked with champagne. I put on a grey adidas T-shirt to accompany my black suit pants and black shoes. Late into the night I joined a group of supporters in the bar and played poker with them and had a few more beers. When I went up to bed, I'd say it was 8am. I went to bed for about an hour, got back up, got showered and straight on the beers again! We flew out of Edinburgh after lunch.

There was a 'do' for the squad that Sunday night in the Intercontinental Hotel in Ballsbridge, and then we went on to The Bridge.

On the Monday we went to Smyths in Ranelagh. The Irish women's team had won the Six Nations as well and I texted Jenny Murphy: *Where are you girls?* I knew Jenny from UCD and they'd been at the function the night before in the Intercontinental and I'd asked them to join us for the day. I don't know how many of us were there, about eleven or twelve players, mostly Leinster boys and a few of the girlfriends as the other lads had all gone back to their provinces. I'd say about twelve of the women's team joined us and they'd already had a few as well. I think they appreciated it, and it was the first time that the lads and the women celebrated something together. We all ended up in Coppers, where there were people dancing on top of bar counters.

We'd earned it and I'd earned it. It had been a long road back. Two shoulder operations. Virtually no rugby going into the Six Nations. Pulling up in the warm-up in Rome. But then playing four games in a row and scoring a couple of tries and being Man of the Match on the day we clinched the title. We were the first Irish team to retain the title since 1949. That's something special when you think about it. I'd worked hard to get back to that place and I suppose I came back at the right time. We were on a bit of a roll and I enjoyed my rugby that year.

Coming back to Leinster was always going to be difficult. When you've been out celebrating for a couple of days, you're looking forward to getting back training in one way, but not looking forward to blowing the cobwebs out.

Two weeks later, in the Heineken Cup quarter-finals, we

were a little lucky to win a shoot-out with Bath. We never really got away from them at all. We were playing what we saw, but we didn't have a good enough plan. At that stage we weren't ruthless enough to suffocate those types of teams.

But we did raise our game against Toulon in the semi-finals in Marseilles, which was a real arm-wrestle. Their back-row was Juan Smith, Juan Martín Fernández Lobbe and Chris Masoe – a Springbok, an Argentina captain and an All Black. When I made a carry early on, Smith came out of the line and almost cut me in half. They were trying to kill us, I think that was their game plan. I know it's in everyone's game plan to hit people, but these Toulon boys just flew off the line and we didn't adapt at all. We let them hit us behind the gain line. We struggled to get any momentum. It was one of the most physical games I've ever played in – all 100 minutes of it, as it went to extra time.

We hung in by the skin of our teeth and Jimmy Gopperth had a drop goal to win the match in the last minute, but it drifted just wide. It was a brave performance, but it wasn't where we'd been in the Heineken Cup-winning years. Bryan Habana scored an intercept try and that killed us. I scored a late try off a maul, but we'd left ourselves with too much to do.

That left us with three dead rubbers in the Pro12, a new experience. It had just become a struggle. We'd developed standards on and off the field, but we weren't accountable enough throughout that whole season. You have to have standards all the time. Otherwise when it comes to the big day, shit happens, and that's what happened through that season. When we came up against big teams, we hadn't got enough to beat them, and then we were scraping by teams that we should have been killing.

We finished fifth in the Pro12 and didn't make the play-offs. For Leinster, that's not acceptable. Then, Mattie got the chop. As players we're not in the know, but I thought it might happen all right. If results are unacceptable, the head coach is accountable. It can happen to any coach.

Heading into that summer there was only one thing on my mind: the World Cup. I resolved to behave myself in the summer and to come back into pre-season absolutely ready to tear shreds off people.

18. The pain

Paul O'Connell met me in pre-season, before the 2015 World Cup, and said that I had the potential to be Ireland captain one day, but that I needed to stop burning the candle at both ends. By which he meant that I was giving too much to the club at home, and that I was having too much craic on nights out as well.

There was nothing unusual about us having a coffee and a chat. Paulie was retiring from international rugby after the World Cup and I'd say it was something that he and Joe had spoken about: who would be the next leaders of the team.

A week before our second warm-up game, Joe came up to me and said: 'You'll be captain this week?'

I said: 'Of course I will.'

It was only a World Cup warm-up game, a friendly in August, but it was still a huge honour to lead the boys out, to be Ireland captain for the one time in my life.

It was also the first run-out of the season for most of the side. You're always blowing heavy and it's hard to get into a flow in those games. But I enjoyed the experience. I just tried to be myself. I didn't try to be more vocal than normal. I spoke as I usually did and I kept it very simple. It was a warm-up game, after all. It wasn't a Grand Slam decider, so there was no need to talk for the sake of talking.

On match day I went about my day as I normally would. At least the game was at home, too, so all my family and friends, bar Mam, were there when I led the team out.

The game was loose. The lead changed hands a few times before Luke Fitzgerald scored the winning try. We had a makeshift side and in the grand scheme of things it didn't matter if we won or lost, but it was good to win.

I did all the post-match media interviews with Joe and the reception afterwards. We had a two-week gap then, until our next warm-up game against Wales, and a few days off as well. So a few of us went out.

We had a good night together as a squad and we ended up in Coppers. I didn't stay too long because some nights there could be too messy, and that was one of them. But I was in great form after captaining my country for the first time. I wasn't messy, but I was giddy out. I met up with a few of my friends in Babylon, a late-night chipper on Camden Street. At my table I remember looking in front of me and seeing a curry cheese chips and two slices of pizza. That was my regular order there and I'd always have great craic with the owner.

I was dancing around the chipper and having fun when 'Time of Your Life' from *Dirty Dancing* came on, and a girl in an Ireland jersey said to me: 'Will you do the lift with me?'

Suddenly I found myself at one end of the chipper, with this girl at the other end about to take off. It's a tough enough lift. She came running down the middle of the chipper, launched herself and I lifted her up over my head at full stretch. It was a perfect lift. Then I dropped her down and the place went mad.

The next day there was a video of all this going around on Twitter, and all you can hear on the video is someone saying: 'He's surely off the fucking squad for this! He's surely off the fucking squad for this!' When I saw it, I laughed. I thought it was quite entertaining. I didn't do any harm to anyone. It was pure fun. Loads of boys in the team shared it around. They thought it was hilarious. But maybe those types of things possibly counted against me in Joe's eyes, and maybe the hierarchy's eyes, when it came to discussions about captaincy.

I'm kind of split on this whole issue because characters are an endangered species in the game nowadays and it's a shame. Granted, you have to be an example to young people and represent your club, your province and your country to the best of your ability. So while other people perceive it to be, 'Oh Jaysus that's terrible, he looks drunk', I don't see what I did that night being different from any other 28-year-old on a night out. What was genuinely wrong with that? I don't think I could have changed the way I was with people on nights out anyway. I always gave people time. I always tried to have craic and that's a part of my DNA.

Maybe it's also part of where I come from, too. When I was growing up, wild stuff went on in Tullow. Everyone would have their tops off in the local pub but there wouldn't be a word said about it, and there wouldn't be a video shared on social media because you were among friends. Most rugby teams, most football teams and most soccer teams are the same. It's a pity that people are so intrusive when videoing things, even when no harm is being done, and then so judgemental. We're humans. We're all going to make mistakes. But that's the way society is now.

In any case, that was my one night out after captaining my country and no one ever pulled me up on it. But I'd say Joe saw it. Joe saw everything. I doubt he saw any harm in it, though, because if he did, he would have said it to me. Besides, I didn't really care who saw it because there was nothing bad in it. I couldn't have been in any better form and I was just having fun.

I thought we were a stronger squad going into the World Cup than in 2011. We hadn't reached the point where you could pick any fifteen out of thirty players, and if we were missing a couple of key guys, the team just wasn't the same. But we'd had a good pre-season and were pretty fit. Our expectations were high. We'd had success and we were hitting form. We had good coaches, and with the World Cup being held in England and Wales we'd have even bigger support than in New Zealand. Things were well set up for us.

Sure enough, pool matches were like home games. In Cardiff there were 68,000 people for our first game against Canada, nearly all Irish. Mad. The place was mental. Roof closed. Savage atmosphere. Streets full of people. Cardiff is a great city for a big rugby match.

We had the bonus point before half-time. I scored the first off a line-out maul and then gave Johnny a return pass for him to score the third. I wouldn't have many better understandings on a rugby pitch than I have with Johnny. Then again, it's hard not to when he's roaring and shouting at me and giving out to me all the time.

I played the last quarter of our win over Romania at Wembley. Tommy Bowe got a couple of tries. Keith Earls became our World Cup record try-scorer. Rob got one. Chris Henry got one. The crowd was 89,267 strong – a World Cup record. Nearly all Irish again. Mental.

It was another Irish full house at the Olympic Stadium when we beat Italy and Earlsy scored the only try. Earlsy was on fire, but Earlsy is always on fire when he's fit and has had a good pre-season. He's one of the best teammates you could have on his day. A brilliant finisher and a class lad.

The Italians had been beaten by France, so Sergio Parisse and his boys were fighting for their lives. It was one that we were never going to lose, but we weren't going to pull away from them either. It was an arm-wrestle, but that probably helped us in the pool decider against France.

All week the French had been saying that they were going to bully us. That was their message. They were going to physically impose themselves. I remember saying a few times during the week: 'No fucking way is this happening, boys.' Paulie also tells the story of me giving the boys a spiel about discipline in the dressing-room beforehand. When Paulie led us out I was about fourth in line behind him and he heard me shout: 'Nothing stupid early on, lads.'

Then, in the first thirty seconds, I hit one of their players in the stomach.

At the time, I genuinely thought I had half-slapped Pascal Papé and I didn't realize how bad it looked until after the game. When he was on the ground, yelping like a child, I thought, what's going on here?

Paulie came up to me and said: 'Did you just hit him a box in the stomach?'

I looked at him and said: 'No, no – open hand.' And I walked away. I wasn't going to tell Paulie the truth anyway because he has this death stare that he hits you with.

I was pumped from the start of that game. My mindset was straightforward: There is no fucking way these boys are beating us today. There had been a lot of chat about the threat posed by Mathieu Bastareaud, and when he came out of the line I melted him backwards.

The roof of the Millennium Stadium was closed again and the Irish crowd was unreal again. We were just on top of them from the start. We were never going to lose that game. There was no doubt. We were on it that day.

Johnny went off early when Louis Picamoles dumped him.

Ian Madigan came on and kicked a penalty to put us 9-6 in front at half-time. But as the first half ended, I looked over at Paulie and I knew he was in serious pain. When he stayed down on the ground you knew there was something badly wrong. But we needed to get into the changing-room and get focused, because it didn't matter who was on the field against France that day, we weren't losing the game. Iain Henderson came on for Paulie and had a big game.

We went after them in the second half and suffocated them. It was time to score a try and it was just a matter of when. Rob Kearney finished well and Conor Murray's smart touchdown against the base of the post finished them off. It was a fairly convincing win in the end, but at a huge cost. All the lads off the bench had big impacts, but we were going to be stretched for the quarter-final.

I got Man of the Match and did some interviews on the side of the pitch. One interviewer began by congratulating me on the win and the Man of the Match award, and then said: 'What about the punch that you threw?'

That was his first question. I just stared at him and said I didn't punch anyone and then I spoke about the game. Off-air, after the interview was over, I said: 'You're some fucking bollocks for doing that.' He got a fright and apologized. I was fuming at that stage because I thought he was adding fuel to the fire, but I suppose he was just doing his job.

I was mad with myself, too, that I had done something stupid. I hadn't taken a backward step and Papé was one of their leaders, but it was the wrong thing to do. He had grabbed a hold of me from behind on my hip and on our side of the ruck. When I hit him, I actually got back out to defend where I was meant to defend. It was an instant reaction and it was meant to be a slap, but it was a closed fist.

That day against France we also lost Peter and Paulie, and Johnny had gone off as well. As it turned out, Johnny would be ruled out of the Argentina game the day before the quarter-final. We'd also lost Jared Payne. After the game I could see that Joe was disappointed in me because I had let him down.

The game was on a Sunday and on the Monday evening I was cited.

I hardly slept that night and on the Tuesday morning myself and our manager, Mick Kearney, got the train from Cardiff to London. The tickets cost £350 or something. The hearing was held in a hotel. It began at 1.15pm and the decision wasn't made until 7.45pm. When we went into that hearing it was bright, and when we came out it was dark. Almost seven hours of my life, and a long seven hours too.

The judicial officer was Terry Willis, an Australian. He liked the sound of his own voice and it was very much his show. It was quite intimidating. I was represented by Max Duthie, a top-class solicitor who specializes in sports. He is based in London and had done a couple of Lions tours. The IRFU had him on standby for the duration of the World Cup.

Max said that I accepted that I had struck Papé and that I knew I shouldn't have done so and that it was an act of foul play. But there were some very important qualifications: it was a provoked strike; we were very sceptical about it causing an injury; I had been trying to get Papé away from me; my focus was on the ruck and the next stage of play. Max said that I should receive no sanction.

The citing commissioner, Dougie Hunter from Scotland, presented video evidence from a number of angles. The first camera angle showed Papé from the ground. The medic came on and put an ice pack on his chest. Max pointed out that there was no evidence of the medic examining him and that the medic didn't lift his shirt. Max questioned whether Papé had just decided to make a meal of it.

(Papé, for his part, had been suspended the previous March for ten weeks after being cited for putting his knee into Jamie Heaslip's back at a ruck. Wayne Barnes yellow-carded him and Papé's appeal was turned down. Jamie had suffered three cracked vertebrae in his back.)

Papé had submitted written evidence saying: 'I received a violent punch on the area of the sternum. Due to the instantly pain [sic], I collapse [sic] to the ground and couldn't breathe any more. I received care from Dr Grisoli. All along the game I felt a violent pain in the area where I had been beaten.'

Max pointed out that he had played until the seventy-third minute.

The camera angle showed the contact, but Papé had clearly dragged me into the French half, and out of position, before I made contact. I had only looked at the ruck throughout, never at Papé. Willis commented that what Papé did was a 'very significant, contributing factor'. In other words, this would not have happened if Papé hadn't grabbed me.

Willis asked when they could get Papé on the telephone. Some French guy said he was training, but Willis said he'd have to interrupt his training session.

Then Max showed another camera angle and said that I hadn't directed a fist at Papé, that it wasn't a punch. Contact was made through the scaphoid, which is a bone at the back of the wrist. There was eight minutes of video and it took over two hours for Hunter, Max and Willis to get through the video. Max said it was 'benign' and not an intentional strike. If I had decided that I wanted to hurt Papé, then I'd have gone about it in a wholly different way.

Willis agreed that it was a swinging arm, which gave me hope. He again asked about Papé giving evidence and was again told that the French were training.

Papé went on to be involved in over forty impacts in the game – tackles, carries and hitting rucks. Max showed some extra clips as well, from the 37th, 41st, 54th and 64th minutes, of Papé going into collisions and he didn't seem to show any sign of 'violent pain'.

Willis accepted this submission, although he noted that players had been known to play on with broken jaws.

Max then asked me a few questions. He began by asking me to explain what had happened in my own words. I said I'd been grabbed from behind and just wanted to concentrate on being on guard from the ruck. I felt I'd been impeded, so I swung out to get him off me. I said I was fully focused on the next play. I said I would take it back if I had the chance.

By then Papé, the team doctor and one of their management team were on the phone from their training base. Willis asked Papé if he remembered the incident when he appeared to make contact with me while running back for a ruck. He denied that he had tried to pull me out of position and said his hand was on my jersey but that at no moment did he pull it. He may have touched me, but he didn't pull the jersey.

Willis asked Papé what he was trying to do when he put his hand on my jersey.

Papé said he was trying to come back onto the French side of the ruck.

Was he not able to come back without contacting me?

Papé said he didn't need to justify it, that there were players around and he was just trying to get back into his own half.

When he put his hand on me, how did he think I would react?

Papé said he had no anticipation of how I would react.

Had he tried to wind me up?

Not at all.

Had anyone ever suggested to him that he should wind up players to win penalties?

No, not at all.

When he was running back, did he recall grabbing an opponent at any stage of the match?

No, he didn't recall.

When Papé was lying on the ground, Dr Grisoli, the team doctor, seemed to lift him by the armpit. Had he explained to Papé what he was trying to do?

Yes, Papé said, the doctor was trying to help him to get his breath back.

Their team manager interrupted to say that Papé had to return to training, but Willis said that he wanted Papé to remain on the line.

When the team manager said they had been told there would be only two questions to answer, Willis suggested he'd have Papé brought to the hearing by car. He said they needed Papé for another five minutes.

Papé said he had been unable to speak to the team doctor because he was completely out of breath. He couldn't remember an ice pack on his chest. Papé again denied that he was trying to gain an advantage by holding me.

Asked if the doctor advised him to carry on playing, Papé said that the doctor didn't advise him to do anything. Once he got his breath back, he carried on. He said that he had told Nigel Owens that he had been punched in the stomach.

Willis asked him if he'd participated fully in the match.

Papé said that he'd really wanted to stay on the pitch, but that he had felt pain for the rest of the match and that he still felt pain.

Did he feel 'violent pain' throughout the match?

He said it had stopped him from breathing in a normal fashion.

Did he have any treatment at half-time?

'Ice.'

Had he made any mention to Seán O'Brien about what had happened?

No.

Had he any marks on his body?

No.

Willis then interviewed Dr Grisoli and asked him if he remembered coming onto the pitch after the incident. When he was asked what Papé had said to him, the doctor said that Papé couldn't breathe and explained his treatment.

Max interviewed the doctor next.

No, he wasn't sure there was no serious injury, but he had decided to leave Papé on the pitch and observe him. He claimed that he had observed that Papé's ribs weren't broken but that he was a bit breathless and in pain.

After the match, the doctor said he treated Papé with ice and paracetamol. While there was no longer any visible mark on Papé's body, the doctor said that there had been a round, red patch of six centimetres at the lower end of Papé's sternum, on the right-hand side.

It was pretty clear by now that they were out to get me.

Max asked them if they'd spoken with match officials after the game.

No, they had not.

Asked how he was now, Papé said that he was still tender,

but that he was 80 per cent certain to play in their quarter-final against New Zealand the following Saturday. (Yeah, he played all right.)

Eventually, there was a summing-up. Max maintained that a citing could be upheld, but that the panel had the discretion not to impose any sanction. Max had dug up other examples of when this had happened. Max argued very strongly that it wasn't a serious enough infraction to warrant a sanction. He said that it was at the low end of the scale, that there were mitigating circumstances and that it would be wholly dispro-portionate to suspend me. He said that I'd clearly been held back and my intention had been to free myself.

Max pointed out that Papé hadn't suffered a significant injury, that he'd been floored but had gone on to play for seventy-three minutes. Willis said it could have been a ser-ious injury. Max maintained that there had been provocation and that, at the worst, Papé had sustained a relatively modest injury.

Mick Kearney gave a character reference on my behalf, saying what a wonderful young man I was, and Willis said that he was extremely sympathetic about the situation in which I found myself. He admitted that it hadn't been a blow to the head, the neck, the back or the groin. I had been look-ing the other way. It wasn't premeditated. It wasn't a punch. It was just a swing of the arm.

My spirits lifted.

We pleaded that I had a good disciplinary record. I've never had a red card in my career and had never had a yellow card playing for Ireland either. I had never been suspended. Willis accepted that I was a person of 'exemplary character' and that I had shown remorse. He felt it was an 'insignificant act'.

Max had argued that a suspension would be a huge price for me and Ireland to pay, but the citing commissioner talked about the image of the game, player welfare, and said that every match is equal – although I don't know how you can argue that an AIL game has the same importance as a World Cup quarter-final.

At about 7.15pm we were asked to leave the room.

At about 7.45pm we were called back in to receive the verdict.

Willis told us that the citing had been upheld and that as it was at the lower end, there was an entry point of two weeks. There were no aggravating circumstances, there were compelling mitigating factors and because of my disciplinary record and remorse, he was reducing the suspension to one week.

Reducing it to one week was no good for me really. Potentially, that was going to end my World Cup. That was part of our case, but I suppose they couldn't be seen to let me away with it. I might as well have punched Papé in the face. After the 'evidence' he gave beforehand in writing and then over the phone at the hearing, I have no respect for him, both for what he did that week and for a lot of what he has done in his rugby career.

The last train had already left for Cardiff, but World Rugby had organized a car, so myself and Mick were given a lift. We didn't get back into Cardiff until around 11pm that night. I was devastated. I knew I'd hurt our chances of beating Argentina. All my family were coming for the quarter-final, too, the whole lot of them, and people from all around home. We were already missing four key men and then there was also one eejit sitting in the stand – who was fully fit and playing serious rugby – because he did something stupid.

I reckon that if I had been playing that day, we would have won the game. Even though we were missing Paulie, Johnny, Pete and Jared, I still think we would have won the game if I'd been playing, and that's not being cocky. I just think the way we defended and some of the stuff we did in the game were terrible. If I was there, I would have had us more organized, particularly in defence. I've always believed that I would have added a lot more to that game.

Sitting in the stadium after that one, I was more disappointed and upset than after most defeats I've played in. I walked into the function room and met my family. I sat down at a table and I couldn't stop crying because I felt I had let everyone down. It had been the nearest Ireland had ever come to a home World Cup, and that's the other fucking disappointing thing about it.

It's one of the things that eats me up inside, because while the 2011 World Cup had gone well for me, it hadn't for the team. This time we had everything in place. It's probably the single biggest regret of my career.

I stayed in the hotel with the boys that night. I didn't go any further and went home the next day. I drove down to Tullow and met James Foley at the Tara Arms. We had a few drinks and ended up going into Carlow, me, James and his brother Darragh – into The Foundry and the Dinn Rí. We didn't realize until we went in there that it was a student night. We weren't drunk at that stage, but then we started having a few shorts in the corner. The tunes were going and it was a good bit of craic. James and Darragh wanted to go home, but I wouldn't go with them. I insisted that I was going on to a house party.

I wish I'd gone home with them. Instead, I wanted more craic at this house party, but little did I know that some people videoed me and someone got my phone as well. I was oblivious to this. I still hadn't overcome the disappointment of the World Cup. For days I'd been whingeing and crying about letting the team and my family down. I came home and went on the beer.

I woke up the next day and ninety-something WhatsApp messages had landed on my phone from different people and groups. 'What happened last night?' was the general gist of them.

I began recalling the night. Yes, I went back to the house party and I remembered walking around the kitchen with no top on and eating a raw potato. But I was also accused of a lot of stuff that was completely fabricated. Whoever had grabbed my phone had broken into my Facebook account and sent messages to people and called them various names. They had sent violent messages randomly to a few people I didn't even know. There was one lad, I think he was sixty-five, who got a message from my phone saying: *I think you are a bollocks.*

Some of the stuff they sent was meant to be funny, but it wasn't funny for those who received it. As I was going through my phone, I remembered a fella who was at the house party and said he was playing rugby with IT Carlow. I contacted him and said: 'What happened last night?'

He said: 'You had your top off and you were going around the kitchen and you were eating a spud, but there was a lad who was at your phone when you left it down on the table. They must have seen you putting in your passcode.'

I remembered sitting at the table with the potato in my hand. I had flashbacks of that, and I remembered my phone being on the table for some reason.

The girl who had sent the initial WhatsApp had messaged

me on Facebook. I messaged her back on Facebook, asking: *Why did you put up that WhatsApp of me drunk and asleep at a table?* She answered: *Oh, I thought it was just fun, but now one of the lads is after sending it out.*

After I messaged her back again, she didn't respond for about ten minutes. Next minute, I received another heap of WhatsApp messages. They were screenshots of my chats with this girl on Facebook ten minutes earlier, which she had also thrown into a WhatsApp group.

Jaysus, I thought to myself, I can't do anything here.

I rang my mam and explained what had happened. I said: 'Do you know what, this isn't worth it. Playing rugby is not worth it for this shit.' I added: 'Look, I shouldn't have gone out. I had been upset for the last four or five days, in a bad place, but this isn't worth the hassle or the abuse I'm getting now. I didn't hurt anyone, but this has gotten completely out of hand.'

She said: 'Look, calm down, it will be okay. It will pass.'

'I'm not sure,' I said.

She was right, it did pass, eventually, but I was disappointed for putting myself in that situation. I held my hand up and spent the day apologizing for my behaviour, and also for messages I had never sent.

I said sorry to James first of all, for not going home with him. 'Please don't go to this party,' he had pleaded. 'You don't know these people.' I was having none of it. I was in that kind of headspace. But he had been right, and I had been wrong.

I was hounded for days because I had been added to all these WhatsApp groups, so I had to change my number. If there was one lesson I should have taken on board, it was not to go out drinking in a sad or emotional state.

There wasn't much of a season left for me either.

In the Heineken Cup at home to Wasps, Leinster were beaten 33-6. A dreadful day – twenty-two missed tackles, twenty-four turnovers. This was Leo Cullen's first season as head coach. Everything was a bit new again in the transition between coaches, and so many of us being away at the World Cup didn't help Leinster and Leo either. One of our worst defeats ever, I'd say. To make it even worse, I suffered concussion and didn't come back out for the second half.

I also missed the Bath game away and both Toulon matches with an ear problem. It wasn't related to concussion. I wasn't suffering from headaches or anything like that. I had a vestibular infection. The hair follicles in the ear open and close like a filter, and thanks to the glancing blow I had received mine were blocked on one side. That meant I had to undergo a series of exercises.

The problem didn't clear up, though. For example, if I stood up quickly off the couch, I was slightly disorientated for two or three seconds. It didn't worry me because I hadn't suffered a proper concussion or a massive impact. I was just puzzled as to why I was feeling like that.

After three weeks I went to see Dr Doug Duffy, a specialist in vestibular rehab. Doug strapped me into a harness, like one you'd wear if you were doing a bungee jump, and put me on a machine that resembled a large weighing scales. It moved from left to right and backwards and forwards. If you have a vestibular problem you'll stumble or fall, but the harness will keep you safe. When I wasn't able to keep my balance, he knew what the problem was straight away. Doug had me lie down on a physio bed and he manipulated my head and neck in about ten different patterns, and the minute I got off the bed the blockage was gone.

In order to ensure it didn't happen again, I had to have a further period of rehab to reset my balance. I'd stand on one leg with my eyes closed. I'd stand on one leg looking into a mirror with a cross on it. I'd stand on one leg and look at a cross on the wall while shaking my head but keeping my eyes on it for one minute. I'd walk along a straight line with my eyes open for a specific period of time.

It was also during this time that I agreed a new three-and-a-half-year deal with the IRFU to take me through to the 2019 World Cup. This time I represented myself. I thought I was in a strong enough position to chat with David Nucifora one-to-one. I agreed with the Union that I wouldn't start looking elsewhere if they offered me a figure that I was happy with.

After being out for six weeks, I was back for the win against Munster over Christmas. We won 24-7 and I put Isa away to score from halfway. Always nice to win in Thomond Park!

I also played the last quarter in the home win over Bath, but missed another big beating by Wasps. By this stage I'd had tendonitis for a year, dating back to when I'd pulled up in the warm-up against Italy in Rome, and it was beginning to flare up more frequently. It's very hard to see a tendon tear on a scan, but it looked like there was a little tear on the top of it. I had managed that for a year, but leading into the opening Six Nations game against Wales my hamstring was at me as well, and I missed that draw.

We had a six-day turnaround before facing France in Paris and that week in training the hamstring was a little achy. With tendonitis, if you dip quickly and try to power off you might get a bit of a bite, likewise if you bend to catch a ball low to the ground quickly. Any forward movement and you feel it.

Once I had warmed up for the game, I didn't notice a thing. It rained steadily in Paris and the Stade de France pitch was poor, but we started well. I nearly scored. I felt good. We went 3-0 up and were attacking again. Conor Murray passed to me and a few French defenders came towards me. I squared up to one of them and went to power off, and the minute I did, I heard a pop and then a rip. I heard two distinct sounds. A pop and a rip. I was in fucking bits straight away and I thought to myself, this is major.

I knew exactly what it was as I walked off and I remember sitting on a physio bed, watching the match on a screen. I had an ice pack under my arse, but after ten minutes the pain was excruciating.

The boys lost the game by 10-9 and I was gutted for them. Mike McCarthy got a bad concussion that day, they roughed up Johnny, and Dave Kearney suffered a serious shoulder injury when hit high by Guilhem Guirado.

I stayed in my hotel room that night and ordered pizza, chicken wings and a heap of food to the room. I was on fucking savage painkillers, in a brace and on crutches, too.

We went home the next day, my twenty-ninth birthday, and the worst was confirmed. Another big injury that required surgery, and a career-threatening one at that because there's always doubt over whether you can come back from something like that. I'd actually torn one tendon off. That was the pop. It was likely the one that had been slightly torn for a year. And I'd ripped off half of the other tendon. That was the rip.

To put this in context, when Paulie ripped his hamstring, he did his three tendons. I'd done one and a half, so it was going to be a tricky operation and rehab.

I went to London for a consultation with my orthopaedic

surgeon, Fares Haddad. He said: 'Yes, this can be fixed.' It's actually quite a common injury in people who are carrying extra weight. If they slip on a wet floor or jolt forward, for example, the tendon can rip off the bone straight away.

In the operation, the surgeon makes a six-inch slit, pulls your tendon back onto the bone, screws it in, stitches it with wire in a figure-of-eight and lets it knit itself back together. It's been brilliant since then, but that was me done for eight months. I knew I had a long road ahead of me again.

The rehab was tricky, and tedious. I had to do a lot of the same stuff over and over again. I couldn't sit on a bike to pedal and build a sweat. I couldn't do anything like that for a long, long time because I couldn't put pressure on the tendon. I could only do bits and pieces. I couldn't lift weights for a while either, even for the upper body, unless I had someone with me.

There have been a few bad ones, but that was one of the worst rehabs that I had to go through. I was still at a low ebb mentally after what had happened at the World Cup. For the next few months, I was not in a good place. Rugby had me beat.

19. I want to be the best in the world

Before the 2016/17 season started, I texted Enda McNulty to arrange one of our usual catch-ups. We'd met once or twice a year ever since Michael Cheika had brought him into Leinster in 2008 and we continued to do so after Declan Kidney invited him into the Irish set-up in 2013. But this one would be different.

Enda had me hooked since the first time he'd spoken to the Leinster squad. We'd just lost to Castres away in December 2008. He told us all to pick a number in our heads of the amount of press-ups we could do without stopping. I think I had fifty or sixty in mind.

'Okay, get down and start doing press-ups,' he said.

I reached eighty or ninety without stopping, and most of us beat whatever targets we'd set ourselves. We could all do more than we believed.

He was off on a runner as soon as he did that.

We arranged to meet in his old office in Clonskeagh on 30 August 2016. We had our usual fifteen or twenty minutes of banter about the farm, the talent coming through at Leinster, business trends and the big GAA games – Dublin had just beaten Kerry to set up an All-Ireland football final with Mayo.

Then Enda asked me what I wanted out of the session and out of the coming season.

I was crystal clear: 'I want to be the best player in the world in my position.'

Enda said that I'd had performances that were world-class but not consistently enough. He asked me how I could get there and what my plan was to get there. He asked me to write it all on the large whiteboard on his office wall.

I was a little vague with my answers, so Enda said: 'I am going to leave you to have a really good, honest conversation with yourself. What you have written on that whiteboard is not going to help you get to be the best in the world. I will be back in half an hour. I expect you to write up a comprehensive plan.'

I started writing down things. Short-term goals. My strengths. My work-ons. The best players in the world in my position.

When Enda came back thirty minutes later, I was buzzing. My mindset had shifted. I had lots of notes written down in my notebook and the whiteboard was also better thought out.

The two of us stood at the board and began to flesh out the plan. We compared me to David Pocock, Sam Cane, Ardie Savea and, even though he'd retired after the World Cup, Richie McCaw. I marked them out of ten in different areas. We looked honestly at where I was stronger and where I needed to grow. In particular, I compared myself harshly with Pocock and McCaw.

We created a table on the board, itemizing each of their strengths and mine. This was a very detailed assessment of me. We went through each aspect of my game and drew up a plan with the following headings: Lifestyle, Strength & Conditioning, Leadership, Defence, Offence, Prehab, Mental Toughness Prep, Communication.

Then we had a twenty-minute chat about lifestyle. I spoke about farming and about the coaching I did free of charge in the evenings in Tullow and for GAA teams. Enda asked me how I was going to be best in the world if this was my lifestyle.

I wrote down the biggest changes I needed to make immediately and my biggest performance 'derailers'. By the end, I had written down an overview of my whole rugby life.

I was in serious shape by then and Enda told me to take my shirt off and he took a photo of me beside the board where we'd written everything out. He said: 'Every time I see you, I want you to be in even better condition than you are now.'

We moved towards the end of the two-hour meeting. Enda said, 'Seánie, it's time to face the brutal truth. Your lifestyle is not good enough. You need to work relentlessly on the basics more. You need to improve all the areas you have highlighted on the board. Seánie, if you want to be the best in the world, you need to massively commit to that now – not a week before an All Blacks game or a World Cup game.'

I came away understanding what I had to do in order to get to where I wanted to be. Too many things were cluttering my mind. The farm was a major one. I needed to prioritize recovery from training sessions and games, nutrition, having a clearer head. I was twenty-nine and all these things had to change immediately.

Within ten days to two weeks I had sold all the cows that I had in Tullow, about sixty in total. When I wasn't on the farm, things weren't being done the way I wanted them to be done. Dad would do things his way. He wouldn't compromise at all. So I decided the easiest thing to do was to get rid of them because it was one less thing for me to be frustrated about. I also decided to stop coaching. These changes meant I spent less time in the car.

Enda also advised me to sit down with the people I trusted and to ask them for their honest opinion of me and my game. He suggested I ask them to reflect on this in advance of meeting to talk about it. Enda said that I should meet with Joe Schmidt for a one-on-one, and we also agreed that I should meet with Johnny Sexton and John Fogarty, the Leinster scrum coach. They were three people who would give it to you between the eyes.

There were similar responses from all three of them. I was giving people outside the game too much time, whether it was farming, coaching, doing charity gigs or just trying to please everyone. For a professional sportsperson, I wasn't being selfish enough. And I was enjoying life too much.

When I sat down with Johnny for a coffee, I said: 'Tell me honestly what you think of me. Tell me honestly what you think of me right now.'

And he said: 'Well, I think you are fucking brilliant, a brilliant lad, a brilliant rugby player and a great friend and everything, but I think you do too much for people. I'd be unsure whether you look after yourself as much as you should.'

From then on, I began to mature a little.

By mid-October I'd recovered from my torn hamstring and was told that I was going to be playing for the Leinster As in the British & Irish Cup away to Richmond in London. Noel McNamara was the coach. I went upstairs into the second meeting area on the top floor of our High Performance Centre in UCD. The room was full of younger guys with whom I hadn't had much dealing, but I embraced what was coming and really invested in that team for that week.

The game itself was a free-for-all. We had a talented team and Richmond trained twice a week. They kicked off to us and we scored, and that's how it continued. We never had to go beyond two or three phases. It wasn't much of a workout, but after eight months to have a few contacts, carries and hits gave me confidence.

They took me off at half-time. I said to Noel: 'Can you leave me on for another ten?' But he was under strict orders.

James Ryan played in the second-row that night. He was twenty years old and scored a try, but I don't remember him playing at all. I'd watched him in the Six Nations Under-20s, standing in the far corner in Donnybrook on my own, and I'd tracked his run before he made an unbelievable tackle against Wales in the far corner under the stand. He was like a back-rower and I thought, this fella is something special.

A nineteen-year-old Jordan Larmour also scored that day in Richmond, and I don't remember him either! It's only when you see them developing and breaking into the senior team that you really start to notice these guys.

The next day, word came through that Anthony Foley had died in Paris. I was at home. It was a complete shock. There's no other way to describe it. A shock that someone of that age, and such a figurehead of Munster rugby and Irish rugby, was gone.

Not long after I made the Irish Youths team, in one of my first media interviews I listed Anthony Foley and Richie McCaw as my heroes. Axel was just invariably in the right place at the right time. A very intelligent rugby player. Even though he wasn't always the star turn, he made the team click. In any good passages of play involving Munster or Ireland, he was usually involved. Good skills, too. He wasn't blessed with pace, but he had everything else. And he didn't need the pace because he was so smart.

The first time I met Axel was in the Shannon clubhouse

bar after UCD had played at Thomond Park in an AIL game. I was in my second year in the Leinster Academy. They had Stephen Keogh in the back-row along with Gareth Noonan, who's a big lump of a man, and Johnny O'Connor, who was as hard as nails.

Axel came over to me and said: 'Well done. That was a great display by you today.'

I thanked him. In later years there were whispers that Munster were after me, so maybe he had something to do with that. In the first few years in the Irish squad, Paulie would rib me about joining Munster and Denis Leamy said I was more like them than Leinster.

Axel was still playing then, but a couple of years later, starting out on his coaching career, he coached me when I played for the Ireland A team. I'm not going to say I knew Axel that well but, listening to his best friends, what a man he was.

A week later I started at number 6 against Montpellier and they took me off at half-time again. They were trying to manage me, but I felt strong and sharp. No one wants to go off when they're in the flow of a game. I was a bit annoyed, but you can't sulk, and I didn't.

Ireland were playing the All Blacks in Chicago two weeks later. I wanted to show that I was up to European Cup level for longer.

That week, Joe re-signed with Ireland until the end of the 2019 World Cup and I was named in a thirty-seven-man squad for the November Tests. There was one more game before Chicago, a full house at the RDS for Leinster against Connacht. We wanted revenge for the Pro12 final the previous May in Murrayfield. There are certain games where you want redemption.

Connacht played a great brand of rugby that whole season when they won the trophy, but we had let ourselves down in the final and that hurt a lot. We had the opportunity to put it right and we were going to take it.

I was yellow-carded for catching Peter Robb's head with my shoulder at a ruck. I didn't actually think that was a yellow. It wasn't as if it was a deliberate shoulder charge or anything, it was just the way it unfolded. I was pretty annoyed about that, but I played well again and was taken off in the sixty-seventh minute.

I thought Joe would have brought me to Chicago and, worst-case scenario, I'd be on the bench. Axel's passing had a profound effect on the Irish squad and would have a massive part to play in the emotional energy of the players as well. It was one of those weeks when everyone was desperate to be involved. But when he took a twenty-seven-man squad to Chicago on the Monday, I wasn't in it. Instead, three hours before the kick-off in Soldier Field, I was playing with Leinster as we kicked off in the Stadio Sergio Lanfranchi in Parma against Zebre. It snowed and I'd say there were barely 1,000 there to watch us. We won 33-10 and I played an hour, flicking the ball on to Adam Byrne to score his third try.

On the flight home the pilot kept us up to date on the score in Chicago. Sitting on the plane it began to dawn on me: fuck me, I am missing out on one of the biggest occasions in the history of Irish sport. That's the selfish thought. But then you also think of it from an Irish point of view: my God, what have these lads done? What an unbelievable achievement.

As a rugby player, you always know the work, the sacrifices and the hardship you put your body and mind through to achieve a win like that, and the abuse you take as well.

Those are the wins that make it all worth it. So, while disappointed not to be there, I was delighted for the lads with whom I'd been in the trenches for years.

The following week against Canada, I started at number 7. Peter O'Mahony was back at 6 for the first time since doing his knee ligaments in the World Cup over a year before, and Jack O'Donoghue was at 8. Jack's a lovely lad and a very good player, he just needs to be more consistent and, for a back-rower, to be more involved and come up with a few bigger moments.

Andy Farrell had come on board before the South Africa tour the previous summer, but I'd had experience of him with the Lions in 2013. I knew what he was about as a person, what he wanted to bring to a set-up and what he expected of me. It was an easier transition for those of us who'd worked with him in 2013. He is a very, very good coach and I've always liked Faz. He has that personal side to him as well. He'd have a bit of craic with you.

As a defence coach, the results speak for themselves. He was a really physical player himself and I think that feeds into his motivational skills, which are exceptional. As is his assessment of other teams' attacks, where you can get at them and how you can win the ball back. He definitely ramped up our line speed as soon as he came into the Ireland squad. He helped to put us in better places and, because we were going forward, to make more impact tackles. And we had a few 'big rocks', as we called them, to make sure that even when we came under pressure, our system never faltered.

That Canada game gave me a springboard into the home game against the All Blacks a week later, when Joe went for me at 7, C. J. Stander at 6 and Jamie at 8, with Josh van der

Flier on the bench. My mindset going into that game was, right, today is the day to be the best in the world. That had to be the mindset against the top players. I did have one of my best games, but I made one major mistake.

They were 14-6 up, but we were on top and had a line-out in the corner. It was a move we'd worked on that week. I peeled off the back from Devin Toner. Dev caught the ball, but he was getting sacked slightly when he passed and I was reaching slightly for the ball. I just didn't hold on to it. My 'ball focus', as Joe used to drill into us, just wasn't where it needed to be. On another day I could have held that. I only had Beauden Barrett in front of me, and he's not going to stop me two metres out with me running at nearly full tilt. If I hold on to that ball and we score there, potentially we go on to win the game.

We were applying a huge amount of pressure. We'd beaten them only two weeks beforehand. They knew we were capable of doing it again. They'd have known they were in a game then, and if it had come to a tight finish, we had learned lessons from 2014. Plus, with the belief we had and with the players we had, we would have been in a good place to win the game from then on. In all other aspects of my game I was really happy, but I probably do kick myself over it a little bit, but, then, that's sport, isn't it?

We'd lost Robbie Henshaw and Johnny Sexton early on, and this is another lesson we learned. The All Blacks were borderline violent that day and people in the media questioned how the referee, Jaco Peyper, let them away with it. It was exactly the opposite. We should have been borderline violent. What do you expect from a team that's wounded, that's not used to losing, that was beaten by this same team two weeks before, and that are away from home? The All

Blacks were always going to come out fighting. So you have to stand up, beat your chest and make sure you don't take a backward step.

I don't think we had enough dog in us.

A week later I was meant to start against Australia, but my knee was sore and in the Shelbourne Hotel the day before the game the doc and physios said: 'No, there's no point in chancing it.' Josh came in for me and he was fit as a fiddle. He's as good a chop tackler as there is around and his work rate is outstanding. Salt of the earth, too.

We lost Rob Kearney, Andrew Trimble and Jared Payne in the first half, and had to put Kieran Marmion on the wing. The team was thrown together by the end, so it was a big win and another incredible day.

Back at Leinster, I had a chance to work properly with Stuart Lancaster, who had come in just before the season started. We also had Graham Henry in on a consultancy basis for a couple of weeks in pre-season, so we were sharing different ideas from good people to get us to a better place. But a fortnight isn't really enough time with someone like Graham Henry. He has an incredible rugby brain and he carries himself in a very professional manner, and I'd love to have had him as a full-time consultant.

Like Faz with Ireland, I thought Stuart's appointment was incredibly smart. He had been treated badly by England. They had beaten the All Blacks, he had had a brilliant win percentage, and he just was very unlucky in the 2015 World Cup against Wales. The England players had to take some responsibility as well, but I didn't hear many of them hold their hands up and admit they didn't execute or deliver. Stuart would admit he became too worried about stuff off the field. What he loves most is hands-on coaching, and he'd stopped doing that with England because of the extra demands.

So Leinster had acquired someone with a good track record and brought him into an environment where he could start doing what he loved again. He's very straight talking. There's no bullshit with Stuart. He's quite detailed, knows what he wants from you and from the team. You have to be fit to work under Stuart. Other coaches wouldn't put as much emphasis on unstructured rugby, but Stuart was all about that, about 'coming alive' when we didn't have the ball.

We trained harder than some of our games, and within the first few weeks of his arrival Tuesdays had already become known as 'Stusdays'. They were forty-five minutes of non-stop match scenarios, from one end of the field to the other. They were tough and they didn't get much easier either just because you knew they were coming every week. We never got Stusdays off. Even if we played a hard game on a Sunday, Stusday could be Wednesday. There was no avoiding it.

In Lancaster and Farrell, Leinster and Ireland were getting coaches who had learned plenty from their time with England. I wouldn't have wanted the Stuart Lancaster who was looking after the off-field stuff in the England camp, but I loved the Stuart Lancaster who coached Leinster.

I started in the back-to-back wins over Northampton in the Heineken Cup, scoring in both of them. I had a good few carries and was feeling fit again and back to myself. Christmas was usually a window for the lads who were playing on the international team to have a week off. I missed the St Stephen's Day defeat by Munster in Thomond Park. I was at home having turkey! I was back for the win over Ulster at home on New Year's Eve. No partying, though, as I was playing against Zebre a week later.

At that stage, I wanted games, but my knee began to bother me again and I missed the win at home to Montpellier and the draw in Castres that earned us a home quarter-final. Even so, the rest did me good and I started all of the Six Nations games.

That 2017 Six Nations was an annoying one. It began with that bloody bus journey to Murrayfield for the opening game. It unhinged us and we were never quite on track again afterwards. The start of the Six Nations is so important, and to come away from that game like that was brutal.

For some reason the bus driver took a different route, the traffic was terrible, and it took us for ever to get to the stadium. As soon as we arrived, we had to get changed and do the warm-up. No time for reading the programme, chilling out or walking around the pitch. We were knocked out of our normal routine. Well, I certainly was. And I'm not excessively into my match-day routine or particularly superstitious, like some players.

I wasn't a good sleeper the night before a game for a long time. If it wasn't my hip or something else bothering me, I'd be awake worrying things over. So I didn't sleep well for periods throughout my career because I'd either be worried about something or in pain. You can go through phases. I'd say almost every sportsperson does. But, tired or not, the adrenalin of the day would get me through it. If it was an evening game, I'd still get up and have my breakfast, but I might go back to bed. That was the only difference.

I'd always want my breakfast early on match day, regardless of kick-off time. No later than 8am. Over the last four or five years I'd always have my oats prepared overnight with milk and water. Sometimes I even brought them with me to away games. Then I'd usually have eggs and bacon, with brown toast and a coffee. I'd stick to my normal routine. I didn't change too much.

Rice pudding has been my pre-match meal ever since I started living with Daniel Davey in 2012. We lived in three different apartments in Mount St Anne's, in Milltown, for five years. I never like to feel too full going out to play a game and I found a bowl of rice pudding, rather than a big plate of spaghetti bolognese or something, worked for me.

On the way to the ground, sometimes I'd listen to music and sometimes I wouldn't. If I was listening to music, I'd listen to Mumford & Sons. They are my favourite band. It wouldn't matter if a really sad song came on or something that was fast. I like them and that's it.

I like to be as normal as I can be around the boys and not get jizzed up too early because certain lads will have seen the way you are for years and if they see something different they think, what's going on here? Some lads enjoyed that part of me and would have the chats. But with other lads, you'd know to just leave them to their own devices.

The moment I lace up my boots is the moment I flick the switch. That would be about five or six minutes before the warm-up. I always liked to chill out and gradually start to get the mind switched on. And then the boots are done and I'm raring to go.

There was none of that at Murrayfield that day. It was gear on, strapping on, headgear on, boots on and straight out onto the field. The headgear comes from having cauliflower ears. That's the only reason. They used to absolutely kill me and were very hard to play with when they were blown up and full of blood.

In any case, Scotland caught us on the hop that day in a big way. Two tries by Stuart Hogg in the first quarter had them 14-0 up. We started slowly, and talking to the coaches afterwards, they could feel we weren't quite on it in the warm-up. They're not going to say that, though, because they don't want to make us panic. Besides, it's up to the players to say to ourselves: 'Let's start getting wound up now. We are not where we need to be.'

Keith Earls scored a try, but then they caught us out with a trick play at a line-out as we had done to them a few years before. We were 21-8 down at half-time but came back to lead in the second half. We should have closed the game out, but maybe it had taken too much effort to get ahead.

It was bad luck for Conor O'Shea and Italy that we took out our anger on them a week later in Rome. We scored nine tries, with C. J. Stander and Craig Gilroy each getting hat-tricks.

We realized that we had let ourselves down a little bit in Murrayfield and that we had to win our remaining four games to be in control of our own destiny. That meant we couldn't lose to France in our own backyard. We just had to muscle up and go and get them. This wasn't Italy. We were going in against the big boys again.

Camille Lopez kicked a couple of early penalties, but we wore them down. Johnny was back from his calf strain and himself and Conor Murray were on top of their game. Mur scored the only try. Nothing memorable about it. Mur's tries are never spectacular, but they're always handy ones.

Mur had become a weapon for us. Like Mike Phillips, he is a big man, but Conor, he has more flair and skill and is a more polished scrum-half in my opinion. He's had a few injuries and a bit of flak in the last few years, but when he's on form he's very hard to handle.

However, Mur was injured and forced off on a frustrating

night in Cardiff when Wales beat us convincingly enough. Playing there on a Friday night under the roof definitely added to their performance. They were kind of a bogey team for a period. They were one of the teams I hated playing against, and, of course, they want you to hate them.

George North had a couple of good finishes, whereas we left points behind, like when Robbie Henshaw joined a maul in front of the ball and Wayne Barnes ruled out a try by Rory Best. That was a correct call by Barnes. He also binned Johnny for not rolling away. To be fair, Johnny wouldn't know how to roll away!

That put us out of the title, but a week later England came to the Aviva Stadium looking for the Grand Slam. They'd sealed the title a week before by thrashing Scotland 61-21. The Lions squad was being picked a month later. That's a pretty good motivational mix for any Irish side.

Heaslip had played his 100th Test match in Cardiff, but he pulled up in the warm-up a week later. Peter came in at blindside, C. J. moved to number 8 and we killed them in every aspect. Pete also played himself into the Lions squad that day, stealing line-outs and winning a few turnovers.

Iain Henderson had a great game and scored the only try. With his athleticism, physicality and strength, he has a lot of strings to his bow as a rugby player. We just need to see it on the big occasions all the time. He's the closest player Ireland have, in my eyes, to Maro Itoje, in being physical, fast and getting you over the gain line. Hendy is also able to move his feet really late at the line and that gets us out of an awful lot of trouble. That's why, when he's on it, Hendy is so hard to handle. But he needs to be on his game all the time because in the last year or two, if he plays well, Ireland usually play well. I don't know if he realizes that.

We didn't know it then, but we'd never see Jamie play again. He was forced to retire a year later. As well as being former teammates for a decade, we are good friends and business partners. Myself and himself, along with Rob and Dave Kearney, bought The Bridge 1859 pub in 2014 and have since bought the Lemon & Duke. The four of us get on very well.

Jamie was the ultimate professional and would do anything for you and for his team. He had his own way of doing things, like everyone. He's his own man, but you could not get a better professional within a squad environment. He always kept himself in the best shape possible and he was a great competitor.

Back with Leinster, we beat Wasps at home in the quarter-final of the Heineken Cup. At one point I overtook Luke McGrath when trying to chase down Christian Wade. Lukey got some slagging about that and I actually couldn't believe that I did it.

I also made a break through the middle, had a look around and there was no one near me. I remember that unfolding in front of me and thinking, surely to God, where's my winger here? To be honest, I was pretty impressed with my own pace.

During the game a stud caught me on the back of my calf. Sometimes those bruises turn into a tear if you train on them. The following week, that's what happened. I missed the rest of the season, including our semi-final defeat in Europe against Clermont in Marseilles.

I was named on the bench in the Pro12 semi-final against the Scarlets, but I had to pull out on the morning of the game. I needed another week, but unfortunately there wasn't another week as we played poorly and lost to the Scarlets in the RDS. It was a huge disappointment because we'd played some great rugby, scored loads of tries and made huge strides. We didn't want to leave our season like that. It wasn't the way we had all envisaged it. But those defeats fuelled us for the following season.

The forty-one-man Lions squad was announced for the tour to Australia at midday on the Wednesday before the European semi-final. It was a day off, so I watched it at home on Sky Sports. You don't receive an email or any kind of advance notification. The players watch it live, like everyone else, which is actually quite exciting.

Even on my own, hearing my name read out as a Lion for a second time was really special. But I also knew it meant that it was time to fulfil that ambitious target I had set with Enda.

20. The peak

When we flew out to New Zealand a week before the first game of the 2017 Lions tour, there were eight back-rowers in the squad, compared to seven in 2013, and Sam Warburton was captain again. But, four years on, my mindset had shifted.

While I had some credit in the bank from 2013, I had been a little quiet on that tour. I decided that I wasn't going to be a foot-soldier again. I wanted to be one of the lads who drove the team on and off the field. I was thirty years old, I had the experience and I wanted to provide more leadership.

Physically, I was in good nick. I hadn't played since that Wasps game on 1 April due to my torn calf, and the first match in New Zealand was on 3 June, but I worked incredibly hard before the tour and looked after myself extremely well. I also benefited from the work I did with Phil Morrow, Paul Stridgeon and the Lions medical staff in the first two weeks in New Zealand. Had I been in the best possible physical shape on the 2013 tour? Probably not. But in 2017? Yes.

Between 2013 and 2017 I had developed a different outlook on nutrition. I learned an awful lot from Daniel Davey, who is the nutritionist for Leinster and for the Dublin senior football team. As a result, in 2017 I was a well-oiled machine. It wasn't anything drastic, more a range of little changes. I cut out some treats. I stopped having a couple of pints after some games. I might go six weeks without any alcohol. I also stopped eating Snickers – and I love a Snickers bar!

You need the odd treat, of course. I love a pizza, and Daniel actually put a pizza into my programme every eleven days.
Whenever I was back in Tullow, on a Sunday evening we'd
often get a Chinese takeaway, be it as a family or whoever
was around. I stopped doing that because if I had played on
a Saturday and I'd allowed myself a pizza or something that
put the calories in after the game, having a takeaway would
have meant backing up something bad with something bad.
By then my motto was: 'If I have something bad, I'll pay for
it the next day.' Myself, Padraig and James always say: 'We
pay for our sins.' So if you have a pint or a takeaway, you get
rid of it the next day. And you don't back up a bad thing with
another bad thing.

My training wasn't much altered. I just wanted to be as
lean and yet as big and strong as I could be. When you know
you are going up against the best in the world, you want to
give yourself every single chance.

I looked at the other seven back-rowers in the Lions squad
and had total respect for all of them, but I knew that at my
peak, fit and healthy and on top of my game, I was the best
of that whole bunch. So my goal was to be in the best place
possible, physically and mentally, and then just implement
what the coaches wanted.

Although my last visit to New Zealand, five years before,
had ended with a 60-0 drubbing, I'd had a good World Cup
there in 2011 and it's a country I like. Many Kiwis are of
farming stock, but whether they are or not they're generally
nice people. And they seem to enjoy the way I play rugby.

We took off from Heathrow on the Monday, arrived on
the Tuesday and went up to Whangarei by bus or car on the
Friday for our first match, against the New Zealand Provincial Barbarians. Watching that scratchy win, and the first

midweek game when the Lions lost to the Blues in Eden Park, I was happy enough to still be training.

On the bus journey to the ground in Whangarei some lads dozed off. They were still jetlagged. It was a tough one to be involved in after all the travel. Sam came off early with an ankle injury and there was speculation he might not be fit for the first Test, but it didn't affect my thinking in the slightest. If he was fit, he was fit, and if he wasn't, he wasn't. But even if he was fit and I was fit, I was going to back myself.

The Blues game drifted away from the boys and after it we said this confirmed that we had to be ready for Test match intensity in every game. We weren't quite at that point yet.

The itinerary, the lack of preparation time and the travelling showed how tough it is to plan and coach a Lions squad and then get selection right. There are so many variables, such as jetlag in the first week, every player is different and they're trying out different combinations, when most of the players have never played together. Realistically, it's about getting to the Test games in the best possible shape without losing too many people through injury, which is the purpose of these tour games. You don't want to lose them, but it's all about the Test series.

We flew down to Christchurch the next day, to play against the Crusaders that Saturday. I hadn't played in over two months, but I had been feeling great all that week. I had done an awful lot of work with Phil and I knew I was ready to rock. Also, if you were picked on this team, you had every incentive to play well against a fully loaded Crusaders side with a good few All Blacks in it. This would be Test match intensity for sure. I was relishing the prospect, and it couldn't have gone much better for us or for me.

We won 12-3, a statement win, and I was flying. I was

sharp. I was using my hands. I was fast. This was the reward for looking after myself so well. Coming back from a two-month lay-off didn't bother me because I knew I had everything done. That gave me confidence to go out and play, and I seriously enjoyed it. Tadhg Furlong, Peter O'Mahony and Conor Murray put down markers that day, too.

We put a big emphasis on our scrum, line-out maul and defence and also on our discipline, and we made sure as a pack that we were on it. Graham Rowntree, or Wig as we call him, is a great man – hilarious as well – and he had our scrum fine-tuned and humming. Steve Borthwick is one of the best forwards coaches I have worked under. He has a good way with people, he's very detailed and he knows exactly what he wants from you. He is softly spoken but, when he wants, he can turn it up too. I really liked his style of coaching. He and Wig were a good combination.

It was on that tour that Sam said two of the best five open-sides he'd ever faced were myself and Tipuric. He also said that back-rowers had to be all-rounders, capable of ticking every box, and had to have at least one exceptional quality. He was right. Even then you needed to have everything as a back-rower, and all the loose forwards on that tour had something special in their own right.

When I look at a young back-row now, I look at his whole game. Can he carry? Can he tackle? Can he poach? Even then you have to add more. I wasn't known as an option in the line-out, yet I could jump. Due to the packs I played in I was rarely used, but it was something I always wanted to do more.

Of those Lions loose forwards, James Haskell had the physicality and he is a smart man. He was plagued with his foot on that tour, but he showed glimpses of his ability to carry ball and to smash people. He was never really a jack-aler, but his clearing at ruck time was his best attribute. In defence I never found him a nuisance really, but he was 120 kilos and if he was coming into a breakdown, he was going to move you. James also knew the game plan inside out. He never made too many mistakes because he had his work done.

Carrying and tackling are the main strengths of Ross Moriarty's game. He loves the physical element of it and that's what you get with Ross. He'll throw his body around for you all day long.

Pete O'Mahony's jackalling and defensive line-out ability are the stand-outs in his game. His athleticism gets him into the air quickly, and when he gets down into that low position over the ball, he's actually quite hard to move. Pete has great hands, too, but the way he's able to operate in a line-out is exceptional.

C. J. Stander will show up and carry and tackle all day for you. I think his defensive game has definitely become stronger over the last few years but carrying and work rate would be his major strengths.

Sam probably evolved his game a little towards the end of his career, in getting onto and carrying more ball. But when he was on top form, even when he didn't get a clean turn-over, he was able to slow the ball down so much, particularly in those Wales games against us. He gave everyone hardship because he dived in so quickly and was on the ball so low. You had to have your eye on him the whole time because if you let him into that position, he was exceptional at slowing or stealing ball. He was also a pretty spectacular chop tackler.

Justin Tipuric is one of my favourite players. Throughout my career, any time I've played against him or with him, he has had the full package and skill set. Tips is not the biggest person in the world, but he hits hard, he's strong over the ball and his skills are by far the best of all the back-rowers that I've played with. He's the complete footballer. He's very quick, so if he gets up a head of steam, you're not going to knock him down easily. He's an all-rounder, and but for his career coinciding with Sam's he would have had a lot more caps.

James, Sam and C. J. started against the Highlanders, with Tips on the bench. It was a really physical, back-and-forth encounter and under the closed roof in Dunedin there was a serious atmosphere that night.

From there we flew up to Rotorua the next day to play the Māori All Blacks on the Saturday. The All Blacks had beaten Samoa 78-0 in Eden Park the night before and this was a dirty enough night in Rotorua. The rain came down heavily in the second half, but there are certain tour games where a statement has to be made. This was one of them. Everybody knew the Māori All Blacks would be fired up. They had some cracking players throughout their side.

Like the Crusaders game, we caused them a lot of grief at the set-piece and were dominant around the breakdown. We just got stuck into them and that set a template for how to beat these New Zealand sides. We had to win the forward battle and we had to be physical to compete with these boys.

I had another good game and I managed to get my hands on plenty of ball. There was a little niggle in it, too, and I was treating it as a bit of a war that night because they had players with a few chips on their shoulders and points to prove.

We turned the screw early in the second half as the rain

came down. We went to the corner and played to our pack. Our scrum stayed at them until we got a penalty try and then Maro Itoje scored.

Maro is an absolute pain in the rear to play against, and I mean that in the best way possible. He's physical. He's loud. He's annoying. He's athletic. He's one of those players you definitely want on your side and not on the opposition.

After that we moved on to Hamilton, and on the Tuesday before the first Test we beat the Chiefs 34-6. That was a more convincing win against another dangerous side, although they were missing all of their All Blacks players. The boys really wanted to send a marker to Warren Gatland and the coaches that night.

Not being involved gives you an inkling that you might be playing in the Test, but you never really know with Gatty. He could do anything. But I was backing myself to start at that stage because I had played two really good games. Where I was going to start was the next question, because Pete had played two good games as well and Toby Faletau was flying. I thought he might play me at number 6, with Sam at 7. Even the possibility of playing at 8 had crossed my mind.

In our Auckland hotel the next day, Gatty announced the team for the first Test. Pete was named as captain at 6, I was at 7, Toby at 8, and Sam on the bench. It's a lovely moment when your name is announced by the head coach for a Test game of that magnitude.

And what an honour for Pete, captaining the Lions in the first Test in New Zealand. He deserved it, the way he had gone about things and how he was playing at the time. I could only be delighted for him.

Tadhg Furlong was nailed on at tighthead. I don't think the Kiwis realized how good he was until that first Test – not only how physical he is for a tighthead, but how mobile and skilful he is too.

Me and Tadhg had a similar pathway, from farming stock through the junior clubs and Youths ranks. Tadhg's place is only forty minutes from my house in Tullow. I met him a few times as a young lad when he was coming through the Irish Youths in New Ross RFC. He's always been a jolly fella with a bit of character to him, and he couldn't be any other way given how he was brought up by his mam and dad. New Ross is a great little club and I've lots of friends down there, the Maloneys being among them, as I lived with Kieran 'Mush' Maloney in our academy days.

No big surprise that Mur was picked at 9. He'd really taken his game to the next level and had become the best in the world. He had it all, and in 2017 he was flying.

Gatty went with Owen Farrell at 10, Ben Te'o at 12 and Foxy – Jonathan Davies – at 13, with Johnny on the bench. I'd say Gatty wanted to go with a real physical backline, but Johnny prepared the rest of us that week as well as if he was starting.

What we'd prepped for during the week with Andy Farrell was to have really good line speed, and if they went deeper we would just keep going after them. But we had prepped for them to play off 10 a lot, whereas in the first few minutes they just kept coming at us off 9. They were targeting our second or third defender from the ruck and kept punching holes. We couldn't come off the line because they were moving onto the ball on a real short pass from 9 to the first receiver. It was just wave after wave in that first fifteen minutes and we were losing the collisions because we weren't able to get off the line. Good tactics by them, I have to say, and they caught us on the hop. We scrambled well and managed it well enough at times, but it definitely wasn't something we'd thought of during the week.

Then, after they'd narrowed us up, they went wide to Codie Taylor to score in the corner. Beauden Barrett kicked well in the first Test and we were 13-3 down with five minutes left in the first half when, as Stuart Barnes described it, I finished 'one of the great Lions Test tries'. It was an incredible moment, I suppose. It can still pop up anywhere nowadays. It's one of those tries I look at and think that, thankfully, I did what every loose forward should do when there's an attack on in broken field – put my head down and chased after those backs.

Liam Williams' mindset is always to have a crack. That's the way he lives his life. So when Anthony Watson gathered Aaron Cruden's kick on the touchline and passed infield to Liam, I knew anything could happen next. Once he stepped Kieran Read, I ran back and arced around onto his inside shoulder. Then he took off past Cruden and I had to get the head down.

Ben Te'o's block on Sonny Bill when subtly turning his back into his path was a significant factor in that counter-attack, as was the fact that Foxy was in support. Elliot Daly had the wheels to get outside Israel Dagg and give it back to Foxy. I suppose I had the easy job of diving over the line, but we'd all gone a long way to get there.

I appreciate it a lot more now. At the time I was like, right, we're back in the game, let's go. That's one of the reasons you don't see me celebrating. The other thing was me thinking, fuck me, I'm absolutely knackered here after running 100 metres! Let me get some air into my lungs quickly and give me some water.

We lost 30-15, but we had chances in that game and that

was the real positive. We missed out simply because we forced a pass or weren't patient enough. On the Monday, the coaches and the players all took confidence from the review. We had broken down the All Blacks a few times. It was about finishing when we got in behind them. We had to make sure that we attacked in waves, that everyone was in motion and that we were playing on top of them.

The last midweek game was a draw against the Hurricanes in Wellington. Iain Henderson was the best player on the pitch until he was yellow-carded, which probably cost us a win.

Hendy was on fire that night. It was one of the standout individual performances, bar the yellow card, of the tour. He was manhandling people, and the Hurricanes were a very tough side. Hendy was unlucky to be picked in that opening game against the Barbarians. He had played well in the next two midweek games and I'd say he was pissed off. He wanted to prove a point. He wanted to have a real crack at getting into the Test 23, so he had a lot to play for. That yellow card didn't help him, but sitting in the stand that night I thought, this is the real Hendy. This is how good he can be. This is the freak of a player that we know he is. He was awesome that night.

Rory Best did a great job as the midweek captain and I know he didn't get the win that night, but it was a nicer way for him to sign off than he had four years earlier.

The next morning the team was announced, with Sam recalled at 6, me at 7, Toby at 8, and C. J. on the bench. That meant Pete went from being captain of the Test side to being left out of the 23. It's crazy how you can go from an extreme high to a low, or vice versa, from one week to the next in this game. I felt sorry for Pete and, because he's my teammate, I asked myself if there was anything I could do for him. But there's nothing you can do. To Pete's credit, he trained well for the rest of the tour, but I don't know how I'd react to something like that, because he did do his job in the first Test.

Sam had done well when he came on and the coaches definitely wanted us to be a little more physical in the second Test given how the All Blacks had caught us on the hop in that first fifteen to twenty minutes. That's why Maro Itoje was promoted from the bench as well. Johnny was back at 10 and when he's in your team, he's all-out attack, all the more so with Owen Farrell beside him. And that's what we said all week: 'We're going to go after these boys and we're going to keep playing.' And there's certainly no better *buachaill* to lead the charge for you. It was great to have Johnny back in the starting side and to have two playmakers on the field.

Myself, Mur and Johnny hadn't played in Wellington since the 2011 World Cup quarter-final against Wales, and I don't think it's a great stadium to play in. The fans are a mile away and the pitch is very exposed when it's wet and windy. But I liked it more after that second Test.

The big talking point, and turning point, was Sonny Bill being sent off. But rightly so. It was a red card all day long and that's rugby. You can't go in with your eyes closed and shoulder-charge someone in the head.

When he went off, and especially when they then took off Jerome Kaino, we knew they were going to keep as many players in their defensive line as possible, and compete less at the breakdown. We also said among ourselves that they were definitely going to come off the line a lot harder. We had to make sure that our ruck was good and that we stuck to our plan. If we did that, we'd break them eventually.

Ultimately, what we had said we'd do at half-time in the first Test we actually did in the second Test. When we got in behind them we kept going after them, kept everybody in motion, and that's where our two tries came from, although our discipline in that second Test was dreadful. I could have killed Mako Vunipola for giving away a few stupid penalties. He caught Beauden Barrett late and then, after I made a half-break and was tackled, he took out Barrett on the ground to get a yellow card. And then we were 18-9 down. That's the type of stuff that can lose you a Test match.

Talking with Mako afterwards, I said to him: 'I could have fucking killed you.'

He just said: 'I know, mate.'

He half tried to justify some of the things that happened, but when you look back on it, the penalties were penalties and the yellow card was a yellow card. It's like me throwing a punch at someone. I deserved to get cited and that's that.

Still, we scored our first try with fourteen men. It was an unbelievable finish by Toby, but before that Anthony Watson carried up the touchline and I barely held on at the breakdown. I kind of nested and took a few hits until Courtney Lawes joined the ruck, but we just barely held on to that ball. Those are the fine margins. If Murray doesn't pick up that ball and pass it when he does and the All Blacks turn it over, we don't score that try. But it was such a well-worked score in the end and the finish was just sublime. You wouldn't want anybody else on the left wing taking the final pass from Liam Williams than Toby. He is so athletic and he bounced Israel Dagg.

Mur also took his try very well to help bring us level after Jamie George made a good carry off a short ball by Johnny.

The key to that try was that Johnny does those O'Driscoll-esque passes in training the whole time. Johnny constantly tells you to always be ready, and in training he was catching people out with that pass all the time.

'Keep your eye on me. I'll hit you with it, if the hole is there,' he'd say, or shout, at teammates in training. That's why that play worked, because Johnny had been barking at players to always be ready for it. 'When I show out the back door, always be ready for the front door.' Owen Farrell would be the same in driving those moves.

Everyone says what a great line Jamie George ran. Yes, it was a good line, but what made it was that Faz was at the back of Jamie and because Johnny carried it to the line and saw the space. It was such a subtle pass as well. Then we were in behind and we did exactly what we said we'd do. We were all in motion. Conor picked up, saw space and another great finish. Thankfully, Faz had his kicking boots on and landed both the conversion to level the match and the penalty to win it.

Charlie Faumuina was a little unlucky to concede the final penalty because it was the pass that made Kyle Sinckler jump for the ball when Charlie tackled him in the air. Charlie is actually good friends with Keiaho Bloomfield, who's been with Tullow Rugby Club for the last ten or twelve years. Charlie subsequently joined Toulouse and I've sat down and had a beer with him a few times after games. He is such a nice lad.

Sinckler also threw a bit of a hissy fit directly after the tackle and there were a few of us around him. I said: 'Sinckler, will you ever calm the fuck down!' He was so wound up and he's such an emotional guy at times.

In the final play we had a good kick chase and I couldn't

believe it when Beauden Barrett kicked the ball to me. I knew then we had it won, but, looking back on it, I wish I'd drop-kicked the ball over the bar.

It was my first time beating the All Blacks in seven attempts, including a few near misses and missing out on Chicago. I was as happy as Larry afterwards. We'd ended their match-winning streak at home of forty-seven matches going back eight years, although it can't have felt like a home match for them. The Lions fans were astonishing, and that definitely was a factor.

It was a class night for everyone. Those are the days you work so hard for, the days that you love. I wanted to beat those All Blacks lads so badly because they were, and usually are, the best of the best. They were the back-to-back world champions. I can only imagine what it was like for the supporters.

We had a few drinks that night in the hotel in Wellington, but the following morning word came through that I had been cited for an alleged forearm into Waisake Naholo's head. I was chasing Johnny's restart after we'd gone 18-9 ahead. Naholo carried back, someone had him half held up and I tried to dislodge the ball while putting him on the ground. It was so innocuous. They had made something out of nothing. I look at things in rugby now and wonder, do citing commissioners actually think that a player is trying to hit another player with a forearm into the head?

So while the rest of the squad flew on to Queenstown, I had to wait in Wellington with Gatty, our Director of Operations Ger Carmody, the Lions' legal officer Max Duthie, our manager John Spencer, and our press officer Dave Barton, for the disciplinary hearing on Sunday evening at 8pm. I knew there was going to be a rollover session in Queenstown and that it was going to be good fun. I missed that, but it was no harm really because my body was sore after the second Test. It made for a long day, though.

Sonny Bill's hearing was on before mine and word reached us that it was running late. He ended up being suspended for four weeks.

We got a couple of taxis to the New Zealand Rugby Union offices. The citing commissioner, Scott Nowland of Australia, had said the incident merited a red card. The panel was made up of Adam Casselden, SC (Chair), David Croft and John Langford, both of whom were former Australian rugby players. The hearing lasted over three hours. When it was my turn to speak, I explained that I was going for the ball, that my fist wasn't closed, it wasn't a stiff arm and that the contact with Waisake's head was accidental.

We were asked to leave the room while they deliberated. Those thirty minutes seemed to take an age before we were called back in. We were told that they had dismissed the citing complaint. Although I had felt sure that I had done nothing wrong, I was very relieved.

We flew to Queenstown via Auckland the next morning and got to the Hilton Hotel by Lake Wakatipu at lunchtime. Some of the lads were still drinking. I thought, what the fuck is going on here? It was Monday. We were playing a once-in-a-lifetime third Test decider against the All Blacks on Saturday. It could go down in history as one of the Lions' greatest series wins. As much as I love the craic, I thought that was a bit much. It rattled me a little.

We also had the Tuesday off before we trained on the Wednesday and I felt we were playing catch-up for the rest of the week. We trained too long on Wednesday because we had plenty to get through and, looking back now, I wonder should we have trained for half an hour on the Tuesday.

That would have made lads refocus sooner, got some of the beer out of our systems and not left us with so much to cover on the Wednesday. But then, I suppose, we were coming to the end of a hard tour after a long season and had just played two incredibly hard Test games, so it's difficult to know.

Before the session, Gatty named an unchanged team, whereas the All Blacks freshened up their side by bringing in Ngani Laumape, who had replaced Sonny Bill in the second Test, Jordie Barrett and Julian Savea.

I only played the first half.

I was on my way into a breakdown for a poach when Jerome Kaino caught me early, and a little bit from the side, on my left shoulder. I was having a small issue with my left shoulder at the time. (It turned out that there was a little bit of bone floating around in there.) My whole arm just went numb straight away. I didn't dislocate it or anything, but I had no power whatsoever. For the next couple of minutes, just before half-time, I could not hit people with my left side at all and I couldn't hold on to anyone with my left arm either.

At half-time, I couldn't stop the physio pulling my arm down. The power just wasn't there. There's no point in being a hero when you are not at full fitness and I felt that I would have let the team down if I had played on. I just wasn't going to be good enough, so I was taken off and watched the second half from the stands. We had been going pretty well and were getting into them, so it was frustrating for me to end the tour that way.

It was a bizarre ending to the series and the tour when, with scores level, Romain Poite originally awarded them a penalty that would have given them a chance to win the match and then consulted with the TMO before changing his mind.

All those weeks of hard work, and all for a drawn series.

At the full-time whistle I didn't know how to feel. Relief that we hadn't lost gave way to a kind of nothingness. It was an anti-climax. Initially no one celebrated. Everyone was a little mystified. No one knew what to make of a draw. Nobody had even considered that possibility until Poite blew the final whistle.

On the sidelines we shook hands and went onto the pitch. Then, I suppose, the All Blacks' players and ourselves embraced it for what it was, but even celebrating together was surreal.

The Lions' fans seemed happier and stayed on longer than the All Blacks' supporters. We may have drawn on the pitch, but I thought they had won off it. To see that sea of red whenever we went out to play on that tour was incredibly cool. I looked around Eden Park and let those moments sink in. The Lions fans were phenomenal. They had out-sung, out-roared and out-everythinged the All Blacks' fans, and were so good in the stadiums and away from the matches as well. Everyone I met was respectful and having a ball, too. I suppose, no less than us, they were on a buzz. As much as we get a kick from playing with new teammates from different countries, they get exactly the same from pitching in together as a diverse set of fans. Like the players, too, rather than hating you, English, Welsh and Scottish people suddenly become big supporters, and not just because they have spent so much money to be there. I feel you have to give them time in recognition of that. I have always tried to give supporters time.

*

A couple of months after the tour, I was in front of the media in Tullow RFC – Bank of Ireland was renewing its sponsorship of Leinster – and I raised some issues about our preparation for each of the Tests.

I said: 'I think we should have won 3-0 with the players we had, we should have won the series. And, looking back, and I could be completely wrong, but if we had a little more structure during the weeks, and more of an attack game plan, as such, driven way earlier in the tour, I think we could win 3-0. If I was being critical of any coach, it would be the fact that I think Rob [Howley] struggled with the group in terms of his attributes of trying to get stuff across whereas Johnny and Owen drove everything the second week, for instance, in our attack and had a better plan in place. So I don't know if it was people were not buying into what he was about or whatever else. That's the hard thing about a Lions tour as well: getting everyone to listen to a coach that was probably set in his ways.'

I didn't mean for it to come out sounding like Gats and Howley were at fault. But what I did feel at the time was that we probably did too much the first week. As a leadership group we said that and it was adjusted for the second week. Before the second Test we had a much better week and we felt a lot sharper during the match. Then, in the third week, we were catching up again. Maybe it's me being an idiot, saying that, because these are decisions that the S&C staff and the coaches think about at length; but that's the way it seemed to me.

I wasn't saying that Rob Howley was a bad coach or that it was all his fault. I was saying that Owen and Johnny had really grabbed a hold of that whole backline and driven it forward, and that's a good thing. The players need to be providing ideas. It was never my intention to make anyone out to be a bad coach or that anyone was to blame. I just said that some things should have been a little different and that you have to try to tick the boxes as best you can. Maybe, on a Lions tour, that's the best you can do, but I felt that it was an opportunity lost for so many individuals because you never get back time, and potentially we could have won a Lions tour in New Zealand.

Gatty and Rob probably feel the same way. I wasn't trying to be nasty. I'd have huge respect for Gatty because his track record speaks for itself. Coming up against Wales so often, I know how tough they were to beat, so of course I'd have respect for both him and Rob, as I would for all the Lions coaches.

I also think Gatty is a perfect head coach for the Lions. He's experienced, he's direct and he knows what he wants. He goes about his business without interacting too much with players, but he's floating around in the background having conversations with coaches and players. And Gats is a very smart coach and a smart man, you have to hand it to him. He treats his players like adults, as people first and as players second, and there was a brilliant atmosphere among the squad on both tours I joined.

There wasn't time for too many down days, but on one of them we were split up into groups and given tasks to do. Each group had to make their own video of their task as well. Myself and James Haskell were on the same team and we got two policemen to arrest me with my top off. It's on the DVD of that Lions tour.

We saw a couple of cops in a shop, pulled in behind their car and asked them would they follow us down the road and pretend to arrest me. They were two good lads. One of them played rugby for Tonga. So they followed us down the road. I was topless and they duly handcuffed me and threw me in the cop car, but then I broke away from them, jumped in the jeep and we took off.

One of the other tasks was to buy a New Zealand pie. One of the media boys, Luke Broadley, was driving a Land Rover on a country road. I leaned out of the back window as Haskell held on to my legs. The camera angle from the passenger seat shows my hands and arms fully extended like Superman, and it looks like I'm outside the car and flying up alongside Luke in the driver's seat. We added the *Superman* soundtrack onto the video.

I tapped on Luke's window and he lowered it down.

Then you hear someone saying: 'Hello, mate. What are you doing?'

'I'm just going for a pie,' I said, before slipping back into my seat and out of view.

'All right. See ya . . . that was so weird.'

It genuinely looked like I was flying.

After the third Test we had a couple of great days. We spent most of the time in the hotel just drinking together because it was so difficult for fifty of us to go out together to a pub. On the Sunday night, though, we did get out to a rooftop terrace bar, all the staff and players, which was really good fun.

Being a player on a Lions tour is everything you could dream of, and more. The way we come together as a squad from four different countries, the memories it provides and the role the fans play all make the whole experience unique. A Lions tour is mental, really, which is perhaps why I like them.

There's no other sports tour or sporting event in the world

remotely like it apart from, maybe, the Ryder Cup. Rugby is so lucky to have the Lions. Recently, on Sky Sports, I watched some of the 1997 DVD and hearing Jim Telfer or Ian McGeechan talking still gives me tingles up my spine and into my neck. I've no doubt that DVD revived the concept of the Lions both for supporters and players. Anyone who is serious about their rugby wants to be a British & Irish Lion at some point.

I haven't given up hope of completing the cycle. If I can get a run of games with London Irish and play at the level I believe I'm still capable of, who knows? You need experience going into that kind of environment in South Africa, and whether as a Test player or as a midweek player, I'd love to be a part of it.

21. The damn shoulder

The 2017 tour to New Zealand was a phenomenal experience. As a player on a Lions tour, you go absolutely full tilt for six weeks, on and off the pitch. I love it to bits, but it does take a lot out of you. I've seen this with other players as well. There is usually a price to be paid.

Myself, Johnny Sexton, Tadhg Furlong and Jack McGrath all returned for Leinster's fifth game of the 2017/18 season, a win over Edinburgh at the RDS. But both my calf and my shoulder were giving me bother and I missed the win over Munster at the Aviva and our opening European wins over Montpellier and Glasgow.

I came back again for the Ulster game in the Kingspan as captain. I played the full eighty minutes and was Man of the Match. I was flying that day. I made a load of carries, a few line-breaks and I did a show-and-go to beat Louis Ludik and then, with a two-on-one, I put Lukey McGrath over for a try. The pain in my shoulder had settled with a few weeks' rest and I had a bit of strength back. It felt good that night.

That set me up for the November series. Ireland's first game was against South Africa. It was my fiftieth cap, so I led the team out for a second time and we won 38-3. It was a class day. One of those purely enjoyable games. We were growing a little more. That South African side actually had plenty of good players, as they would show at the 2019 World Cup, but we just clicked and executed everything as we'd prepared to do. I had loads of involvements, at the breakdown, in carries and tackles, and I felt on top of the world. It was one of my favourite days in an Ireland jersey.

We wore a pretty cool slate-grey kit that day. They were different and went down a treat with the lads, although we didn't see them again. I still have that one at home. I'm not sure how many jerseys I have kept. I get asked for jerseys every single week. I've kept most of the good ones. I gave my first Irish jersey, my first Heineken Cup jersey, a Lions Test jersey and Richie McCaw's jersey to the rugby club.

Bundee Aki made his debut that day and put down an early marker, with Johnny's help, when he made a big hit on their prop, Coenie Oosthuizen, in the first play of the game. It was a good statement by Bundee to get his Ireland career up and running.

I have no problem with C. J. Stander, Bundee or anyone else playing for Ireland through the residency ruling. It's the same rule the world over, and if Joe Schmidt, or whoever is head coach, is picking them, then these players are progressing the team in their positions at the time. They probably do block other lads coming through. For example, if it wasn't for C. J., how many more games might Jack O'Donoghue have played for Munster and even Ireland? How good would he be? But that's just the nature of it. C. J. works incredibly hard, he knows his detail and keeps showing up for us. The foreign-born lads do exactly the same work as we do and they are just as much a part of Irish rugby as we are. They move over here for another life, some of them start families over here, and good luck to them. They earn what they get.

That day marked the arrival of a new wave. As well as Bundee's debut, Jacob Stockdale and James Ryan played their first home Test, having made their debuts on the summer tour to the USA and Japan. Every team is re-energized by new, young players coming through, and that day confirmed what all of us already knew – that James and Jacob were going to be the future of this Irish team.

I don't think Jacob is the finished article yet by a long shot, but if he gets his defensive stuff sorted, he could be one of the best wingers Ireland has ever produced. He has a bit to do, but if he can get that right, he'll be phenomenal.

As well as definitely being a future captain of Ireland, James could be a future Lions captain as well. At some point Ireland should give James the captaincy and let him develop in the role before the next World Cup. He does what he says he's going to do. He is a good lad, he has a good head on his shoulders, he minds himself well, he's a very good professional, he's fit and he's very smart. There are a lot of strings to his bow and that's what I like about him. He's also hardy. He's not going to sit back and get bullied too often. At times we might be missing that with Ireland. I think we can let teams bully us a little, but James is one of those lads who is not going to get bullied too often.

Two weeks later, Jacob scored a couple of tries as we beat Argentina 28-19. That win was a little bit more comfy than the scoreline suggested. We gave them some soft tries, which wasn't ideal, but we were really starting to build something under Joe. We could sense it. Unfortunately, and I wasn't to know it then, I'd only win another five caps for Ireland.

From the start of the 2017/18 season I was rehabbing my shoulder regularly. It was fine for the November Tests, but after those games my hip was killing me too. By that stage I was limping badly. I went to Leo before the December Heineken Cup back-to-back games against Exeter and I said to him: 'Look, I'll give you the next two weeks against Exeter, whatever I have.'

We had them away first and we went to Sandy Park and won 18-8. I lasted the full eighty and I actually felt fine. I played some of my best rugby in a long time in that game. But two days afterwards I was crippled with pain from my right hip and had a limp again.

I didn't train at all in the week of the return game at the Aviva Stadium. I did absolutely nothing, got an injection into the arse and played that game. I felt okay, but as the game wore on my hip became more agitated. I couldn't go top speed, but I was still strong. I was trucking well in that one too until just after the fifty-minute mark, but then I had to go off.

That put me out of the start of Ireland's Six Nations campaign.

I watched our first game, in Paris, from my couch at home in Tullow on my own. My brother William was living there too, but he knew better and went to watch it in the pub. Everyone leaves me alone when there is a match on. I hate watching games. I'd rather listen to it on the radio or keep tabs on it online, really.

Before Johnny lined up his drop goal I was cursing at the TV because I didn't like that zigzag pattern that we had got into. Then when Mur turned and passed to Johnny I thought he'd gone too early. But when I saw Johnny strike the ball, I thought he'd made it. His connection was so good. Only he could kick one from that far out, in that situation, and I don't think he could strike another one like that again.

When William came back from the pub, I said to him: 'The boys will win the Grand Slam, after that game.' They had the squad to do it, and they had belief from that point on. Also, all the other teams would have watched that and said: 'Jesus, how are we going to beat these fuckers?' In truth,

France had thrown the kitchen sink at us that day and I was disappointed in our performance. We should never have been in that position. Then again, we weren't going to play that badly again. No way. Of course, my frustration also came from not being there. Those are the games you train so hard for, the exceptional ones.

I had my hip cleaned out and rehabbed it intensely. As the boys went on to beat Italy, Wales and Scotland, I knew I had one chance to be a small part of that Grand Slam. Eight nights before Ireland played England at Twickenham, I attempted to prove my fitness away to the Scarlets in the Pro14. I thought if I could come through that game, I would be in the match-day squad at least in Twickenham, which would have been something.

I wasn't at all worried about my shoulder. The only thing I hadn't done going into that Scarlets game was actually plough into someone in training. I hadn't done much training with the team, but it was my last chance to get some minutes before Twickenham.

It was only the second breakdown I'd hit when my shoulder went again. It just got caught in the wrong position, very like the incident with the Lions in the third Test. I knew straight away. I had no power again. The first thing that came into my head was, next week is gone. The only thing I could do was hold my jersey. I didn't even make it to the half-hour mark. There was no point.

So I ended up watching all of the Six Nations games at home. The Twickenham one was the hardest to watch because I knew that if I'd played a good forty or fifty minutes against the Scarlets, I'd have had a chance of being brought back to camp and being involved. But it was also class. The boys started so fast and the way they had been playing since

Paris, I never thought for a second that they were going to be beaten.

When the full-time whistle went and Ireland had won a Grand Slam, I wished I was there. I should have been there, but I wasn't. I was delighted for the lads, especially when I looked at Johnny and at Devin Toner, for instance, someone who doesn't get much credit. It was great for the squad, Rory Best, the whole lot. That's what they live for. They live to win Grand Slams. I live to win them as well, but it just hasn't happened for me.

For a month after the Scarlets game I rehabbed my shoulder. Two weeks after the lads dismantled Saracens at the Aviva in the Heineken Cup quarter-final, I played against Treviso at the RDS. I think it was about three minutes into the game. There was a breakdown right in front of the subs bench. One of their players went in for a poach and I went in to melt him. I hit him with my left shoulder and . . . *ding*. It was gone straight away again. I stayed on until half-time but I wasn't hitting anyone or anything. There are clips of me trying to hit mauls with one arm. It looks ridiculous. I just had no power again. So that was the decision made for me.

No regrets, though. I knew those Exeter games were two of the most important games of the season for us. They were going to be our toughest pool games, and the back-to-backs usually define our season. If I could play them and help get us over the line, especially the first one away, I knew it would be significant.

I thought if I got my hip under control, I would be fine for the rest of the season. At that point there was no question about my shoulder. I thought it was strong because I had done all the rehab, but then we discovered there was a piece of bone floating around inside the shoulder. That had to be fixed, so while I was getting that done, I had my hip scoped as well. But the shoulder operation was scheduled first, with Hannan Mullett again in Santry, because it was causing me the most pain.

I had a complete clean-out of the shoulder joint in April 2018. It gave me some relief. They found eleven or twelve osteophytes, which are tiny pieces of bone that chaw at the cartilage and upset the joint.

After all the ops, my shoulder looks like one of those old leather footballs with the lacing on the outside.

Shortly after the shoulder work, I had another hip operation. They used an instrument like a cheese grater that resurfaces everything in the joint.

Six weeks after that I had an operation to have stem cells inserted into my hip. That one is quite sore. They go into either side of your stomach, take out a little bit of fat, spin it and inject it into your hip. That was done by Professor Griffin at BMI Coventry.

All the operations I'd had made for a busy summer: I hardly stopped rehabbing. I did two weeks of rehab, had a week off, back for another week of rehab, had four days off, back for two weeks of rehab, then had seven days off. I don't really take holidays if I have injuries, but I did that summer because I needed a break mentally as well.

Three days after the operation in Coventry I went to visit my brother Stephen, his wife, Lucy, and their three kids in Gibraltar. My girlfriend, Sarah Rowe, was with me for the first four days and then Josh van der Flier came over and the two of us trained there together. Josh wanted a quiet holiday and I wasn't going away on a lads' holiday or anything. I wanted to mind myself. So we just did some rehab together as he was rehabbing his ACL. It's easy-peasy to get on with Josh.

I came home from there, did another week of rehab, chilled out in Corfu for a week with Sarah, then did two weeks of rehab, then went to Jack McGrath's wedding for three days in Portugal and then spent three days in Lagos with Daniel Davey and Gary Kenny.

The first few months are the worst mentally, simply because you know it's going to take so bloody long.

Along the way, Leinster's quarter-final performance against Saracens was possibly the best of the season. I watched that from home, but I was in the stands in my suit for the two semi-finals and both finals. We were good in attack when we beat the Scarlets in the Heineken Cup semi-final at the Aviva, but there was so much more in us – we could have set down a marker for the final.

I was in Bilbao when they beat Racing in the final, in the RDS when they beat Munster in the Pro14 semi-final and in the Aviva when they beat the Scarlets again in the final. I couldn't run, so I couldn't even be a water boy for those games. I'm a far better player than I am a spectator. Racing were a good team but I just know that if I'd been playing, we would have performed so much better. Physically we weren't standing toe-to-toe with them. They were making a show of us at times. Nine times out of ten the team that wins collisions wins the game of rugby, but not that day.

The boys stuck at it, Johnny kept probing and probing, Robbie Henshaw and Garry Ringrose made some inroads and Isa Nacewa took over the kicking to land two late penalties. The game hinged on Teddy Thomas not playing the percentages when going down the blindside and being tackled into touch by Jack Conan and Dan Leavy. Even then they had a drop goal to take the game into extra time but missed it.

We had perhaps been in those big, tight games more often than Racing and our experience came through at the end of the game. But sitting in the stands and watching those games is dreadful, especially the ones that are tight, when I know I could make a difference.

When the full-time whistle went and Leinster were European Champions again, I was delighted, but it was so different. Walking around the pitch with the rest of the lads, I thought: I'm not part of this really. Yeah, I played my part in those back-to-back wins over Exeter, but I still didn't feel that sense of achievement. Something was missing.

It's just not the same when you haven't added much value the whole way through, like I had in 2011 and 2012. Although I hadn't missed any meetings and I'd chipped in with my own little bits when I'd needed to, it's not the same as being out on the field. It's as simple as that.

Because we hadn't gone to the well against Racing, I felt there was no way we could lose the next week against Munster. We hadn't been physically punished. The players might say differently, but I always felt confident that the lads would beat Munster and the Scarlets in the Pro14 final a week later.

In the Pro14 final, Johnny McNicholl ran amok. That was down to our system as well. We weren't doing the right things. But I never felt at any point that we were going to lose the game.

I went around the pitch with the boys afterwards, but it felt the same as Bilbao. Most of the fifty-plus lads that we'd used during the campaign had played a bigger part than me. Between the double and the Grand Slam, Leinster and Ireland had won everything that they could have won that season. Had I missed out on a season like that earlier in my career, I probably would have thought it was a disaster, but I just had to accept that it was what it was. I was thirty-one and I'd learned that there are some things that are outside of my control.

That night away to the Scarlets was a low point, and the torn hamstring in Paris in 2014 had me particularly worried because of the way I play. I kept wondering, will it heal properly? Will it stitch right? But I suppose as you get older, you suffer bigger injuries and you think to yourself, how many more can I take?

Over the years I've suffered a broken leg, injured both ankles and had two operations on each of them. I've had a few clean-outs on my knees, just scopes, nothing major. I've had four hip operations, three on my shoulders, both thumbs done twice, a broken arm and a few broken fingers. But other than that, grand!

I don't remember the last time I played pain-free. But you get runs and you don't think about it. I was in great shape on the Lions tour in 2017. I felt as strong as an ox and as fit as a fiddle until I got that slap in that third Test. I've missed out on big things, but that's just the way it is. That's the hand I've been dealt. You get on with it and try to get better, so that you can do it all again next season, until you retire. That's sport.

22. The hardest decision

The plan was for me to make my comeback against Connacht at the end of September 2018 in the Sportsground, but a week beforehand Leo Cullen had second thoughts.

'Look, I don't know if I'm going to go with you against Connacht.'

I said to him: 'But that was always the plan, if not against Edinburgh then Connacht a week later.'

'Yeah, but I don't want to set you up to fail,' he said.

'Well, I'd rather fucking fail in the Sportsground than fail in the Aviva in front of 50,000 people.' And I added: 'Don't worry about someone going down early or anything. I have that sorted.'

Maybe that swayed him. He put me on the bench against Connacht. I actually felt in better shape than I had been on the Lions tour. I figured that if I could play twenty or thirty minutes against Connacht, and an hour or so against Munster, then I should be on fire for our first European games against Wasps and Toulouse. Just in the nick of time for November.

Connacht had beaten us 47-10 when we'd gone down there in April, in John Muldoon's last game. Muldoon taking that last conversion himself was shown in the team room during the week, but I didn't think it was insulting of him. I'd have done it if it was me. It was his last game. He's given everything to Connacht over the years, so fair play to him – and they won the game. We were more embarrassed by our performance that day and decided to travel to Galway the night before for this one.

Connacht are a very talented attacking team. Our plan was to keep the ball and play on top of them, which is exactly what we did. I was meant to play fifteen to twenty minutes, but I said to one of the S&C staff before the game: 'I bet you someone will go down here after ten minutes.' Sure enough, Rhys Ruddock got a dead leg early on and I played for an hour.

In the dressing-room afterwards, Stuart Lancaster said some nice words about me being in the gym before most of the squad almost every morning for the previous five months. The lads demanded a song, so I sang the first verse of Pat Shortt's 'The Jumbo Breakfast Roll'.

I went to Ballina after the match, as Sarah was there – watching her first-ever game of rugby. She was with her best friends from home, Noreen Moran and Kate Sullivan, and her dad, Alan Rowe, and his friend Gerry O'Donnell. Alan and Gerry are heavily involved with Ballina Rugby Club. Sarah hadn't a clue what was going on, but her dad had ref-ereed for years and talked her through it. None of my family could make it, but my buddies Gary Kenny and Daniel Davey were there and it was nice to have that support.

Sarah and I had been going out since 2017. For about three months she kept popping up on my newsfeed on social media. A cheeky head on her. One day I said to James: 'I'm telling you, she would be serious craic.' I was somewhere in Ranelagh, having a pint of Guinness, and I sent her a mes-sage saying: *Are you out tonight?* My first words to her. Big cheeky bastard.

She responded and we arranged to meet the next day for lunch. She was doing a presentation for her graduation, so she arrived in a suit. I arrived in a pair of grey shorts and a

T-shirt, hair a bit messy and a beard. We met in the Gourmet Food Parlour in Santry for an hour and a half. We had a good chat and a right laugh. That was it. That was the start of it.

Sarah was a serious soccer player, all the way up to winning a senior international cap, before focusing on Gaelic football – and, more recently, Australian rules football. I try to get to as many of Sarah's games with the Mayo Ladies team as possible. My sister Caroline and her husband, Willie, were always very good at attending my games, and I think it means something when you have people you love there to watch you play. I like it when Sarah comes to my games as well, which she does whenever she can. I think it makes the day a little more special.

Being with Sarah has meant I've formed an emotional attachment to the Mayo Ladies team. I've been to plenty of their training sessions. I've chipped in and helped some of the girls with mindset stuff when I could. For the 2019 Championship they picked their own leadership group and they have taken more ownership than before.

I see the effort they put in. Some of them are living in Dublin and are leaving work at 4pm or 5pm to drive cross country for training and then not getting back to Dublin until 1am or so. Top Oil have come in as sponsors and given them fuel cards with a certain amount of petrol per week. But otherwise it all comes out of their own pockets. They don't get any expenses.

Sarah plays full-forward or corner-forward, but she can play anywhere. She is a complete professional. She's quick, she's athletic, she's very smart and she reads the game very well. And she's able to score, given the opportunity. She works incredibly hard at her game. When she's in Dublin, she might do some kicking on her own – take twenty or thirty frees, whatever it may be. She looks after herself very well and is very disciplined.

I wouldn't say I was nervous before that Connacht game, but I was a little apprehensive. I hadn't played an hour's rugby since the previous December. My body was very sore the entire week of the Munster match. I played the first hour of that win, and then I played the last quarter when we thrashed Wasps at the RDS.

Perhaps the Wasps game was too much of a walk in the park. It gave us a false sense of security that Toulouse were happy to bust apart.

I was on before the twenty-minute mark at Toulouse. I did some good things, but I missed a tackle for one of their tries. It was a wake-up call. They were a little fitter than we thought they'd be and better than they'd been in previous games. The away changing-room was not a nice place afterwards. Everyone was very pissed off.

It had been a bit of a slow burner for me with Leinster, but I was excited to be back in the Irish squad for the November Tests. I hadn't been part of one for a year. In the meantime, I was happy to put in another hour's shift away to Treviso on a dirty day. The ball was greasy, as ever they were a big bunch of lads, and we ground it out.

I was one of those who stayed back in Carton House when we beat Italy in Chicago, and then we had Argentina and the All Blacks at the Aviva Stadium. The training was tougher, mainly because it was that bit faster. But there wasn't a bother with my hip and I felt sharper. I even made a few breaks in training for the first time in a long time. I'd taken another kilo off myself and I was running fast again.

I took an anti-inflammatory on the morning of the

Argentina game. Being in the Shelbourne Hotel and walking out to the team bus reminded me how much I'd missed it. It had been a year since I'd played in the win over Argentina.

My sisters, Alex and Caroline, my two nephews and my buddy James Foley were at the game. During the anthems I looked for them in the crowd and thought about family and other people I care about.

Five minutes before half-time, Tomás Lavanini received the ball and ran straight towards me. I couldn't hear anything coming from my inside or my outside, so I kind of half waited for him rather than attacking him. When he came close enough, I went to tackle him. Suddenly, he dropped his head straight into me. I knew immediately that my forearm was broken. A lump shot up like a golf ball and I couldn't move my wrist.

The team doctor, Ciaran Cosgrave, came on and although I knew it was gone straight away, I asked him to leave me on for a minute or two to see if it started working again. I think I managed another thirty seconds before the next stoppage. The nurses X-rayed the forearm in the medical room, but I knew I would be missing another shot at the All Blacks a week later. Even so, when they showed me the X-rays, I broke down. Fuck me, not again.

I waited for the lads to go back out for the second half. I didn't want them to see me. I went into the changing-room, showered, was put into a back slab and went out to watch the rest of the game.

Ciaran said it would be an eight- to twelve-week job, and before the game had finished he had set up an appointment with Hannan Mullett for the following morning.

I know Hannan way too well at this stage, but he's a lovely man and brilliant at his job. He wasn't scheduled for operations that Sunday, but he came in and did me at 7.50am. I remember looking at the clock when they were giving me the good stuff. By 4pm I was home on the couch, feeling rough. It was the first time I'd ever been sick after an operation, and this was my eighteenth or something ridiculous like that.

I watched Ireland beat the All Blacks at home in the pub with my friends James and Padraig, and my brother-in-law, Willie. I didn't want to go – didn't want to be reminded about missing out on another crack at them with Ireland – but it was a great game to watch. That series was always about the All Blacks and the lads played unbelievably well. They exited really well, they controlled the game, and Johnny's kicking took a lot of pressure off the rest of the lads. There were some outstanding performances – Peter O'Mahony, Josh van der Flier and James Ryan, in particular. You couldn't say anyone didn't play well, and the bench made a big difference. It was just a really clinical performance. The All Blacks looked like breaking us down a few times with their unstructured game, but otherwise we were in control. I felt we could have scored another two tries, actually.

Sarah came home from her first stint with Collingwood in Australia for two weeks over Christmas, and that cheered me up. She loves it there. She is very focused, trains hard and was incredibly fit when she came back. So was I. My return target was Leinster's game against Ulster on 5 January 2019. I did three, sometimes four sessions a day. Mondays, Wednesdays and Fridays were the big days, the running days, so I was always in at 7.30am. Charlie Higgins was first in every morning. He's our Head of Athletic Performance, who came to us from the Western Force in 2016. I've been in there at 6.30am doing bike sessions and Charlie would already have all the lights on. I'd say him and Leo are the last ones to leave as well.

I usually do forty-five minutes of rehab with Fearghal Kerin, our rehab physiotherapist, to start off the session. Some mornings it was still dark when he took me out onto the field for sprints and endurance runs. Hugh Hogan, our contact skills coach, would also design match-like conditioning sessions for me – hitting pads, getting up and down off the ground, sprinting, getting into a defensive set, getting off the line, back into a poach, into a barge. That session would be about forty minutes long and I'd get in more hits and more high-speed running metres than in a game. I liked to do those sessions before the team meeting, after which we broke into unit meetings. I did my normal gym session then. When the boys went outside for their full session, I did something else, like a bike session, and after lunch in UCD that was the day done usually.

I often went for a recovery swim in the afternoon, and on Monday and Thursday evenings I went into Griffith College from about 6.15pm to 9.15pm and worked on a couple of modules of my business degree. It was tedious. I didn't want to be there, but it was something I wanted to get done.

It's always a grind when you're rehabbing. No one understands. You do four times as much training as you do when you're fit. But I wanted to win trophies with Leinster and Ireland, so I had to commit to it. And I had one motivation above all else then: to win the World Cup.

At eight weeks the arm was still sore and the surgeon said he could still see a very light crack where the surgery had been performed, enough to be cautious with it. At ten weeks, I was given the green light.

For our final Champions Cup pool game away against

Wasps, I knew Jack Conan was struggling, and as I'd been named on the bench I'd prepped for all three positions. On the morning of the game, Leo came to me before breakfast in the team room at our hotel in Coventry and said: 'Jack is out so you'll start.' I just said: 'Fair enough.'

That week I'd fired myself into a few contacts and I'd done a little bit with the coaches at full belt to make sure everything was fine. I was happy to play for fifty-six minutes in a tough contest. I felt good, carried well and was happy with my contribution.

When we got to Birmingham airport for the flight home, I rang Joe. I wanted to play the following week, as we'd planned, against the Scarlets, to put myself in the frame for the first Six Nations game at home to England. But as I'd played nearly an hour against Wasps, he said I'd be better off coming to Portugal with the rest of the Ireland squad that week. Another flight the next morning to the Algarve wasn't ideal recovery, but that was a great week's training. I felt really sharp and all the different calls and systems came flooding back.

As various players were carrying knocks, Joe didn't announce the team until the Thursday. While that added an edge to training, it wasn't ideal for preparation. I was named on the bench and felt I'd earned it after all my hard work. I wasn't completely match fit, but I was well conditioned. In Portugal, I had a meeting with the coaches. They asked me what I was going to bring to the table. I said my leadership and communication skills and that I'd make sure I was as well prepared as possible. I did think the group was very quiet during the week of the England game, but it's very hard, coming back in, to be bossy and barking at lads when you're on the bench, especially when you've played only once in almost fifteen months. And this was my first Six Nations game in two years.

I thought we were possibly too focused on the detail side of it. Whether playing for Ireland or watching from the side-lines, I always felt pride seeing us going after teams and beating them up, in wave after wave, whether it be attack or defence. But we just didn't do that against England. There were snippets of it, but not enough. We should have hated England more. The physicality should have been at an all-time high. I think that would have negated a lot of the things they did that day. As it was, they kind of bullied us.

The start of games can have a massive effect, like a boxer going out in the ring and getting one in the jaw. If the first few minutes go badly, you're a bit wobbly for a time. Maybe Jonny May's try in the second minute had that effect on us. Our carrying game went nowhere and I detected a lack of energy. There was no one tipping anyone on the arse when winning little margins or plays. We didn't play in the right areas of the field either. We were trying to do stuff in our own half and putting pressure on ourselves rather than on them, and they had their tails up.

You don't mind losing if you put in a good performance. It doesn't hurt as much. But going out and playing like we did in front of our home fans, against England, was just not acceptable. You have to be prepared to eat humble pie after a defeat like that. Speaking to one of the English players I'd toured with on the Lions, he told me that Eddie Jones had been constantly at them about how good Ireland were, that nobody was giving England a chance. 'He had us fired up for the last two weeks.'

I went into the Shelbourne Hotel, chatted to a few people, went up to my room, got changed, drove home to Tullow and flaked out. On the Sunday morning I went for breakfast with James and took the dogs for a walk. I rejoined the Ireland squad in Carton House that night and then on the Monday evening I signed for London Irish.

Negotiations with the IRFU had started in November. My contract would be up at the end of the World Cup. The Union probably wanted to wait until they saw how I went in the Six Nations before making a commitment, but that was too late for me. I needed it sorted sooner. By this stage, Ryan Constable from Esportif was representing me. A couple of English Premiership clubs were interested in signing me, and maybe one club in France. That wasn't on the table yet, but it was an enquiry, and I had definitely one and possibly two options in Japan, to stick around there after the World Cup.

I had employed Ryan because I had entered the last phase of my career and needed a different approach. Esportif have people all around the world, in Japan, England and France, and I found Ryan very good to deal with. The last time I'd been negotiating my contract, I'd had the power. I was in a good situation. I'd played a load of games. I was fit. This time, it was different. The Union probably felt they hadn't got the value they'd wanted out of me, which was fair enough from a business point of view.

In November, Ryan contacted David Nucifora, the IRFU's High Performance Director, and told him the situation, that there were two offers on the table. David was a bit taken aback by that. He hadn't really thought about me at that stage and was heading back to Australia. After Christmas, David got back to us and said that they hadn't budgeted anything for me going forward after the World Cup, that they would wish me well if I was leaving and there'd be no hard feelings. He wanted to reassure me that it wouldn't affect my World Cup chances.

Ryan had informed me that London Irish were interested, so I chatted with Declan Kidney, the London Irish coach, that same week. I've always been completely honest with any manager or coach, and I promised Deccie that I wouldn't kick the can down the road too long: 'I'm not bluffing. I'm not using you as a tool. I've never done that.'

People might have had different ideas about the Toulon offer in 2014, but the truth is that I'd signed a pre-contract with them and told my family that I was leaving. I think a lot of people thought I'd just played Toulon for a better contract here, but I hadn't done that.

I spoke with Deccie a few times and agreed in principle to join London Irish. He asked for time to speak with Joe and the Union. He wanted to be completely clear and honest with them. I said: 'Yeah, hundred per cent. You take your time, whatever you want to do.'

In the meantime, while he was doing that I called in to see Guy Easterby, Leinster's Head of Operations. I told Guy about the contract that was on offer from London Irish, that there was another offer from a Premiership club, but that the challenge Deccie was offering me at London Irish appealed to me more. I told him about the Japan offer, but said that it was too far away for me. 'Right,' he said. 'I'll talk to Nucifora.'

Ryan spoke to David again and told him what was on the table, and again David said the Union were not going to get anywhere near that money. If they were to offer me anything, it would probably be an extension after the World Cup for eight months, until the end of the 2019/20 season, and it would probably be for around half of my existing contract.

By contrast, London Irish had offered me a two-year deal, starting from the time the World Cup finished. This was now the end of December 2018 and Dave was in Australia at this stage. Ryan messaged him twice asking: *Can we have a discussion about Seán?* No reply.

In the last week in January, while I was in Portugal for Ireland's pre-Six Nations training camp, Ryan texted me one day to say that the London Irish CEO had been on to him, and that the offer was coming off the table at midnight. I rang him and told him I needed more time, because I'd had no word back from the Union at this stage, so I couldn't say yes or no.

By then I had talked to Sarah, to my sister Caroline and my brother Stephen, but I hadn't spoken with Sarah for the previous three days because she was in Melbourne and the timings were wrong. We kept missing each other. I was falling asleep when she was waking up, or vice versa. That evening I went up to Robbie Henshaw and said: 'Are you free? I'm in the middle of a conundrum here.' Robbie may be younger than me, but he has a good head on his shoulders. I also spoke to Rob Kearney about it. I had told no other players at this stage. I'd mentioned it to Johnny, but he'd said: 'Just wait until after the Six Nations.' I said: 'I'm not doing that. I can't do that. I can't afford to do it. The offer will be gone.' After talking to Robbie and Rob, I rang Alan Rowe, Sarah's dad, who is a businessman. The thing I love about Alan is that he is so straight. He's black and white. He thinks about things for an hour or two and then he'll come back to you.

In going through it forensically with Alan, he reaffirmed my thinking. If the Union really wanted me, they'd have come to me fairly rapidly after being informed there was another offer on the table, whatever it might be. I rang Ryan and said: 'Ryan, I'm going to do this, but for what they want me to do I am going to need more time.'

'What do you mean?'

'I'm committing everything to them, my life, what I have built in Leinster. I need more commitment from them and I need a bit more time to do what they want me to do.'

'I'll see will they give you another year.' He rang me back half an hour later and said, 'Yeah, it's done.'

I was happy then. It gave me the security I needed. Two hours after Ryan's initial text, after those discussions with Robbie, Rob, Alan and Ryan, and thinking it through in my room in Portugal, I texted Ryan back: *Yeah, I'm in.*

And that was it.

I texted Deccie: *Looking forward to the challenge. Thanks for giving me the opportunity.*

I sent Sarah a big long text because I knew she was in bed asleep. She woke up in Melbourne to a text saying: *Love, I'm moving to London for three years.*

The following morning, we finally had a long conversation on Facetime. I was upset and so was she. We'd just bought a house in Dundrum, and Sarah had this picture of us coming home and settling down in Ireland. I tried to explain everything, what had happened over the preceding twenty-four hours and how I'd basically had a gun to my head. I'd had two hours to decide whether to take a contract that was worth serious money to me, that offered me a great rugby challenge at a good club, and that was an hour and a half away from home.

There was another complication between me agreeing to join London Irish and actually signing the contract, namely Brexit. We had to get on to Ciarán Medlar in BDO Ireland, who had advised both me and Esportif in the past, to discuss whether I'd be able to claim the sportsman's tax relief if the UK was no longer in the EU by the time I retired. If that was jeopardized, we couldn't have gone ahead with the deal. Ciarán gave us confirmation that it wouldn't be an issue.

The following week David Nucifora got back to us. I met him in Starbucks in Ballsbridge on the Wednesday before the opening Six Nations game against England. When I started talking about what I wanted, he said they'd look into an extension for a year at half of what I was currently on but would incentivize it to get me to a good level again with appearances and so on. There was a stipulation: if I wasn't fit for the extended year, the Union wouldn't have to go with it. I said: 'Yeah, you do up something and get back to me.'

I had made up my mind that I was going to London Irish but, out of curiosity, I wanted to see if they did come to me with something, although it probably would have created a shitstorm for me and Ryan if they had.

But then he said: 'I'll have to have a conversation with Leo.'

'Why?' I asked. 'What's that about?'

He said: 'You know, you could be blocking some of the younger lads from coming through.'

I said: 'Do you think I am trying to stop Scott Penny or Josh or any of these younger lads coming through? Who does all the video work with them, or meets them? You don't see any of this.'

'I understand you are doing that.'

I added: 'You look at the last few weeks. Josh, Jack Conan, Dan Leavy, all these class players that were all injured over the last five weeks. There wasn't one week where we'd all six back-rowers fit. That's just the way the game has gone. If you think I am going to be blocking the younger lads coming through, you're joking me.'

I'd say I was only with him for half an hour because I was so direct. I wasn't entertaining any bullshit. But what really pissed me off was that if I was to stay, he said in return he'd want Leo to move two younger lads to other provinces. In other words, he might have a contract for me, but only on condition that Leinster compromised in order to keep me. I thought that was disgraceful. Knowing Leo, and the environment and the culture at Leinster, I knew he wouldn't agree to do that. If I was Leo, I'd never agree to it either because it would be damaging for the future of the club. That wasn't an option as far as I was concerned, so that was it, done and dusted.

As far as I can see, Leinster are producing players for the rest of Ireland. We work in a fickle industry. You are a piece of meat at the end of the day. However, from the Union's and Leinster's point of view, I think there has to be a plan in place for players who have given their entire careers to the province to be kept on when they drop down from an international contract.

I said I'd ring David on the Sunday after the England game, but when I rang he didn't answer. On Monday at 9am I rang him from Carton House, where we were beginning our preparations for the Scotland game, and he told me that there was no offer on the table for me. He said: 'We're not willing to offer you anything.'

'That's grand, good luck.'

That's all I said to him. I didn't want to be somewhere I wasn't wanted. Not that Leinster didn't want me. I knew they did, because they did see the day-to-day stuff and they knew what I could bring.

So that was it: I was out of the club to which I'd given fourteen years.

Andy Farrell was taking over from Joe after the World Cup, so I had spoken to him before Christmas and I'd told him what I was willing to stay for. The Irish squad were having a meeting at 10am that Monday and before it started I walked up to Andy and said: 'Just so you know, it's done. I'm not staying. I haven't been offered anything.'

'What?' He stood up from his chair. Face to face with me he said: 'I didn't hear anything about this.'

I said: 'How did you not hear about this?'

'I was talking to David yesterday. I was talking about other things, but he never mentioned anything to me about it.'

Andy couldn't believe it. He asked me if I'd signed for London Irish yet. I told him I was signing that night, that James Downey, who works with Ryan Constable, was coming to Carton House at 8pm with the contract.

At about 7pm Joe came up to me and said: 'Can I speak to you for a few minutes after dinner?'

'Grand.'

I was in the lobby when Andy came over first and said: 'How are you feeling?'

I said: 'It is what it is now.' I was pretty upset. I was about to sign the contract and that would be it. It would be done then.

Joe came over to us and said: 'Can you give me a day?'

I said I couldn't.

'When are you signing the contract?'

I said: 'In half an hour.'

'Where? Here?'

'Yeah.'

Their attitudes changed then. 'Well, look, this could be the best thing for you.'

They started to put a positive spin on it. Suddenly, I had the feeling that they didn't want me either. I'd say they saw me playing to the World Cup and then they'd have got enough out of me. That was fine, but if it was the case, then the Union should have just said that at Christmas. They should have said: 'The World Cup is your time and best of wishes to you after that', rather than stringing me along. That was the first time Joe spoke to me about it, but it had nothing to do with him, really, as he was finishing up after the World Cup himself.

In my conversation with Joe and Andy, I tried to keep it together, but my bottom lip was quivering because it was genuinely such a hard thing to do. It is definitely the hardest decision I've ever had to make in my life. After I had signed the contract, I said to them: 'I want this announced next week, during the break. I want it done and dusted.'

I was back at number 7 against Scotland in Murrayfield the following week. We did very little in our Captain's Run because we thought the Scottish side were watching us. I didn't tog out, which led to media speculation that I was carrying an injury. But it's a case of knowing your body. If I do the Captain's Run, I could be stiff on Saturday. If I'm twenty-four hours away from a game, I want to rest, and I've been doing that since I was twenty-six or twenty-seven. Waking up on the morning of the game, I was giddy with excitement. I went down and started a bit of craic in the team room, to make sure the lads were awake and happy, and I probably had a little too much to eat.

Throwing on the gear in the dressing-room and going out for the warm-up, I was still as full as a bull. My intention was not to say much, but then I became a bit emotional in the changing-room beforehand: 'I'm after watching more fucking games in the last twelve or fourteen months and the biggest thing for me and how proud I'd be of watching you lads is seeing you fucking smash people with wave after wave in defence, and wave after wave in attack and getting over the gain line. Let's make sure we put these fuckers to the sword today.'

The first ten minutes were played at 100 miles an hour. Scotland started well, and we were just too tight and couldn't get off the line hard enough. Then we scored two tries in quick succession, but lost Johnny after he took another hit when taking the ball to the line and putting Jacob through.

The key was a massive defensive set before half-time. Three minutes and twelve seconds, and twenty-five phases. Everybody chipped in, everybody made tackles. But I looked back at it the next morning and we were very tight at times in that set. If they had gone out the back at all, we probably would have been in trouble. Joey Carbery had a mixed game, but his piece of magic teed up Keith Earls for the try that won it. Joey just glides. He's always looking for any bit of space and away with him then.

We won a bit of a shitfight. I played sixty-four minutes and I felt I grew into the game. But, sitting in the changing-room, I knew there was so much more in me. Speaking to Sarah later, she made me realize that, not having played much at that level for so long, I shouldn't be too hard on myself.

Back in the hotel, I was rooming with Peter O'Mahony and he suggested we go down to the team room for a glass of wine. We went down, but I didn't have any wine. I'd promised myself that I wasn't going to have a drink until after the Six Nations. So I chatted with the boys for about an hour and a half, went back up to my room at about 11pm and watched Netflix until about 2am. I drove home to Tullow the next day. On the Monday, my move to London Irish was announced.

Joe told me on the Tuesday morning before the Italy game that I would be starting, which was reassuring. We trained well and I trained well that week. I had rarely been so excited about a Test match, but rarely so disappointed afterwards with my performance.

I made a bad pass to Mur at the start of the match. I dropped my right hand a little bit. Then Tito Tebaldi took the ball off Mur and I lined him up, only to miss him. Then I half fell over Chris Farrell when they scored. No one played well, but I sensed after the game that Joe would start Josh against France two weeks later. This seemed even more likely when I was sent back to Leinster while most of the squad went to Belfast for a two-day camp.

The week of the France game was a tough one because I knew it was potentially going to be my last home Six Nations game. When I went into camp on the Monday evening, I met Joe and admitted: 'I'm incredibly upset and pissed off at the way I played personally.' He said there were a few things that he was disappointed in all right. I thought I'd be on the bench, but Joe never even came to me beforehand to tell me I wasn't going to be involved at all.

The game was on a Sunday, and I was determined not to sulk, and to help prepare the lads as best I could. But when we went into a 15 v 15 as part of Friday's training session, I was on the opposition team, attacking as France, and I had a row with Johnny. I stepped over a ruck, he thought I was holding him down with one leg (it was actually Andrew Porter's leg) and he swung a punch at my other leg. I gripped him while he was on the ground, he got up and tried to get away from me and I tapped him on the chin as a parting shot. That really riled him and we had a running feud. Joe had a cut off me at one point, and when Johnny was still mouthing me at the end of the session, I was so furious that I had to walk away.

Faz followed me off and asked what it was all about. I had to go to my room and ring Sarah to calm down. I had too much external stuff going on in my head. I was incredibly disappointed that I wasn't going to get a chance to play my last Six Nations game at home. All my family were going to the game, brothers, sisters and cousins, on the presumption that I was going to be involved, but they didn't go in the end.

Players have fights in training all the time, but that one upset me more than most. Johnny texted me a peace sign that night, and I sent him back a thumbs-up. I'd say he was still as angry as I was, but we'd started to cool down.

I went down to Clonmel to do a gym session with a friend of mine, Eddie Whelan, and had dinner with him on the Saturday. Then on the Sunday I watched the France match with my brother-in-law, Willie, and my sister and their two lads. I knew from the way training had been going that the boys would start well, and after two minutes I knew France weren't up for it.

We were assembling in Carton House on the Monday night. I arrived early to do some pool work and look at videos. I met Joe at around 5pm in a corner of the team room and we cleared the air. We talked about my performance in Rome. He said he didn't think my attitude had been great in the week of the France game. I disputed that. He accepted that I'd trained well, but said he was talking more about my mood in the team room. When I pointed out that it would have been my last home Six Nations game in front of my whole family, I could see in his face that he hadn't thought about that at all. The row with Johnny was never mentioned.

Although Josh had gone off injured against France, I came away from that meeting thinking I mightn't be involved again because at the end of it he said to me: 'Well, I don't know what I'm going to do this week yet.'

Dan Leavy was back in camp as well, but when Joe announced the team on the Tuesday, I was back in. We trained well, although we were fighting a battle with the pitches in Carton House throughout the whole Six Nations because they were so wet and heavy. We never really had one fast, sharp session and we underperformed in training some days. But training was relatively sharp on the Thursday before we flew over to Cardiff. We stayed outside of the city for a change. I was rooming with Pete, which was perfect. The leadership group voted by 4 to 2 to have the stadium roof open, and Joe wanted the roof open, too. Had we started well, it could have been a different story. We could have kicked a lot of ball, played on top of them, put them under pressure to try and play their way to the Grand Slam. Instead, they scored a try in the second minute from Gareth Anscombe's chip, even though we'd practised for that during the week.

When they went 10-0 and then 13-0 up, we had to try and create something in the rain. But we didn't have much shape or momentum on the ball when we were carrying. Occasionally during that Six Nations, I thought we were playing set-plays almost for the sake of it, when sometimes there was space that we could have attacked straight away. We also played too much between the two 15-metre lines. But I genuinely didn't think we'd peaked. I still believed that, when we got it right, we had the quality to beat any team.

We got nothing from Angus Gardner that day either, but

our discipline was shocking. I was disappointed to be taken off because I thought I was moving better than I had moved before, certainly against Italy. I was doing my fair share of work. Watching the rest of the game, I knew there was no way we were getting back into it at that stage. I congratulated all the Welsh lads I knew from Lions tours. You just have to grin and eat humble pie and get out the gap. Fair dues to them, they did what they had to do and we didn't.

Leinster still had another double to aim for, and potentially nine more games to play. Going into the Champions Cup quarter-final against Ulster, I was conscious that if we lost, it would be my last Champions Cup game with Leinster and possibly my last at the Aviva. I didn't want to go out of the competition by losing a derby match in front of all our fans. The atmosphere was electric. I felt strong in contact and put in a few good hits at the start when we set a bit of a tone physically. But they threw the kitchen sink at us and we were probably 5 or 10 per cent off. Ulster pushed us all the way, and the turning point was Jacob losing control of the ball as he was about to touch down for a try. Johnny said it to the referee and to me: 'He hasn't grounded that.' That would have put them 18-11 ahead with a touchline conversion to come. But it was only five minutes into the second half. I never felt like we were going to lose that game at any stage. If they'd scored there, we would have scored again. The key try by Adam Byrne was set up by a piece of brilliance by Jack Conan – a pick-up, break and offload. I was taken off then. Leo told me later that was always the plan, to bring Dan Leavy on.

The downer for everybody was Dan's knee injury. We all knew in the dressing-room that it was really bad. He came in on the stretcher and he was completely out of it on gas and painkillers. We went over to him, but he didn't even know we were there, I'd say, he was in so much pain. Not a nice thing to see, but if anyone will come back from a thing like that, it will be him. He's very strong-minded and has a lot of things he wants to tick off in his rugby career. I texted him afterwards: *There's not much I can say to you at this stage, only that I know you'll be back and I know you'll be better than ever. One day at a time now.*

I'd love to have played in the same back-row with him more often. He's an athlete, a big strong rugby player, an all-round back-rower, and he's developed his carrying. We haven't seen the best of him yet. I think he is going to be a phenomenal player. He doesn't lack confidence, but he's not cocky and he's a good lad. He'd do anything for you. He's possibly a bit cracked, but sure you could say that about us all.

Leo made me captain for our Pro14 game against Glasgow at the RDS. We played some nice rugby that day, but we became way too narrow in defence. We had a lot of younger lads on the field and it was the quietest pitch I have ever been on in my life. They're good players, but their communication skills still needed to be developed. My nephews were there because it was potentially my last one in the RDS, and it was nice to have them in the stands, watching and cheering.

We turned the page on Glasgow pretty quickly and on to a massive week, playing Toulouse in the European semi-finals at the Aviva. There was a big focus on their ability to score from anywhere, and we had that covered off on the Tuesday. That was a really hard, tough session, an unbroken, totally unstructured forty-five minutes. And then we had twenty minutes of units afterwards.

I spoke to the team twice that week. On the pitch after Thursday's training I reminded everyone of the group we had, how special it was and how rare these opportunities were, how watching for much of the last year had made me so envious and that it would be a crying shame if we didn't do this. Johnny spoke passionately on a few occasions, too, about doing the basics well, and when Johnny talks you get revved up a little bit because he talks from his heart.

During the pre-match warm-up I was thinking, fuck me, it's boiling out here! I was blowing hard and after a couple of minutes I had to get rid of the scrum cap for the first time in years. I thought I was going to explode.

We were always in control, both with and without the ball. We also said we'd just let Wayne Barnes do his job. No chat. We played with our poker faces that day because a few of the Toulouse players can be a bit lippy. Nothing major, but we weren't going to get rattled like we did over there in the pool game. Wayne had come over to me in the warm-up and asked about London Irish. 'Yeah,' I said, 'you'll be seeing more of me next year.' And he laughed. Johnny was also really in control of himself in the way he managed the game with Wayne. Sometimes you don't know how it's going to go between Johnny and referees.

I captained the side for the last fifteen minutes, after Ross Byrne came on for Johnny, and we won 30-12, three tries to nil, which was a serious effort against that Toulouse team. They would go on to win the French Championship.

That was my last game for Leinster at the Aviva. Sarah was there, as were Caroline and Willie and my two nephews, my brother William, James and his girlfriend Anne, another good friend Eddie Whelan, and Stevie Cahill and a lot of people from Tullow. But I didn't go over to them afterwards because I knew I wouldn't be able to hold it together. I was just about able to speak to the players on the field afterwards about how proud we could be of each other because we'd really showed what we are about in that game – brothers, and all our values. I said to them: 'The job is not done yet.' We had to make sure we finished it against Saracens.

It turned out to be a good way of signing off. I didn't know it then, but that was my last home game for Leinster, and probably my last game in Ireland.

23. The little moments

On the Tuesday before the Champions Cup final against Saracens in Newcastle, I was struggling. My hip wasn't great at all. The most mundane tasks had become so difficult. Even tying shoelaces had become brutal. The pain just shot through my groin to the top of my hip like a dart. It was bone on bone.

By the Thursday, it felt better. I got through that session in UCD relatively okay, although I wasn't feeling as well as I had been before the Toulouse game three weeks earlier. That semi-final had been only my second full eighty minutes of the season. I was in bits for two days after it. The pain in my hip was becoming worse at night-time, waking me up regularly. That week was a struggle physically, and mentally I was trying to get myself in the right state to kill Saracens!

Yet it was also an exciting week. Our fifth Heineken Cup final in a decade. We knew what we wanted to do and we knew our game plan. It had been a good week. Nothing out of the ordinary. Everybody had prepared well. We talked about fine margins. We knew how difficult it was going to be but felt that if we all played to our potential, we'd get there. When we dissected Saracens in our video analysis, we felt that we could hurt them in a way few other teams could do, and that if we played our game, they'd struggle to manage us.

The 5pm kick-off made for a long day. After breakfast and coffee we had a little bit of a walk through. I chilled out in the room for most of the day. Match days are very lazy. Have a shower, go down for strapping and then I'm ready to rock.

I used to get nervous on match days, but not in recent years. The more games I've played, the more I've learned to go with the flow, especially if I feel I've prepared well. And with experience you learn to prepare well. But I've rarely experienced a pre-match atmosphere like the coach journey into St James' Park on the day of the final. I really haven't. There were blue waves of cheering and singing Leinster fans everywhere. Arriving at the ground made the hairs stand up on the back of my neck.

'Right, we're here now. Let's go do this.'

The stadium was packed and it was rocking. The sun was shining. The pitch was cut nice and short. Conditions were perfect. The scene was set.

We couldn't have started any better. From our first pattern of the day we played for a penalty. We'd seen how they had tried to creep up and shoot up off line-outs, so it was a dummy off the top from Devin Toner, who instead pulled it down and gave it to Luke McGrath in one motion, and Saracens were already offside. In the changing-room we'd told the referee, Jérôme Garcès, that we were going to do this. Johnny Sexton made it 3-0, just as we'd planned.

For ten minutes after that there was plenty of kicking and we were competing well. James Lowe chased a box kick by Luke, and Johnny was first onto the loose ball. We had seen in their semi-final against Munster that they were slapping balls back rather than catching them, so we had to make sure we contested in the air and flooded the channels to have players around the ball.

Their attack stressed us at times. Their system means they can always go both ways to pods or out the back to go wide.

But when Luke tackled Alex Goode the ball went loose, Jordan Larmour picked up, stepped Billy Vunipola, chipped ahead and kicked on. The linesman, Pascal Gaüzère, said Jordan had knocked on, which gave them a scrum, but he hadn't. That was a big call, and a bad one. We were on the wrong end of several calls, which can happen some days.

We were relieved, though, when Romain Poite raised his flag from the touchline and a replay showed Brad Barritt led with his shoulder into Scott Fardy at a ruck on our line. It was an arm-wrestle at this stage, but I wasn't feeling too bad. They're so big and strong that it's very hard to stop their momentum. We just weren't winning enough collisions.

You make a tackle. Get up. Make another tackle. Get up again. They're big men. You have to try to move them around. It's hard work, and my hip was starting to give me jip. After about twenty minutes I got a kick to my right calf. No idea how I got it. I remember running and thinking: fuck, this is tight. It might be torn! The right hip – my bad one – just locked up.

It was hard going for both teams. There wasn't a hint of a break. But then Rob Kearney cut through their defence and we hammered at their line. Maro Itoje was penalized and binned for offside. We could have gone for 6-0, but we decided to go for the scrum. We had a call off the scrum that is called a 'Chiefs'. Jack Conan picks up and hits me back inside if the scrum is square, but the scrum wasn't square. It was a mess, and with Garcès refereeing it was a free-for-all. He said 'Play on' when it should have been another reset.

Instead of me, Jack had Fards on his inside and if he hit him, it was a try. From the ruck I picked and went, but George Kruis got a good hit on me. It would have been nice to score, but then Tadhg picked and muscled over. A good finish.

When we get inside our opponents' 22, we expect to score. We strangle teams. Our mentality is to stay patient and eventually we'll get something out of it. We'll get either three, five or seven points. Sexto's conversion made it 10-0 to us.

The chat among us was 'Next ball now'.

We had said all week that we were going to keep attacking these boys, no matter what happened. We had a set-play inside our own half. A four-man play. I was outside Jack. Johnny transferred it to Garry Ringrose, but Ringer shuffled a high pass to Jack. He had to reach for it, couldn't keep his stride and was hit well by Alex Lozowski. We scrambled and recycled the ball, but, as a consequence of not getting the first and second phase right, we didn't get the third phase right either and Kruis shot up and put in a good hit on Sexto. Garcès pinged him for not releasing and Owen Farrell kicked their first points.

We were still 10-3 up when Itoje came back on. The 40 was up and we had ruck ball in the middle of the field. We went for the box kick to contest on their 22, but Garcès pinged Rob for not rolling away. It's easy to say in hindsight that we should have kicked the ball off the pitch at 10-3 with the 40 up, as some pundits said. But if the referee looks back on that penalty against Rob, it's a scrum to Saracens. Nothing more than that. Rob is completely trapped. I said it to Garcès at the time.

'He's completely trapped.'

'No. He has to try to move.'

'How can he move?'

Rob had 140 kilos on top of him. Chest to chest. It was a harsh one. I genuinely don't think Rob could have moved. If

Garcès doesn't award that penalty, they probably kick it back to us or they just kick it dead and we go in 10-3 ahead. Instead, from the penalty they attacked off the top from a line-out and hit up Barritt. Johnny and I tackled him. I was holding on to Barritt's feet.

I had a conversation about that moment with Johnny on the bus back to the airport. Johnny didn't think I was involved in the tackle and he was saying to me at the time that I needed to be giving him a hand. Johnny likes to choke people more than chop them, so I had Barritt's legs and Johnny was trying to hold him up. A few Saracens players came in around Johnny and they drove Barritt on another three yards beyond where we should have stopped him. They got momentum off first phase and then got around the corner on us. We were chasing our tails a little.

They're the little moments that we let slip.

If I'd gone off the line a little bit harder and me and Johnny had made a better hit on Barritt and stopped him on the gain line, it would have made it much easier for us to go at them off the next phase. But we didn't do that then, or in the whole game really. We didn't knock them backwards enough. I could probably have got better entry and gone a bit harder. Normally we have that seam between me and Johnny sewn up. Then it's just about winning the wrestling part of it. Between the two of us, we could have done a better job.

They pounded us from then on. We defended really well on our line. Lukey somehow stopped Jamie George at full tilt. But then Jordo made the mistake of biting in as Owen Farrell put Sean Maitland over. He's young and he won't do that again. On another day, maybe he doesn't do that and we defend it. They did well to finish it. Farrell's conversion made it 10-10. There was an extra spring in their step as we all headed off the pitch for half-time.

There were certain aspects of the game that we hadn't really been in control of and that we tried to fix during the interval. The key messages were to go harder off the defensive line and to win more collisions in 'D' and then, in attack, to start playing to the edges.

At half-time I told one of the physios I had a dead calf, then took a breath and gathered my thoughts. I wasn't exactly leaping out of my skin at half-time. I was suffering a little. There was a general sense of frustration that we hadn't played the way we wanted to play. I looked around and saw a few grumpy heads.

We managed early parts of the second half quite well. We should have scored again. James Lowe came off his wing and linked with Johnny up the middle. This gave us inroads. From the recycle we had a five-on-two. I was one of those outside Ringer, but he didn't throw the pass. The following week he would throw the pass to Cian Healy, and Tadhg Furlong would be the link for Seán Cronin to score. But not that day.

It was a great chance to score. I could have relayed the information to him better, and so could the lads outside me. At the time I felt, we're on here. Watching it on the video again, if I get that ball, I walk it in, regardless of the three lads outside me. It doesn't matter who gets it, we walk it in.

In another big moment, Liam Williams flew up to win a turnover from Garry. But Williams didn't release and he put his two hands on the ground. That should have been a clear penalty to us under the posts. That was a poor one by Garcès because it was so easy to see. If it was a back-rower, I'd say he would have pinged him because he'd have expected a back-rower to try it.

They were off the hook again.

Tadhg also had the ball ripped from him close to their line. They're the moments that matter in their 22, especially in a final. And ten points was never going to beat them.

Then they started to get their runners going. Jackson Wray, Will Skelton and Itoje all made big carries in one attack, and Fards was pinged and very harshly binned for offside.

They opted for a penalty to make it 13-10.

Then Billy Vunipola intercepted a pass from Johnny. James Tracy stepped out of the line when he should have been running at Billy's inside shoulder. He would have been through. Instead, Johnny only had one option, to hit me. Again, it let them off the hook.

That was my last involvement. I'd done a few okay things, but I was also pissed off that I hadn't added enough while I was on. You're always unhappy to be replaced with almost twenty minutes to go, particularly in a European Cup final. Still, coming off I thought, let's go and win the game, boys. Rhys Ruddock was as fresh as a daisy and I knew well what he was going to bring.

I watched from the sidelines as they came at us in waves. With a penalty under the posts, they opted for a scrum. We had practised for this all week. Billy Vunipola was never going to pass the ball. We knew what was coming. He actually broke his bind, and we were just too honest. As soon as he broke his bind we needed to go. We should have been looking at the ball. If Rhys had his time over that scrum again, he'd come off the scrum harder and meet him full on. You just need to go and get him. Fire yourself under the bus. Stop his legs and let Johnny have a go at the ball. Even if you put in a great shot up high, his legs are still going to move. He was only four metres out. And Johnny missed him at the angle. He didn't get a shot at him. By the time Lukey and Lowe arrived on the scene, it was too late. Vunipola is such a big man and so powerful.

Now they were two scores ahead, 20-10, and there's no tougher team to chase a game against. The endgame was horrible to watch. We tried to run everything from our own 22 because we had no choice. Full credit to them, Saracens are some outfit. They took their chances and we didn't. We lost too many moments, little and big. And we weren't nasty enough in our collisions. That was the story of the game.

On another day we might have played a different shape so that they couldn't bluff as much. Play a bit closer to Lukey at 9 and to Johnny, and everybody be in motion at the line rather than the middle man getting the ball. We could have used our hands a bit more with tip-ons. We had practised that, but they were just coming so hard at the first man and the second man and the third man. Dev gave me one in the second half and I said to him: 'What the fuck are you doing?' It was a suicide ball, whereas he actually had momentum. Small things like that. We were just off by 5 per cent in everything.

But even though we hadn't exactly played the way we'd wanted to play, we did have our chances. We'd turned over the ball three times in their 22 very easily. If we hadn't done that, if we'd even managed to score off one of them, it could have been a different game, even though we didn't play that well.

There's not much worse than losing a Cup final. You think of so much throughout the week. You think of performing to your very best. You think of having your hands on the trophy. You think of your family. My nephew, Will O'Toole, was having his communion that day in Ballon/Rathoe, and

Dad, Mam, my brothers and sisters were all at that, although they were able to watch the game back at the house. But my best friend, James Foley, and his parents had taken the ferry and driven over and I thought about them, watching us lose.

It's a horrible feeling. You and your teammates have worked your bollocks off all season to get to that place. And then it's over. I'd rather get knocked out in the group stage than lose the final. It's the worst place to lose.

I shook hands with every one of the Saracens boys. I knew several of them through the Lions, but I didn't get into conversations with any of them. Watching on as losing finalists as the winners receive their medals and the trophy is not a nice place to be.

It was the first time any of us had lost a Champions Cup final. We'd won all of our four previous ones, as well as a Challenge Cup final. The dressing-room was quiet. Everybody was pissed off because we knew that we hadn't played to our potential. That's the most annoying thing as a player – knowing that you've left something behind. You need a bit of bloody luck as well and we didn't get any.

But we had a Pro14 semi-final against Munster at the RDS in a week's time. So we spoke about getting the bodies right and going again.

24. The Leinster endgame

The problem with my right calf and hip kept me out of the Pro14 semi-final, but on the Thursday beforehand I gave a presentation to the lads on the breakdown. It was a chance to speak to the whole group one last time. I knew we'd beat Munster because I didn't think they had the quality we had. And I thought the lads would be hurting so bad from the European final that losing just wouldn't be an option.

Leo announced the team pretty early in the week and Johnny wasn't starting, so he was like a bear that day. He got over it pretty quickly, though. I want Johnny playing the whole time, but I liked the idea of bringing him on as a sub because you know he'll light up the place, which he did that day. And we needed a bit of freshness after losing to Saracens. Ross Byrne is a good lad, and in terms of standing in for Johnny you'd never doubt him at all. You know exactly what you're getting with him.

Despite my bad hip, I couldn't stop myself jumping up from my seat when Garry Ringrose, Cian Healy and Tadhg Furlong combined to put Seán Cronin over. Nugget had a bit of a chip on his shoulder going into that game as well because of the perceived pecking order with the national team that had him behind Munster's hooker, Niall Scannell.

A typical James Lowe finish sealed it. Johnny said to me afterwards that when he saw Mike Haley sitting off, he called 'Hands', so as to get the ball out to Lowe. James is unstoppable from less than ten metres.

Everyone was happy in the dressing-room afterwards. Recovery. Get the head down. Get ready for a big final against Glasgow, in Glasgow. And let's go and win it.

The night before the Pro14 final, Johnny sent me a lovely text from the team hotel. I had been out for dinner in the Clonskeagh House with a few other guys who weren't going to be involved in the final – Jack McGrath, Devin Toner and Josh Murphy. Then we had a couple of beers in Ranelagh, but I didn't stay out and was home at 11pm.

It was during the meal, at about 9.30pm, that I received the message from Johnny: *Sorry you're not going to be running out with us tomorrow. Sometimes people get the fairytale ending and sometimes not, but it doesn't take away from your legacy at the club. You'll go down as the best forward ever to play for Leinster in my eyes. The best forward that I've ever played with. Injuries were cruel on you right up until the end but when you play like a warrior that's what happens unfortunately. It's been a pleasure to play with you and if we win I want you to lift the trophy at the end of the game on your own and for it to be the last thing you do in a Leinster top. I won't take no for an answer. See you at the end of the game on the pitch. Try not to be too drunk so that we can do it. Sexto.*

I texted him back: *You're the best in the world and you'll bring the lads with you tomorrow. You're on a different planet in everything you do compared to anyone I've ever played with, and I can't explain to you how much I love and respect you. You're Mr Leinster and I'm happy to have been a part of that journey we've been on. It's been an honour every step of the way. Blue Blood.*

I rate him that highly. He's the standard-bearer. He set us up. Everything he does is for Leinster. From that day against Munster in the Heineken Cup semi-final in 2009, Sexto has been the heartbeat of Leinster. He and I have had our run-ins. We clash because we both want to win so badly. But he knows how much I respect him and I know how much he respects me, even though he might call me a few names now and then, and vice versa.

When I came home, I told Sarah and she agreed that it was a very classy gesture. And a very genuine message. But, then, Johnny's a very genuine man.

The playing squad had travelled to Glasgow on the Thursday. I flew over on the morning of the game along with a dozen other players who had played in the Pro14 that season but who wouldn't be involved in the final, and some of the management as well. We had to be in the airport at 11.15am for check-in. I had texted Daniel Davey, our nutritionist, the night before saying that I'd pick him up at 10.30am. But I completely forgot. He texted me at 10.50am.

Where are you?

I'm just going through the tunnel now.

So that left him in a bit of a scramble to get to the airport on time.

We met up with some of the players' parents at a pre-match function in a hotel in Glasgow. Myself, Fergus McFadden and a few of the younger lads were there for two hours. There were canapés and chicken curry, and we also had four or five schooners. I chatted with Eoin Reddan's father, Don, with Leo's parents, with Bryan and Ed Byrne's parents, with Seán Cronin's dad and father-in-law, and with Tadhg's dad.

Some of us had to make 'appearances' in corporate boxes before the game, but the traffic in the rain to Celtic Park was very heavy and we were late getting to the ground, too late for some of them. I ended up doing only one, for Virgin Media, at pitchside.

I felt grand. It would have been very different if I'd been forced to pull out the day before. But from the Thursday before the semi-final I had known my fate.

It was always going to be an extremely tough game, playing a good team like Glasgow in a huge stadium in their home city. But I was thinking to myself that if we got stuck into them early on, they had individuals like Stuart Hogg who would go off script and try to do something themselves. It was Hogg's last game for Glasgow, and it was guaranteed he would try something from his own half. That said, they're always a hugely dangerous side. And that was the worry. Once they got any kind of momentum, they were hard to stop.

They stressed us and scored first, too, going 7-0 up. I wasn't too concerned. We had said during the week that it was probably going to be tight. A one-score game. The game plan was: no matter what happens, let's learn our lessons from the Saracens defeat. Whatever we say we're going to do, do that, and keep doing it as best we can.

We were in a shitty enough viewing spot, behind the dugouts. I don't know how soccer fans watch games from there. You can't see the pitch. I found a few free seats further up to the right of the coaches' box before the game and I moved Don Reddan and Leo's parents up there because they had even less of a view than I did. I watched more of the game standing than sitting.

Looking at the lads after that early Glasgow try, I could see that there wasn't a bother on them. They were grand. They weren't rattled. Of course, to hit back with a score straight away was the perfect response. There was a massive chase from Johnny's restart, and two good sets in 'D' – good hits. Then Lukey McGrath did what Lukey does, bringing energy to the whole thing. He and a few other lads went after Hogg, who had a tendency to take two steps before kicking the ball. Lukey made the charge-down and Ringer was the first onto the spinning ball for the try. But if it hadn't been him, it would have been any of three others.

They did have us under pressure a few times. Jordo and Ringer got us out of jail once, and Adam Hastings blew an overlap on another occasion. They went to the edges, and we didn't get there as often as we wanted to.

Behind 10-5, we went to the corner. The boys kept it nice and tight, and after sixteen phases Church scored. He can't be stopped from that close in. We'd prepped for this all week, too. Get into their 22. Choke teams. Keep the ball. Either we'll score or they'll give us something. Whatever team we have on the pitch, there's a belief within the players that we'll score eventually.

Johnny kicked the conversion and a penalty for a 15-10 lead at the break. Before the start of the second half I went up to the coaches' box. We'd kicked a few balls back to them that had gone astray and we'd said during the week that we wouldn't do that. I said this to Leo, that we needed just to kick it off the field, because Glasgow live off broken play. Whenever we didn't find touch from our 22, they were launching their attacking game. That's when they get into their shape, whereas we would be more in control of what's coming at us off a set-piece.

They had us under pressure again when Ringer's read and line speed forced a turnover and he broke up the pitch with James. Their centre, Kyle Steyn, was binned and we took the penalty to make it a two-score game. We probably should have taken another three points when we had another penalty under their posts but we opted for a succession of scrums instead. The boys wanted to take them on in the scrum, which is grand, but in a low-scoring final in the rain an eleven-point lead is a big lead.

When Rob was yellow-carded for taking out Hogg in the air, it could have been red. At least he kept his eye on the ball. Also, it was the sixty-seventh minute, so red or yellow didn't make much difference at that stage.

Suddenly, the noise levels rose again and they were energized. We were back in a scrap. They worked a good try on the edge and it was 18-15 with five minutes to go.

We had a light-looking bench, but I thought they did well. The lads ran down the clock well. I hate the pick-and-go with Owens reffing, but we stayed on our feet and saw the game out. As the clock passed 80, and Lukey passed to Ross Byrne to kick the ball dead, I threw my arms in the air, hugged whoever was near me and made my way down to the side of the pitch.

I hadn't thought about the trophy presentation too much throughout the day, not until it was actually happening. Sexto came over to me on the sideline and we hugged. 'You stay with us now over here.' I didn't really. I stayed on the sideline. But after he called the whole squad together for the presentation, he took the trophy from Gerald Davies and called me over to him. I suggested that we do it together, but he insisted I lift it on my own in front of the rest of the squad.

So I did as I was told. I lifted the trophy. It's an honour that has been afforded to very few Leinster players over the years. It's normally shared. Only Leo and Isa have done it. It was brilliant, definitely one of the nicest moments of my career. Except for being saturated with a bottle of prosecco down my back. I think that was James Lowe. I had to take off my jacket and shirt. The smell of booze off me was disgraceful. I borrowed a T-shirt from Rhys Ruddock for the journey home. If he'd had a spare pair of trousers, I'd have borrowed them too.

Afterwards, in the changing-room, we all jumped in for one group photograph, but those of us not playing stood back to let the boys who had played continue their celebrations. I stood in the corner of the changing-room on my own. I didn't talk with anyone. I just took it all in, soaked and alone with my thoughts. And I had loads of thoughts. All sad thoughts. Fuck, I'm not going to be back here again, was the main one.

We were getting the bus to the airport before the boys. If you were playing, you'd be having the craic. I was starving, and tucked into some chicken skewers while the boys were giving it some welly. You let them do their own thing. They're the ones who won it. It's not the same as having played and we were ushered out after about fifteen or twenty minutes.

Myself and the other uninvolved players, management and committee members were back in the airport forty minutes before the boys, and the beers were already flowing. The departure area was nearly all blue, and smiling.

When we got back to Dublin, we went to the Intercontinental Hotel, where a room was reserved for the extended squad, family and friends. Sarah and I were chatting with Johnny and Laura, and Ringer and Ellen. We moseyed around the room and I had a beer with nearly everyone. There was a nice, intimate, buzzy atmosphere in the room, but there were plenty of tired eyes as well. We hit the road at about 3.30am. It had been a long day. I was wrecked. And still sodden.

The next day, we met in The Bridge at around 2.30pm.

We'd cordoned off the upstairs for the players. Food, music and serious craic.

We've had a few deadly nights at Leinster. There was one in Johnny's house, and the night after we beat Racing in Bilbao in the 2018 Champions Cup final was definitely the best night out I've ever had in my life. That was in The Bridge, too. Mental. Great craic. Music. Dancing. Lads singing together. All helped by a few characters almost running the whole thing, like Max Deegan and James Ryan when they get a few beers into them. James walks around like Forrest Gump when he's had a few drinks. Max is good at putting on stupid songs and getting people dancing.

This time we actually had to tie the lights up in The Bridge, after we broke them all that night after the Racing win. At some point we moved on to Cassidy's on Camden Street – at least forty of us. A trad set started up as usual in there. I had been keeping an eye on things in The Bridge. I'd kept my wits about me to ensure the place wasn't broken up. In Cassidy's, I felt like I could blow off a bit of steam.

As well as being drunk, I had also been an emotional wreck all day. There were a few things. Not only was I never going to play for Leinster again after a dozen years with the club, I knew this was my last match weekend with Leinster. As the singing and dancing took off in Cassidy's, I was thinking, this is great, but I'll never have this craic again.

We were all down at the back of the pub and the place was absolutely mobbed. Two days earlier, the day before the final, I'd formally booked the hip surgery I needed, so I also knew that was awaiting me. There were a few too many tears that night. All in front of the other lads, mind. Some of them don't remember any of this, but I remember.

So what happened then? I was sitting down beside the

musicians. The toilets were about seven yards away, and I was going in and out of the loo basically after every pint. On one occasion, all the urinals were in use. I was bursting, and turned around to have a piss in the doorway. I turned around and a fella was staring at me.

He said: 'You're after pissing on my leg.'

'I didn't piss on your leg.'

He goes: 'You did.'

'Well I might have splashed you,' I said, 'but you weren't here in front of me.'

What I knew for sure was that I hadn't deliberately or directly pissed on anyone. There were a few verbals then and I was like, 'Will you fecking relax. I didn't mean to do it.' One of his friends started to get a little more aggressive. So that was me done with Cassidy's. Out the door and into a taxi. I was pretty upset when I got home and I wasn't making much sense. I was mumbling, whingeing and crying. Sarah thought it was a mix of being drunk and the emotion attached to it being my last real weekend with Leinster.

I didn't really think of the incident again until I looked at my Instagram and I had a message from yer man along the lines of 'lawyer up'. I thought that maybe he'd been a little drunk himself or fired up when he'd sent it, but everything took off from there and spiralled out of control a little.

It was suggested in some media that the incident had taken place in the main bar. Not true. It was suggested that Tadhg had had to step in to prevent a fight. Not true either. Tadhg was around that area, but he didn't have to stop a fight.

Leinster HR got in contact with me and I had to meet with their representatives and the Union's HR department as well. They had recommended that I enlist a solicitor for advice, so I did that as well before going in to tell them my side of the story. They subsequently sent me back their find-ings, which amounted to three things. One, I had 'urinated in public, and splashed a member of the public', an action that 'could reasonably be regarded as bringing the player, the province, the game or the IRFU into disrepute'. Secondly, their findings also viewed my verbal exchange with this member of the public as bringing the game into disrepute. (Not that I said much to him at all, other than asking him to get out of my face.) The third finding was that I had my top off in public.

On 11 June I had to go to the BMI Meriden Hospital in Cov-entry for the hip operation. Professor Damian Griffin had done my last two hip operations, in 2018. He's absolutely brilliant. He talks you through everything first.

He didn't want me to get it done immediately because he wanted to talk me through the options first. In fact, I spent three hours with him one day, following the first scan. I had been feeling severe pain in the hip and he talked me through every single aspect of the operation. There was the possibil-ity of it going terribly wrong. The hip could break and then I was looking at God only knows what. Where they insert the pin in the femur, if it does break, there is still room to put in a full hip replacement. I knew there were risks attached to it, but I also knew it would be worth it if it worked. Professor Griffin also told me there would be a ceramic version of the pins in another three months' time and they might possibly last longer. He suggested I could wait for that. But I wasn't waiting.

He rated my chances of playing rugby again at fifty-fifty. The same operation was performed on Andy Murray by a dif-ferent surgeon. Obviously, the key difference between Andy and me is that rugby is a contact sport and I'd be getting impact hits on my hip. However, the UFC fighter Sean O'Malley has had the op, and he's had no problems with his either. A couple of decathletes have also had it done. Now, I was going to be the guinea pig for rugby players with the op.

They had to dislocate my hip at the outset of the operation. Professor Griffin had admitted to me that this would be his biggest task, aside from the risk of my groin being torn. He had some rooting to do while I was asleep. All I could do was hope everything went all right. I was told I'd be out of pain straight away, and I was looking forward to that.

The surgery lasted five and a half hours. When I woke up, at around 7pm, I actually thought they'd dislocated my left shoulder. It was completely numb. I pressed against it and felt nothing.

'Get me morphine or get me a doctor,' I said to a nurse. 'My shoulder is out.'

She said: 'No, no. It couldn't be.'

'There's something wrong with my shoulder.'

Little did I know, I'd been lying on my left shoulder, my bad shoulder, for the whole length of the operation.

The operation usually takes about three and a half hours, but when I spoke with Professor Griffin the next day he told me he'd been extra cautious with everything and taken five and a half hours, because he didn't want to risk cutting through any muscle, especially in my glute and my quad. By not disturbing any muscle there, it should stand to me in the future, and I'll be incredibly strong around those areas.

When he first walked in, I had my two knees bent up on the bed. He looked at me with a slightly puzzled expression, and said: 'Have you range in that already?'

I said: 'I've no pain. I know there's plenty of painkillers in my system from the operation yesterday, but I've no pain in my groin or hip at all.'

He grabbed my leg and manoeuvred it. He was surprised how much range I had. I asked him what range I'd had in external rotation on the operating table. I'd had zero degrees for a year and a half. Immediately after the operation, I had 35 degrees. So my hip was moving perfectly. Previously, when my hip was bad, I could only bring my knee up 80 degrees, but within days of the operation I had it right up to my chest. All of which merely shows how fucked the joint was.

That evening I was on the bike in the physio room in the hospital. I started rehab straight away. Very static stuff. Before and after, I had an ice machine and a movement machine on my hip all day, just to get it moving as quickly as possible. I felt great.

On Sunday, 16 June, my sister Caroline flew home with me. I was in a wheelchair for most of the journey, and on crutches for the flight. I had intended going straight to Mayo when I landed, to be with Sarah. I'd even arranged a lift. But I had to cancel those plans because my IRFU disciplinary hearing was scheduled for the following Tuesday. I could have said to the Union that I'd already made plans to go to Mayo after my operation, and that I'd see them in three weeks' time. But I didn't do that. I wanted it finished with, because of the amount of flak I was getting on social media. I needed it to end.

Caroline brought me home to Dundrum. I couldn't climb the stairs to the bedroom, so on Monday I slept on the couch. On the Tuesday morning I had to be in the Union's offices at 9am, so I'd booked my taxi for 8.30am.

The first person I met was Denis Hurley, the former Munster player who is the Rugby Players Ireland representative. I didn't feel well at all after walking in on the crutches. I nearly passed out, and apparently I was as white as a ghost.

I then met the head of the Union's HR department and the head of their legal department. They asked me for my side of events again. I told them the story, precisely and in full, again. They asked me to draw a diagram of the toilet in Cassidy's and show where the incident had happened. They asked me if the offence was on a low, medium or high scale, in my opinion. I said that in my opinion it was on a low scale. If I'd done it intentionally or if I'd turned around so that I was facing him, then it would be a high scale. No doubt about it, I said. But that hadn't been the case. I told them that the one thing that sickened me about all of this was that it had been suggested that I'd done it intentionally, that I'd deliberately pissed on someone in the middle of a bar for the hell of it.

The hearing lasted about thirty-five minutes.

I went back to Tullow that day. Ed and Bryan Byrne, the Leinster front-row twins, were driving down that way for a family event and dropped me home. I stayed in the cottage until the Friday.

Two days after the hearing, the Union rang me with their verdict. They agreed with me that it was on the lower scale in breaching my code of contract and issued me with a fine and a warning.

I'm sorry it ever happened. It shouldn't have happened and it was my fault.

My legal advice was not to respond on social media or publicly. Sometimes saying nothing is best, while knowing you're not the type of fella that some people think you are or make you out to be. You just have to content yourself with that.

*

Four weeks after my hip operation, sitting on my couch at home in Dundrum, I was pain-free for the first time in eighteen months. It would take four or five months to know my fate, but I felt fully confident. The only bit of discomfort I was experiencing was when I rolled onto my right-hand side, where the scar was.

Of course, the downside of all this was that my Ireland career was over. I'd finished with fifty-six caps for Ireland, as well as five Tests with the Lions, and it could have been 100 but for injuries. Should have been 100. There were 126 appearances for Leinster over a dozen years, which could have been 200. Although I'd lifted the Pro14 trophy in Glasgow, losing to Saracens in my last game and playing the way we did was not how I'd wanted to finish with Leinster either.

Not ideal, but that's the way it is. As Sexto says, you don't get to write your own fairy-tale ending.

Four weeks after the operation, my weight was up to 110 kilos. My ideal fighting weight would be 106 kilos. It was bad weight, too. I find it impossible to keep fat off me if I'm not training. It's not that I eat badly. In that eight weeks without training I'd say I had three or four 'chippers', max. I drank eff-all. I picked at sweets, things that wouldn't be in my normal routine when I'm training, but I didn't overdo it. It's just my genetics when it comes to weight gain. I can't afford to stay away from training for too long. I wasn't worried, though, because I knew I'd have that extra four kilos off me within three weeks.

I began the rehab in Leinster, and then spent a week in Mayo with Sarah. I had a physio call to Sarah's family house every day – Gerry May from Ballina Rugby Club. I went to a gym in the town for a daily bike session but nothing else initially. Sarah and her mum looked after me really well. They cooked for me and 'picked up my bits', as Sarah put it, because I wasn't very mobile at that stage.

About four weeks after the operation, I started driving again, so I was able to rehab at UCD Monday to Friday. Then I drove back to Ballina on the Friday and had a relaxing afternoon at the Ice House Hotel with Sarah, enjoying a massage and the jacuzzi.

I drove to Limerick the next day for the replay of the Connacht final between Mayo and Galway. It was the first of a double-header between the counties, as the men's teams were facing each other in the final round of qualifying. It was a long drive, two and a half hours, and on bad roads as well. I got back at 10.30pm and Sarah was back at 11pm. We chatted about the match for about half an hour.

I went for breakfast with Sarah and her teammates the next morning. I had suggested to them that they didn't do enough together, so they were trying to generate more of a team bond. Sarah organized that and we all went to a café called Pudding Row in Easkey, County Sligo, that looks out on the Atlantic. It's the best place I've ever been to for breakfast. I'd drive from Dundrum for it. I really would.

About fifteen of the girls joined us for breakfast, and then a few of them chilled out in the Rowes' house for the day before I cooked a barbecue that evening. I hit the road early on the Monday morning, and was in UCD at 7.50am for the first of my daily rehab sessions. I wanted to be back in the Leinster environment, even if I was training on my own.

For several weeks I had to do a Wattbike session every morning. It's a bit harder than a normal spin. I did about forty-five minutes of that every morning and then an hour of rehab/physio, as well as three upper-body weight sessions each week. For the first few months, that was it.

A month on from the operation I was very happy. I only took painkillers for three nights after the op, a blood thinner for eight days, and I hadn't taken an anti-inflammatory since a week after it. I felt great, with no pain except for the scar tissue, which was natural. London Irish knew my situation and there was pressure on me to return to playing before February. That gave me a six-month block to prove my fitness from the time of the operation.

Continuing my rehab in Leinster while the boys were preparing for the World Cup was a little strange. The second warm-up game against England didn't look great, but talking to a few of them afterwards they said they'd had a big week in Portugal and were heavy-legged going into the game.

I didn't agree with Jean Kleyn being picked for the World Cup squad ahead of Devin Toner because I didn't think he'd done enough. Dev had his injuries, but he knows how to run a line-out, he's a good scrummager and he would have brought a lot of experience. He had been such a big part of everything the team had achieved. I was disappointed for him. The back-rowers picked themselves and I felt for Kieran Marmion, but Luke McGrath deserved to be brought in, based on his season with Leinster.

I was in Las Vegas when the World Cup began, and watched the Ireland v Scotland game in McMullan's Irish Bar after midnight with my two brothers, Stephen and William, and a few mates from home. It was Stephen's fortieth birthday and I didn't want to be in Ireland. There was a great bunch of supporters in the bar, about fifty Irish and twenty Scottish. It was better than watching it at home on my own. Every time Ireland scored, I sang 'Flower of Scotland' for the craic.

We looked fresh for the first twenty-five minutes and it

was the Scots who looked heavy-legged. We played at a high tempo and it looked like we were on it, although we fell off in the second half. But we defended well. A good start.

I watched the Japan game at home in Tullow the following Saturday at 8.45am on my own. We fired our shots early on and then dipped straight away. I sensed we were in trouble. It looked like we were tired again. We were soaking yards in contact and things weren't going our way. Japan fired the ball around and made us continually run and tackle. It was tough to watch. You were just waiting for them to score the decisive try.

The lads dug deep, but we just didn't play enough when we had the ball and we didn't win enough collisions. They came off the line and splattered our first ball carrier every time and we were going backwards. Then we were trying to force things and it just didn't work. Johnny was carrying a knock from the Scottish game, but I still think Joe should have had him on the bench at least because I think he was fit by the end of the week. He would have driven standards and got everybody doing their basics well. It looked like we had become more dependent on Johnny, partly because the other leaders in the team were a little bit off it.

I watched some of the Russia game. A few of the boys in Leinster watched it between meetings in UCD because it was a mid-morning, Thursday game. The Russians were emulating Japan, coming off the line and being physical. And they were big lads. But if you're just playing off 9 and between the two 15-metre lines, then the defending team will keep lining you up, knowing you aren't going to get to the edge. We should have been able to outsmart them better, like the All Blacks would do to us. They had two runners running at the line and the 9 pulls it out behind them for the 10 to hit the midfield. The defending team has to respect those inside runners. A two-sided attack forces defending teams to make smart decisions. I thought we should have played more of a wide-wide game against Russia. Run them around. Little plays out the back. We never got into a flow.

I was worried then because Samoa went well against Japan and Scotland. It was going to be their last shot and they were going to be physical. Against that, they were always going to give us penalties. And that's what happened.

I watched the win over Samoa in Caroline's house. They showed glimpses of what they could do in attack, but I still wasn't filled with confidence that the way they were playing was going to get them over the line against New Zealand.

That one I watched in Jersey at 11am. I went there for a couple of nights with Sarah and did a media gig for a financial company called Rathbones, taking in England's quarter-final against Australia beforehand. I thought there was a big performance in the lads, but I did say: 'We'll know where we are after five minutes in this game.' And after five minutes, it was clear that we weren't the mad Irish we'd seen before against the All Blacks.

There were a few plays we absolutely messed up. We created space, but lads ran into each other, or took the wrong line, or didn't give the pass. There were chances to get us into the game early on and on another day we probably would have taken them. It didn't help that the All Blacks were completely on top of their game, even down to Richie Mo'unga keeping Johnny's long penalty into the corner infield. People on social media had a cut off Johnny for 'not making sure of it'. But it was actually a superb kick and incredible play by Mo'unga. Not many players could have done that. It's the fine margins in those games.

We didn't win the early moments like we did in Chicago and in the Aviva in 2018. We had them, but we didn't win them. The All Blacks moved the point of attack very well and made us make decisions in defence, and they got to the edges so easily, which was very worrying from the off. We needed one big flat line and more line speed, particularly on the outside. They had us sussed out. They sat down our first three or four defenders with those two runners off 9 and just went out the back continually. Then it was hit a pod in the middle with a tip-on pass and they were on the front foot the whole time.

When Rob Kearney ran into Johnny, and Beauden Barrett scored off the turnover, it was 22-0 after thirty-two minutes and game over, when it could have been 17-10. Again, we had created space, but that was another chance gone.

I felt for the lads then. You're looking at it and thinking, what can be done here? To make matters worse, I was surrounded by a heap of English fans and a few Kiwis as well.

I don't think we reverted to a more conservative way of playing in 2019. In 2018 we had played with a ferocious intensity and the trick plays got us scores. If anything, by the end of 2019 not much had changed. The way it ended shouldn't tarnish Joe's name or his time in Irish rugby. It's not the way Joe wanted it to end and it's not the way the players wanted it to end for him either, because of what he did for us as a group for almost a decade. Maybe more of us should have led the charge with him on that.

25. An Irishman in London

On 26 November I emptied the house in Dundrum, packed up the Hilux and headed for Tullow. I unpacked some stuff I needed to leave behind and picked up other things I needed for the move to London. I locked up the jeep and was ready for the ferry the next morning at 8.45am. I left the house at 6.30am and was in Rosslare in plenty of time, but I was feeling a bit under the weather. I'd been chasing my tail and was a little stressed out the night before because I'd been seeing people for dinners, or coffee, or a few drinks. It had come upon me so fast. Suddenly, I was leaving.

It didn't help that the boat was delayed. I didn't get on board until 9.30am. When we finally got underway, the crossing didn't make me feel any better. I settled down with Joe Schmidt's book to pass the time, although that wasn't the reason I felt ill! The water was a bit choppy, especially for the first hour.

It was a four-and-a-half-hour journey, so I got through most of Joe's book. Learning more about his mindset as a coach was interesting, how that mindset was formed as a young man in New Zealand and the different experiences he'd had. The discipline that was drilled into him by his parents and teachers made me understand the person and the coach he became. Then he became a teacher himself, and they are more process driven, which explains why he liked to be in control so much. That was always a part of him, even when he coached in Mullingar. He didn't just finish playing and then suddenly invent himself as a coach.

I felt worse as the journey wore on. We landed at 1.50pm in Pembroke and I hit the road for my five-hour drive to the Richmond Hill Hotel, where I was staying for four or five nights until my flat in Teddington was ready. I stopped for some food and arrived at about 7.30pm, by which stage I was feeling pretty lousy. I had a snack, went to bed and woke up in the middle of the night coughing and spluttering, veering from hot to cold sweating. It was a rough night.

I wasn't due to train with London Irish that week, but I popped my head into the club the following morning to tell them I wasn't well and to ask if there was a doctor around. I don't get sick very often, but when I do it knocks the stuffing out of me. I knew I needed antibiotics.

I met the doc, who gave me a prescription, and I stopped off at a pharmacy before going straight back to bed in the Richmond Hill. Wednesday and Thursday were bad days and bad nights, and the weekend wasn't much better. I drank as much fluid as I could force into me.

On the Sunday I went for a walk around Richmond to get some air into my lungs. Going down the hill was fine. No problem at all. Coming back up I was absolutely gasping. I had no energy. I was glad nobody saw me, least of all anyone from London Irish.

When I made it back to the hotel, I forced some breakfast into me – my first food in days. I had no appetite at all, but I needed some energy. I wanted sleep so badly, so I went for an afternoon nap before I packed up my bag for my new home.

I checked into my flat in Teddington at 11am and then went to the London Irish training centre to go through my rehab programme with physio Nick Hess and head physio Brian O'Leary, who is a Corkman. I had wanted to continue my rehab and training at a relatively intense level, but they could see I hadn't the energy for much that day. What a shitty start to my London Irish career.

Although Wednesday was a down day, I met some of my new teammates. Then I went back to the apartment, tidied it up, unpacked and got the TV going.

My landlady came by to introduce herself. She had the place spotless and her family were into rugby. She told me that I wouldn't have Wi-Fi up and running for almost three weeks.

It was quite lonely, on my own in the apartment. I wasn't used to this. Most of the London Irish lads have their own scene – wives, families, girlfriends – and some of the younger lads live together. But I quickly learned that Teddington is a nice village. Everyone around here has a dog. That's the main subject of conversation.

London Irish has a good rugby environment. There's plenty of desire within the squad to achieve and to win, but there's so, so much work to be done. In my first three weeks I went to every player meeting and every contribution I made was about the breakdown. There was no point in me trying to fix four or five different pieces.

The one thing I had noticed in our breakdown work was that we were stopping at the ball all the time, whereas over the last ten years I would have been coached to get to the breakdown as quickly as possible and then get past the ball. At London Irish there was an awful habit of just putting our foot beyond the ball and so slowing things up for our scrum-halves. Initially I was hesitant about speaking, not having played a minute for them. But there was no point in biting my tongue and saying nothing, not if it could help the team to improve. That's why I offered to do a little bit of coaching as well.

We've started scouting the opposition a little more, too. London Irish had romped through the Championship the previous season and there were still some bad habits, whereas in the environment I came from, and in the Premiership, you don't get away with bad habits.

London Irish are based in their purpose-built Hazelwood Training Centre at their old Sunbury-on-Thames base. It has everything a club needs: four pitches, a High Performance Centre, meeting rooms, a kitchen, the works. And it's only twelve minutes from my apartment. Leinster's day started earlier, and that's what I was used to, so in those early weeks I was usually the first, or one of the first, there, at around 7.40am. I'd set my alarm for 7.15am and grab a flat white on the way in at a place called Woof. Good coffee. They open at 7.30am and within a few days they had it on for me before they unlocked the door.

Getting to the training centre early gave me half an hour of my own prep time before going to the physio at 8.30am to get loosened up for a forty-five-minute run three mornings a week. After a shower I'd have my overnight oats and then a team meeting around 11.30am, followed by unit meetings, and then we were on the pitch for an hour-long session. Some days we had weights sessions after lunch. I stayed a little longer than most lads, maybe doing videos or review-ing training, but I was generally back in my apartment by 4pm. Wednesday was a freer day. I did some upper-body weights and a Wattbike session in Hazelwood and was gone.

A week before Christmas I met my hip surgeon, Professor Damian Griffin, as he was in London for the day. We chat-ted for an hour and decided to take out the two screws that were holding in the bony part at the side of my hip, where they had extracted my hip joint and inserted a cap. The screws were there to fix the bone in place. They'd served their purpose by now and I could feel them through the skin.

They were removed two days later. I met the physio at 5am, got to the hospital at 7am, was on the table at 10.30am and out again at 3pm. A good day. I was happy to have those screws removed. I didn't want to return to playing in February or March and aggravate those pins when being knocked about.

That meant it was all systems go for the New Year. The plan was four or five weeks of conditioning and movement patterns, then another four weeks of rugby training and then back playing by mid-February. That would be ahead of schedule, but the surgeon was really happy with the movement in my hip.

A few days after that minor operation, I saw Andy Murray post on his Instagram account: 'Comeback of the Year'. I said to myself, feck it, I'll chance it.

I sent him a message: 'Andy, what you've done in the last year has been brilliant. I watched your documentary and you're a credit to yourself and an inspiration to me and the rest of the lads getting back from the same operation. Looking at the work you do and how you push yourself, I shared your emotions in that documentary over the last two years. It's been an emotional rollercoaster. Some people have seen the same in me at training, getting emotional about the pain, but people outside the game wouldn't know what you're going through. It takes a lot of guts to do what you've done. Undergoing a hip replacement is a massive decision, but now that you've done it and beaten it, it's exactly what I was hoping for as I've had the same surgery.'

Within ten minutes he messaged me back. 'Sean, it's great to hear from you. Yeah, I heard about your surgery and I was speaking to one of the boys and we were thinking of meeting for dinner one evening if possible.' He gave me his number and said to give him a ring that weekend, that he'd give me some advice based on his rehab.

I spoke with Andy a couple of times on the phone after that. We compared what was working best for each of us with regard to rehab, and we had pretty similar programmes. The main difference was that he hadn't really put an emphasis on strength work throughout his career, until this happened. Realizing how much gym work he had to do was a massive eye-opener for him, but other than that it was exactly the same rehab for both of us. It was great to have that kindred spirit to bounce things off and compare progress.

I trained hard for another week and then we had a squad Christmas dinner, which was also to mark the departure of Ruan Botha, a South African lock who was on a short-term loan and was leaving to play in Japan. Botha is 6 foot 9 inches (2.06m) and weighs 19½ stone (124kg). He's some unit, and a very good rugby player. By then I was starting to bond with my teammates, although a few of them, the younger lads especially, didn't know what to make of me.

I went home for a break on Christmas Eve. Me and one of the other Irish lads, Conor Gilsenan, were on the same flight and Dad picked me up from the airport. I dropped my bag at home, sprayed on some deodorant and went down to the local with him. I hadn't had a drink in a few weeks, but I was home by 11pm and up the next morning, as fresh as a daisy, to do some farming on Christmas morning. I fed the pheasants, walked the dog, had lunch at my sister's and slept for a couple of hours on the couch before driving to Sarah's place in Mayo.

I spent five days in Mayo and then came home again for a

couple of days before returning to London on 2 January with Sarah. She left for Australia on 4 January, for another stint with Collingwood. Our days together went by quickly but it was lovely, and I trained every day.

Friday, 17 January, was a landmark day for me: my first contact session since the hip operation, in fact since the previous April. It felt good. I wasn't hesitant at all. I was straight in. Poaching. Getting buried. Hitting pads. Running with the prowler sled. A tough thirty-five minutes. Good for my confidence.

It was just little unit sessions, along with some skill work for a few more weeks. This progressed to full pitch sessions at the start of February, but even by January I already felt as strong as I'd ever felt in my whole career. In fact, I felt stronger than ever. I was lifting the heaviest weights I'd ever lifted. I knew then I'd be in my best shape ever when I started back, even better than for the 2017 Lions. I was cooking well, eating well and looking after myself. I was pain-free for the first time since November 2017. When your body is right, you can get so much more out of it.

It had been seven years since I'd worked with Declan Kidney, but I'm glad to say he hasn't changed. He's still very good at man management. He has been very honest with me and I've been very honest with him. I'm able to have tough conversations with him when they need to be had. That's good. With some coaches you might be hesitant, but you can talk to Deccie, thrash it out with him and come up with a good plan.

The majority shareholder of London Irish is Mick Crossan. He's from Mayo but has spent most of his life over here, and he's the majority shareholder of Powerday, a waste management and recycling business in London that is also the club's main sponsor. London Irish is Mick's passion, and, from what I've heard, he's been unbelievable for the club over the years. Mick's a bit of a character. He's a good man and looks after everyone well. He engages with the players, and that's important. He wants the club to progress in the right way.

I've met most of the board of directors and they're all enthusiastic as well. Kieran McCarthy is the chairman. He's a great character from Cork who's been around the club a long time.

Another of the directors, Michael O'Hagan, has been very welcoming to me since I've arrived over, always checking in on me. His son, Sean, was in the Ulster Academy and played out-half on the same Irish Under-19 team as Jacob Stockdale. I actually presented Sean with his jersey at the Carlton Hotel in Blanchardstown at the time. He was also the out-half for Richmond when I played for the Leinster As in that British and Irish Cup game in 2016. Rugby is a small world all right.

After I'm finished my day in the training ground, I go to Nutfield, about five minutes down the road, for a swim and a sauna. When I get back to the apartment I usually start cooking. I'm working through Daniel Davey's *Eat Up, Raise Your Game*. That's been good because I know what I'm eating is healthy and it has helped make me strong and fit. After dinner I'll watch something on Netflix and head to bed at about 10.30pm.

If I was at home or in Dublin, I'd be racing around doing something all the time. Living on my own in Teddington and not having much to do has been a bit of a blessing. I have made enquiries about coaching a team in the area and I've also looked into doing a leadership course. I do miss Sarah and I do miss home, but being only an hour from Dublin is good. It's a different kind of life for me, but it's working well.

I miss the Leinster lads. I would have been really close to some of them and I miss the craic I had with them. I text a few of them, Ferg, Nugget, Johnny and Johnny O'Hagan, who, like Rala, is one of the best characters in the whole set-up. I miss talking to him. Like Rala, he's very positive, he's seen a lot in rugby and he has to be on his game, too. A good kit man makes our jobs a lot easier, and he has to put up with all the lads taking the piss out of him.

I sent Sexto a voicemail when he was made captain of Ireland, to tell him that it was a great achievement and thoroughly deserved. I asked him one favour, that he let me be the mascot the first time he leads out Ireland.

But for the most part I've tried to remove myself from their world. You just move on and get on with it. London Irish is where my job is now.

My delayed debut after the hip operation was to have been the London Irish v Wasps game at the Madejski Stadium on Sunday, 1 March. I trained fully from the start of the week, but after three wins on the bounce, Deccie was reluctant to change a winning team. We'd beaten Northampton and Harlequins away, and then Gloucester at home. Also, we had a five-day turnaround to the game away to Sale the following Friday. We trained on the Tuesday and I didn't know if he was going to start me against Sale, but after the defeat against Wasps he had to refresh the side.

Playing my first game in ten months and my first for a new club, I wanted to make sure I knew all our plays from early in the week. I wanted to be clear on all the detail so I could be physical against Sale, because they're a big team and they were flying at the time. I was buzzing that week. I brought some energy to the gym and onto the training field. The day before the game I was relaxed. After training we left at 1pm and travelled by coach for almost six hours to Salford.

On the day of the game I was a little nervous. It wasn't that I was afraid of my hip, more that I was anxious about going into an unknown. But once we got to the AJ Bell Stadium and pulled on the jersey for the warm-up, I felt good. With experience comes calmness. Some of the boys said it would be a tough place to go, but there wasn't a massive crowd. It's usually wet and rainy, but this was a good night for rugby, until it became a little breezy in the second half.

There was no point in me running around like a maniac. I didn't give away any penalties, I made twelve tackles in forty-eight minutes, I had six carries, my breakdown stuff was good and I won two turnover penalties and I ripped another clean one in the tackle. It was good to get a few hits and be knocked around. I put a few in, too. My first good shot was on their South African prop, Coenie Oosthuizen, about twenty minutes in, and I absolutely melted him. That felt good.

We were very competitive defensively, but we threw two intercept passes to be 12-0 down at half-time. My hip flexor was a little tight, so I was content to get forty-eight minutes under my belt. But they had a stronger bench and scored four tries in the last quarter to win 39-0. Because of the result, I didn't think of my achievement. Looking back on the video, though, my work rate was high and I did some good things in that game. But the very best thing was that there was no reaction from my hip.

In the days afterwards, I came to realize that I had done something that no other rugby player had ever done, through the operation and the ten months of intensive rehabbing. I hadn't really thought of this until I started receiving texts about it. But I wanted way more. We were eighth in the table after that weekend and I wanted us to be a top-four team. Most of all, I wanted to be one of the lads and just get on with it. Be a rugby player again.

We came back straight after the Sale game to Hazelwood at 3.30am and then I drove to the apartment. It's hard to sleep on a long bus journey after a game. You can't stop thinking about it and your body is a little stressed.

We had a team 'social' the next day, meeting for brunch at midday and then moving on to a pub to watch the England v Wales game. We had a great day and I was home by about 11pm. It felt like my London Irish career had properly started – and started well. A good feeling.

On the Sunday morning Sarah's granddad passed away. I was coming home anyway on a flight at 10.10am. Simon Clark from the gun shop picked me up and we went straight to a clay pigeon competition before I was dropped home and did a bit of farming.

I fed the pheasants on the Monday and then hit the road to Mayo for the wake that night and the funeral the day after. Sarah couldn't make it home from Australia because she was preparing for a game, which was sad because she had been very close to her granddad.

I still hadn't recovered from my first game back when I returned to Tullow on the Tuesday. I was fatigued for the week and, as usual after a comeback game, I came down with something. I took the dogs for a walk on the Wednesday morning and shot a few crows before Dad brought me to the airport for my flight to London.

I filled myself with vitamin C and was back training on the Thursday. I did the majority of the weights session, but a few people were out sick with flu symptoms. I said to Paul Cremin, one of our physios: 'Paul, I'm not feeling well. I'm going to get out of here in case I have flu.'

I spent the afternoon on the couch, but after a day's rest I felt considerably better. I didn't go to training on the Friday, when several other players and staff stayed at home as well. By then the Covid-19 virus was starting to spread and precautionary measures were being taken at the request of the club, so I had to self-isolate for seven days in the apartment. I ordered a Tesco delivery online and stayed in the apartment for a week, cooking and eating and watching Netflix. I also had a Wattbike delivered to me on the Tuesday evening.

When the Premiership was suspended, I rang Deccie and asked him could I go home. Cabin fever was setting in. By that stage, the club had been closed up and we had all been sent our individual training programmes by Rob Palmer, the head of S&C. I would have gone crazy in the apartment in Teddington and I knew I could maintain my fitness, and my sanity, far better at home on the farm.

I left there at 7am on Thursday, 19 March, after my week in self-isolation. As the club was going to be closed for a good few weeks and the season was going to be canned for at least a month, instead of flying I drove the five hours to Holyhead and got the ferry home at 2pm to the East Wall in Dublin. I was back in Tullow by 7pm.

I was able to work on the farm, do a bit of shooting and do my training at Tullow RFC and on the local GAA pitch. I had put a load of equipment in the gym and I had it and the pitches all to myself.

My career had come full circle, in a way.

I also had my own weights platform and I could go running with Padraig and other lads all within two kilometres of home, on the GAA pitch, while maintaining our distance. I could keep myself very busy, and I did. It was far more beneficial for my fitness than staying in Teddington.

I spent eleven weeks on the farm, my longest stint there since I'd joined the Leinster Academy in 2005. I was flat out, too. As well as a bit of calving that had to be done, I was renovating a cottage that myself and my brother Stephen had bought before I left for London. I also did a good bit of shooting in the evenings. I enjoyed being home and I was happy out.

I now own a pub in Tullow, The Irish Bar, on a corner site in the centre of the town. It was the only rugby pub in town and the pub where I had my first beer. I also bought the pizzeria beside it, which I plan to make into my kitchen for the pub. The owner of the backyard also had right of way, so I bought that too, and then last year I added the old hairdressers behind the pub. So I've the whole block there and the plans include a pub which will be the full length of the building and five two-bed apartments. I'll let someone I trust run it for me, probably my sister Alex. It will be nice when it's done, but it's going to take time.

When I look out on the main pitch at Tullow RFC, the only difference is that there used to be a timber rail on the side of the pitch and there's a galvanized rail now. Even some of the advertising signs look like they've been there for the last twenty-five years. Slaney Eggs is still there, and Rathwood and Dawson's.

Above the scoreboard – Tullow v Visitors – is an ad for Swordfish, a dental-supply company owned by Bernard O'Neill, who has always been good for the club.

The clubhouse, with a big function room, hasn't changed. On a rainy day you could squeeze 150 people into that function room. But a minis team would have filled one of the old changing-rooms. I don't know how fifteen grown men did it when I first started playing Cup games with Tullow. It was ridiculous.

Not before time, those old changing-rooms have been redeveloped into a gym, and we now have six good-sized changing-rooms with showers which were built in 2013. The club has also added on a small training ground with floodlights behind the main pitch, along with a stretch of grassland to the side of the pitch from the main entrance of about 1.3 acres. I actually lent them the money to buy it in 2015, and they've paid me back over the six years.

A grant has been approved for a full-sized Astroturf pitch, which is scheduled to open in 2020. Then, hopefully, the main pitch is going to be turned and that will give us three pitches facing the same way where before there were two.

The club has good neighbours. Along the laneway beside the main entrance are Jim Curry, his wife, Catriona, and Patrick 'Puddy' Curry and his wife, Deirdre. The Currys have been there a long time and Jim has done a huge amount of work for the club, as has Puddy, who is a former player. John O'Connor and his wife, Jennifer, are also on this laneway, and, as they are both gardaí, the club is in safe hands.

On the other side of the club we have Tom and Michael Eustace, who are involved in the club with their families. Also on that side is John Brophy, who sold us that bit of land from his farm, which adjoins the club. Tullow RFC's expansion wouldn't have been possible without these friendly neighbours, and hopefully we'll see their kids going through the club for many years to come.

The club has grown hugely since my playing days, which is down to the success they've had at all levels, and the catchment area is bigger, too. There are players coming from as far as Baltinglass, which is half an hour away, or Tinahely, forty minutes away, in Wicklow. There are over 250 mini-rugby players on Sunday mornings from under-8s to under-12s in the club now, whereas we were lucky to have maybe seventy when I started. They have the guts of eighty senior lads as well as under-14s, 15s, 17s and 19s. There's also a ladies' section, with under-15s, under-18s and senior teams.

I've been coaching in Tullow since I was eighteen, and I'd say I've coached nearly all of them at least once. I also sponsor the Tullow ladies' team. My sister Alex plays for them. She can play 8 or 12. They lost to St Mary's in the AIL Cup last season in one of the best games of rugby I've ever watched in my life. Mary's had a few internationals and Tullow had none, but they batted way above themselves. It was try after try after try, and so physical, some belter shots! Caroline also played with Tullow for a year before doing her cruciate playing football.

I've coached them too, but mostly I've coached the men's senior team on and off for the last dozen years. We've been holding our own in Division 1B of the Leinster League and have reached four Towns Cup finals since 2008, never having reached one before.

That 2017 final, when we beat Skerries 20-3 in Athy, was the best day in the club's history, without a shadow of a doubt. Grown men, all former players, were crying on the sidelines and on the field. Men like Pat Nolan, also known as the Red Lad, who was one of the best players to come out of Tullow. And all the O'Briens, not related, who have been stalwarts of the club. Sammy O'Brien was one of the best junior players in Leinster on his day, and Ger was actually part of the coaching ticket that season. There's also the Browne family, including current club president Paddy, and John, who was also one of the best junior players in the province. They've contributed hugely to the development of the club, and Louis Kilcoyne, whose mother is a Browne, played one of his best games in the Tullow colours that day.

I looked around the sidelines and saw how much it meant to people like them and Mark 'Sprocket' Coady, who have given their whole lives to Tullow, that the club had finally achieved this success. Sprocket was one of the best scrum-halves in Leinster and one of the best players Tullow ever produced. He must have played in three Towns Cup semi-finals and lost in all of them. I can't remember any year when he wasn't involved coaching either the firsts or the seconds. He is Mr Tullow.

One former player, John Bolger, jumped down off the bank to run out on the field at the full-time whistle, and broke his ankle.

There could be more Seán O'Briens in Tullow. I know it. But they're falling out of the system. While I give the Schools credit for developing class players at a rapid rate, if you want another Trevor Brennan, Niall Ronan, Shane Horgan, Tadhg Furlong or Seán O'Brien, then club and Youths players need more investment in facilities and time. Because players from the clubs are not training every day of the week, they don't have the same skill sets, but they could develop them if given the chance.

In my opinion, it requires three years of development in the academy for a Youths player to be prepared for professional rugby. A Schools player might only need one or two years because his game knowledge, his strength and conditioning, and his athleticism are all more advanced.

Leinster should be screening kids from all over the South-East, and should have ten lads from Tullow training in a high-performance centre two or three times a week, along with lads from Enniscorthy, New Ross, Athy and Carlow.

There are lads playing on Tullow's first team who, if they'd been given that opportunity when they were younger, God only knows how they might have progressed. There might only have been two lads in the entire Tullow senior squad who had the right attitude, a big frame and were athletic, at any given time. But they were never given a chance. Players from the schools have so many advantages in terms of facilities, coaching and time.

I was very lucky. I made it despite the system rather than because of it, thanks largely to Colin McEntee in the Leinster Academy taking a punt on me. That was the break I needed.

So many people have helped me along the way. As well as Larry Canavan and Vinnie Mahon in Tullow, there was Pat O'Keefe, who always looked after the gear and the water, as well as Ger Kavanagh. He wasn't much of a rugby player himself but had a fierce interest if one of his lads was playing. They were all very good to me, and Dad too, although I think he came out to Tullow more to socialize!

I'll always keep that connection with home, no matter where I end up living. If things go the way I hope with Sarah, my hip and London Irish, I could see myself living in London for a couple of years, or until the hip falls off, and then Dublin could be our home for the foreseeable future.

I love going to Mayo. I really switch off and relax when

I'm in Ballina. I also absolutely adore Enniscrone, which is about fifteen minutes away in Sligo. If I could build a house there, I would – either a holiday home or a family home. It's peaceful, with a long, safe beach, and nice little places to eat and drink.

My home life will, of course, be related to my work life, whatever that may be. And as my rugby career nears an end, I'm still not sure what that will be. As I'm making more plans for the future, I also have to take into consideration what Sarah is doing with her life. Whenever I retire, it won't be just about me.

I think I will definitely go down the coaching route to some degree, and see how that pans out. Other than that, I'm not sure. I've to finish off my business degree. I like dealing with, and chatting with, people, so I could see myself being a relationship manager, or in that line of work. My uncle owns a new lending firm called Sancus, and I might work with them.

On Father's Day, Sunday, 21 June, I took the ferry from Rosslare to Pembroke and came back to London. They were difficult weeks because things were so all over the place. Due to the Covid-19 restrictions, there was no real structure to my life. We had to train in smaller groups and maintain physical distancing, and the club's facilities were closed off, so there wasn't the same craic. Tough on the mind, to have a lot of time to yourself, sitting around the apartment alone.

But, still, I feel optimistic about the future. I'm in great condition and I will have more opportunities to get proper rugby into my legs and proper conditioning now that we know my hip is good again.

When you sign a contract, you don't see anything like a

pandemic coming at you. For the lads on smaller contracts it will be tough, especially with the cost of living in London. In due course there will be reductions in salaries for the season. Like most clubs, I'd say, the reduced-salary cap and the financial losses will mean a leaner squad, which means players are going to be playing more games. But that's sport, as I've said – unpredictable to the end. I can't complain, though. I'm one of the lucky ones.

I love rugby. I love the structure of the week and the competitiveness of the weekends, the shared enjoyment of playing and of winning. And the dressing-room and its values. The respect between players and teams.

Back in my first season in the Leinster Academy, 2005/06, I first heard Brian O'Driscoll say: 'You don't have to be the most talented or the best player on the field to work hard.' He trained and played like that. I'd like to think I've always tried to do that, too, and that I've been a good teammate.

And I'm not finished yet. I've two more seasons at London Irish, and possibly a third. There's a Lions tour to South Africa next year, too. Who knows, there might be another chapter or two in this story yet.

Acknowledgements

Seán's Acknowledgements

I would like to take this opportunity to thank all the people who have helped to make me into the person I am today.

To start, I have to thank my entire family for their support and love throughout my career to date. My mam's love has been unwavering and she has done all she can to provide the best life possible for us as children. My dad developed in me a social character and the fun element of life that people need. Both of them together have showed me that you need to work hard in life.

To my brothers, Stephen and William, for their support. To Stephen for his advice, and for being that bigger brother to me throughout my life. To William for being himself – a character to rival my dad! And to Caroline, who drove the length and breadth of the country to bring me to every sports event and training session, and has followed me with her family all over the world. I can't put into words how much that has meant to me to have you there on those big days. And to Alex, the youngest in the family, who has a big heart and is mad into sport too. She is mature beyond her years and plays the type of game I love to play as well. In that respect I'd like to think some of me has rubbed off on Alex!

It would be remiss of me not to mention by name Willie, Caroline's husband, and Lucy, Stephen's wife, who have, when needed, provided sound advice throughout.

I owe all my family a huge amount for the part they played on my journey.

Special mention too for my five nephews, who I take around the farm and kick a ball with, namely Caroline and Willie's lads, Patrick and Will, and Stephen and Lucy's boys, Donnacha, Lochlan and Conan.

I would also like to thank all of my friends from Tullow, the Fighting Cocks and the surrounding area for the support they've given me throughout my career.

I'd especially like to thank Tullow RFC for keeping my feet firmly on the ground as my career progressed and for all the people in the club who helped me. There are just too many to name who helped me in my early days, when things were tough financially, and they believed in me when maybe some didn't.

I can't go through these acknowledgements without mentioning my good friends James, Padraig and Daniel for being a constant set of ears for me through thick and thin. For your support and loyalty to me in the good times and the bad I'll be forever grateful. Indeed to all my friends that I have grown up with and friends I've met along the way, I couldn't have done any of it without any of you.

I'd like to thank Leinster Rugby and Colin McEntee for bringing me into their system when they did, and also UCD Rugby Club for giving me the opportunity to lead a professional lifestyle as an eighteen-year-old. I'll be forever indebted.

Leinster has been life for the guts of fifteen years and I've made lifelong friends in that club, along with creating some unbelievable memories that I will cherish for ever.

Without Leinster I wouldn't have the opportunity to play for my country, Ireland, and the British and Irish Lions. I'd like to thank everyone associated with Ireland and the Lions – unforgettable memories with both of them.

The Lions was, I suppose, the pinnacle, but getting my first Irish cap, as well as playing in those Lions tests, will be days I will always treasure. Again, there are too many coaches to name here.

I've suffered my fair share of injuries and as a result have spent a lot of time with physios, doctors, surgeons, and strength and conditioning coaches. As with all the coaches who have helped make me the player I became, there are too many to name, but I would like to thank all of them for their patience and assistance in getting my body back to where it needs to be to play rugby.

Sarah was also a huge part of my later career, not least in helping me through the tough times over the last three years, for her patience, support, friendship and love.

I would like to thank Gerry for the huge amount of work he put into researching and writing about my life. Throughout it all we got on so well and that, hopefully, is one of the reasons we've written a great book. I would really like to thank you for being there for me. You probably know me as well as anyone else at this stage. When Michael McLoughlin in Penguin asked me who I had in mind to write my biography, I said any article you've ever written about me was always exactly what I said and how I said it. Thank you for how you've written this book and how you've portrayed my life, so far, in my eyes and my words.

I'd also like to thank Michael, Brendan, Rachel and all the people in Penguin who I think have done a great job with this book. I wouldn't have wanted any other publisher to publish it, and after meeting Michael and Brendan, my mind was at ease that it was going to be a brilliant book.

I'd also genuinely like to thank every player I played with for their hard work and honesty throughout my career. Without them I wouldn't be where I am now.

Finally, sincere thanks to every supporter out there who has sent me a message, or that encouraged me, or was at a game I played in.

I always thought I was, firstly, honouring my family, my loved ones and my close friends, but, secondly, people from my club, my province and my country.

And it's been one hell of a ride.

Gerry Thornley's Acknowledgements

When Michael McLoughlin's name popped up on my phone I immediately wondered if he had a book in mind. But when he said the words Seán O'Brien I was genuinely taken aback and more than a little honoured. Seán has been, in my view, a properly world-class Irish rugby player, in the very top bracket. 'No' wasn't an option.

He also has a story to tell and for this I'd like to thank him most of all. Seán could not have been more helpful or forthcoming over the many hours of interviews. If readers do not enjoy this book it is not your fault, Seán. Sincere thanks again.

I'd also like to thank Michael, Brendan Barrington, Rachel Pierce and all the staff at Penguin Random House Ireland for their patience and guidance, and the wonderful job they have done on this book.

Sincerest thanks to Kaye, Stephen and the rest of Seán's family for their hospitality, friendship and constant availability and help. Likewise to James Foley for the revealing tour of Tullow.

Many others could not have been more helpful in giving their time towards my research, among them Charlie McAleese, David Eakin, Hendrik Kruger, Colin McEntee, Enda McNulty, Mick Kearney and Ryan Constable.

Thanks to Malachy Logan and Noel O'Reilly in the *Irish Times* for their understanding.

Special thanks to Marian for her love and support, and not least for making time. To Dylan, Evan and Shana for their love and encouragement, and to Fergal for 'making' the office just before lockdown. And, as ever, I couldn't have done it without 'the team', particularly my sister Yseult for the transcribing and proofreading and, our guiding spirit, Petria.

Index